Rooted and Renewing

Rooted and Renewing

Imagining the Church's Future in Light of Its New Testament Origins

Troy M. Troftgruben

Fortress Press

Minneapolis

ROOTED AND RENEWING
Imagining the Church's Future in Light of Its New Testament Origins

Cover image: Shutterstock 2019; Monochrome parasol pine tree with sunburst and church roof in the background By Fortgens Photography
Cover design: Alisha Lofgren
Typesetting: PerfecType, Nashville, TN

Print ISBN: 978-1-5064-3976-1
eBook ISBN: 978-1-5064-3977-8

To my mother
Judith Fay Troftgruben
(April 6, 1941–February 9, 2019)

CONTENTS

INTRODUCTION

Why Church Roots Matter

The origins of Christianity have excited deep curiosity since the second century. In modern times no ancient phenomenon has been the subject of such intensive research. Yet its beginnings and earliest growth remain in many respects mysterious.

—Wayne A. Meeks

What comes to your mind when you think of "church"?

For many today, it's physical things like church buildings, architectural symbols, worship spaces, and tangible elements like water, bread, or wine. For others, it's music, artwork, singing, and creative expressions. For still others, it's the people associated with church community: children, adults, pastors, worshipers, shut-ins, and so on. For others, it's formative experiences associated with church communities: funerals, weddings,

Figure 1. "Loaves and Fishes Mosaic in the Church of Multiplication" (fifth century). Photo by Avishai Teicher, Wikimedia Commons.

baptisms, worship, faith formation events, shared meals, and the like. And for others still, it's leaders like pastors, deacons, teachers, godparents, and mentors. For most people, whether the associations are positive or negative, things that come to mind associated with "church" are rich and multifaceted—not neutral and drab.

For ministry leaders, other things may come to mind in thinking about "church." Many leaders may think of programs and offerings. Others may think of staff people and volunteers. Still other ministry leaders may think of pragmatic things like budgets, fundraising campaigns, and building maintenance. Still others may think of social dynamics like pastoral care needs, instances of conflict, and power dynamics. And others may think in terms of weekly responsibilities, from preaching to meetings and visitations.

Some of the things that may come to mind in relation to "church" are new to our day and age: church websites, online teaching resources, phone numbers, and the like. But most of the things we think of are not new at all: worship spaces, the sacraments, pastors and leaders, people of various ages, baptisms, sources of conflict, shared meals, neighborhood ministries, visitations to homes, grieving death together, addressing community needs, and hearing from God in various meaningful ways. In fact, many of these things were no less central to the experiences of church people centuries ago.

In many societies of the Western world today, people believe dramatic change is soon to come—and is in fact underway—for the church as we have known it. In the United States, for example, abundant forecasts predict declining participants and resources for churches, as well as increasing indifference among the populace at large toward religious faith. Certainly, if these forecasts are correct, changes are coming for church communities. Many fear these changes a great deal, thinking they represent the death of authentic church life and a turn to something much worse.

But will these changes truly replace authentic Christianity with something alien or artificial? News stories predict "the death of the church," but such dramatic reports are exaggerated. Changes will come—in fact, the historic church has rarely been *without* significant changes afoot—but the communities of

Jesus Christ have seen more difficult days than church people today fear.

At its very beginning, the small Jewish sect we now call "Christianity" lacked big numbers, social influence, and even a name. But within a few centuries, not only did it catch the eye of the Roman Empire at large, it transformed and rearranged the empire's entire worldview. At the outset, the fledgling community had neither dedicated buildings nor consistent leadership patterns, but it ultimately took root in the shadow of the highest offices in the world. This dramatic turn of events, in the face of major obstacles, suggests Christianity has tended to flourish most when facing its greatest challenges.

Most important, a lot of the things most central to church communities—in antiquity and today—are not passing fads. Church communities in the first century gathered, worshiped, ate together, listened for God, and empowered people to live out faith daily. Church communities in the twenty-first century also gather, worship, eat together, listen for God, and empower people to live out faith daily. The things most central to being "church" today are not so radically different from the things central to first-century believers.

Church Community: Then and Now

Certainly, some things today are different from the first few centuries. Even a casual comparison between church communities then and now shows a host of things that have changed: today the church has over two billion adherents, leadership hierarchies, power dynamics, historic traditions, social divisions, negative stereotypes, static buildings, modern conveniences, standardized leadership training, printed resources in abundance, the internet, cell phones, and many other things. Some of these new things are desirable, while others are not. Likewise, some features from earliest Christianity may be desirable to recover today, while others are gladly left in the past.

> The things most central to being "church" today are not so radically different from the things central to first-century believers.

Despite the differences between ancient and modern churches, there is a continuum between them. The church of today is, finally, a direct descendant of the churches of New Testament times. This makes questions about the earliest churches today, at least for Christians, questions about our family history.

Many church people today are asking, "What does it mean to be the church in the twenty-first century?" And many factors play into this question, from the well-founded to the fearful. Questions about the church may be interesting to anyone, but those of us connected to church communities today have skin in the game. Our questions come from a place of personal significance as we strive to be faithful in cultural contexts that are rapidly changing.

Whatever the church is called to be today, it is neither brand new nor unrelated to how it began. In fact, the questions raised by changes today compel us to reflect not only on future forecasts but also on where we came from. In other words, the changes we face today lead us, as church, to ask not only "Who will we become?" but also "Who are we?" and "Where have we come from?"

Whatever the church is becoming today, it must keep a clear sense of its distinctive character—what has persisted at its core throughout the centuries, despite the changes in contexts and cultures. Whatever the church hopes to be in the future, it must start with revisiting its roots. To know better who we are, we must begin with where we have come from.

Why Should the Church Today Care about Its Historic Roots?

It may not be clear to you that the history of early church communities really matters. You are not alone. Even in church communities, among leaders and others, many people think we ought to focus on far more pressing areas than church history. With boundless information available to us today, why bother with the past? Why should we approach our church questions today with such deliberate reflection on our historic church roots? Let me give four reasons, for starters.

First, many of us in the twenty-first century have forgotten the past. A familiar adage suggests, "Those who cannot remember the past are condemned to repeat it."[1] Certainly, the more informed we are about our past, the more discerning we are about our future. For many people today, inside and outside Christian circles, notions of the earliest church are vague at best.

And so we do well to revisit—if not learn for the first time—some basic facts like the following:

- The earliest followers of Jesus were Jews.
- "Christ" was not a last name but a title.
- The earliest apostles did not believe they were starting a new religion.
- The name "Christian" came well after Jesus's day—likely as an unfavorable designation.
- The earliest sources on church communities are Paul's letters in the New Testament.
- The portrayals of the church in Acts are not "pure history" by twenty-first-century standards.
- "Scripture" for the earliest churches entailed nothing from the New Testament.
- In the early centuries, the New Testament writings were not *read* as much as *heard* (read out loud).
- The earliest communities did not meet in church buildings but in homes and other locations.
- Women likely played roles of leadership in these communities.
- Most early church people could not read.
- Some of them were people of means and social status.
- Most of them were not martyred under mass, systematized Roman persecution.

This is just a sampling. But these points alone show how different the world of the earliest believers is from ours today. To enter that world is to make a major cross-cultural shift between now and then.

Our primary sources for early church communities are the New Testament (NT) writings. Among these are the letters of Paul (ca. 49–62 **CE**), which tell us a great deal by what they assume, imply, instruct, and ignore. The Acts of the Apostles (late first-century CE) narrates a distinctive story of the birth, growth, spread, and controversies of the earliest church. Other NT writings are the Gospels, whose teachings address later first-century church experiences; the **disputed letters of Paul**, such as the Pastoral Epistles (1–2 Timothy and Titus), which depict increased structure in church leadership roles; and the General (or "Catholic") Letters (James, 1–2 Peter, 1–3 John, Jude) and Revelation show how communities reacted to external and internal threats. In addition, writings outside the New Testament give later glimpses into early practices of the faith communities (e.g., the Didache, 1 Clement, Pliny's *Epistles*, Justin Martyr, Irenaeus). Although mostly later than the NT, they flesh out a bigger picture of church expansion and development beyond the earliest decades. These sources do not all paint the same picture. But together they offer a more accurate, composite portrait of what the earliest church community looked like.

This leads to a second reason to revisit our historic church roots: to clarify *how* they are relevant today. While some people today undervalue these sources, others show an opposite tendency: they assume the earliest NT patterns are the blueprint or "instruction manual" for churches of all times and places, period. For example, a recent book on church-planting proposes that the NT shows "the divine pattern" for effective churches today, one that is "handcrafted by God Himself."[2]

Defining Some Terms

CE and BCE: the Common (or Current) Era and Before the Common (or Current) Era, respectively. Numerically, these abbreviations mean the same thing as AD (*anno domini*) and BC (before Christ), without assuming a worldview oriented around Christ as Lord.

Disputed letters of Paul: six NT writings attributed to Paul whose authorship is today disputed among interpreters: Colossians, Ephesians, 2 Thessalonians, 1 Timothy, 2 Timothy, and Titus. The authorship of seven other writings of Paul is not widely disputed, making them the **undisputed letters of Paul**: Romans, 1 and 2 Corinthians, Galatians, Philippians, 1 Thessalonians, and Philemon.

Certainly, the NT portrayals of church are instructive. But is it truly *possible* to reproduce these models in our vastly different contexts today? Our experiences are worlds different from those of the first-century believers: most of us can read; we assume access to public education; we often work at different professions than our parents; we have traveled more than ten miles from home; we know things about China; we expect to live more than forty years; we value women and children as equal to men; we condemn slavery; we value democracy; we do not condemn charging interest on loans; we value private ownership of goods; we think saving money for the future does not necessarily imply a lack of faith; we encourage saving for retirement; we expect fair taxation; we are concerned about caring for the environment; we have advanced medical care; we do not associate ailments with demons; we distinguish religious matters from "secular" ones; we tend to approach the world individualistically; and we think Jesus might not return before we die. In short, our world today differs profoundly from the world of the NT believers.

To use the NT portrayals of church as a blueprint for universal restoration is not only unfair, it is impossible. The first-century models cannot be remanufactured pristinely. Instead, they must be understood within their historical contexts, appreciated for their distinctive contributions, and read with discernment for our contexts today. Certainly, the NT examples of Christian community are relevant today. But their relevance shines most clearly when they are read not as scripted recipes but rather through ongoing dialogue and discernment. This book aims to be a resource for precisely this kind of back-and-forth engagement.

A third reason to approach church questions today in view of our historic roots is because what we "know" about the past keeps changing. Although our sources are sparse, our knowledge about these communities is not stagnant: our interpretive reconstructions are constantly developing, shifting, and being further refined. For example, just over a decade ago a scholar could confidently say "nearly all NT scholars presently agree: early Christians met almost exclusively in the homes of individual members of the congregation."[3] That assumption is now being reexamined.[4] For another example, not long ago most scholars characterized the earliest churches as egalitarian.[5] That too is being challenged, since signs of more stratified leadership are visible even in Paul's earliest churches.[6] In addition, questions about the extent to which women participated in leadership in the earliest communities are as lively as ever. So are questions about the extent to which Paul's leadership models reflected surrounding social norms. These are but a few examples of ongoing debate on highly significant issues. Though our sources are sparse, our interpretive reconstructions are constantly being revisited and revised. For this reason, our resources need not only be accurate, they must also be *up-to-date*.

A final reason for approaching church questions today in view of our historic roots may put the proverbial cart before the horse, but it is still worth naming: interest is *high*—and for many reasons. At the seminary where I teach, I regularly offer courses on Acts, 1–2 Corinthians, and the historical world of the New Testament. In these courses, we spend significant time on the ideals, characteristics, and experiences of the earliest church communities. Outside my seminary, I also often engage people in various settings with the book of Acts and the study of early Christian communities. And in all my years of teaching, I have been pleasantly surprised at how widespread and active interest is in these topics.

Among seminary students, pastors, congregations, and people of all kinds, I have seen many responses to the NT portrayals of early church community: surprise, wonder, interest, skepticism, appreciation, pessimism, and inspiration, just to name a few. I have seen readers of vastly different church experiences uniting in shared reactions of fascination. I have seen people who have been burned by church upbringings that overemphasized reenacting the first-century church today, who find themselves still wrestling with unresolved questions. And I have seen many people struggling with major questions about the church and its future who find this topic a refreshing opportunity to step back, reflect, and dream.

> "Now they devoted themselves to the apostles' teaching and to the community, to the breaking of bread and to the prayers. Awe came upon everyone, and many signs and wonders took place through the apostles. All those who believed were united, and they held all things in common. They would sell possessions and goods and distribute the proceeds to all, just as each had need. Daily they devoted themselves with one accord to gather in the temple, and at home they broke bread and ate with gladness and simplicity of heart, praising God and experiencing the favor of all the people. And the Lord added daily to their number those being saved." (Acts 2:42–47, author's translation)

What I have not found in these experiences is *apathy*. Although it may exist, it is rare these days. Interest in where the earliest church communities came from is high—and not just among church people. And since the cultural landscapes of church and society are undergoing some significant changes right now, apathy toward these NT portrayals is not likely to increase. As major shifts take place in the demographics and leadership of faith communities in the Western world and elsewhere, questions about the roots of church community are alive and well—and increasingly important. As uncertainty about the future increases, our interest in the past only becomes more focused and intentional.

These are the kinds of questions and concerns that prompted me to write this book. They come from ministry leaders and church people of all kinds, who share their questions with me and yearn to know more about how to respond. They ask because these questions matter to how we do church today, and even more to how we continue in the future.

What This Book Is

This book springs from a core conviction: *As church, where we came from truly matters to where we are going. As Christian communities, our roots not only inform our present and future, they help us discern who we are.* Although many factors play into questions about church and ministry practices today, most of these questions are not new to our day. The most relevant discussions of ministry practice today may—and should—be informed in thought-provoking ways by revisiting the roots of church community.

> As church, where we came from truly matters to where we are going.

This book is an engagement with questions of church ministry today from the lens of the earliest NT church communities. In attending to both questions of ministry practice today and informed research on early Christianity, I want to show how ancient are our questions and how relevant are our roots. In this book, we will raise questions that reflect on modern church practices and challenges, but in ways that tap into the practices, realities, and experiences of the earliest followers of Jesus. In doing so, I think we will find that our experiences today are shared by a much larger cloud of witnesses than we may have assumed.

The chapters are organized by specific areas of significance: (1) the relevance of sacred spaces, (2) the sense of (comm)unity our churches share, (3) the significance of just social dynamics and leadership, (4) the core activities that are most essential, and (5) the call to bear distinctive witness in the world today. Although I am in regular dialogue with the works of NT scholars throughout the book, the focus here is dialogue with church people and leaders of all kinds, so my citations are sparse, questions abundant, and suggested resources sufficient for those who want more. My intention here is not to shift the fulcrum of scholarship but to engage today's questions of church ministry in a way intentionally informed by the best of historical research. In doing so, I hope to provoke ongoing conversation among both church people and leaders in various settings for years to come.

Chapter 1 ("Sacred Spaces for a Church on the Way") explores what "sacred space" truly is, whether associated with church buildings or not. Although ministries today often experience both blessings and burdens with owning buildings, the earliest Jesus-followers experienced church differently. The earliest church communities gathered in homes, and sometimes in other public and multipurpose spaces. Wherever they met, early church communities esteemed practicality and adaptability in their spaces, placing value more on those who gathered than on designated spaces. This raises questions for us today, including how we may recover a sense of the gathered community as "the church," and ministry as primarily what happens in the lives of people outside of designated buildings.

Chapter 2 ("Being True Siblings in a Divided World") points out how prevalent divisions are in society today and in some people's experiences of church. In view of this, some specific church communities (Corinth, Rome) inform our thinking, particularly by how broadly they included people from larger society and how strongly they emphasized a shared unity. Though conventional interpretations have characterized early house church communities as independent congregations, Paul emphasized a more fundamental, far-reaching unity than the idea suggests. In these early communities, we find men and women, slaves and freed people, children and the elderly, and many others. Amid this diversity, Paul's use of family language ("sisters and brothers") implies a unity that ran counter to conventions in society at large. This raises questions about how churches today carry on this vision of unity in Christ in a world increasingly divided.

Chapter 3 ("Being a Body in a Stratified Society") considers social dynamics around leadership in our church communities, with an eye to how the earliest communities approached these things. Early believers lived in a world rife with social divisions: patron-client relationships, patriarchal systems, and the price of public honor. How they dealt with these realities informs our own wrestling with social dynamics today. Conventional interpretations have held that early church communities were egalitarian, but that is a bit exaggerated. Rather than put past models on a pedestal, we must strive for just visions of unity and equality in Christ today. Leadership roles in early church communities were more contextualized than universal, making it difficult to pin down *the* biblical leadership model. Jesus and Paul simply emphasized leadership as service and stewardship—not roles of honor and prestige. How we implement these ideals today is a pressing matter, especially in view of ecclesial abuses of power.

Chapter 4 ("Practicing the Things That Matter") reflects on spiritual practices that most build up church communities, starting with what the earliest believers did. Detailed evidence for early Christian worship and service is sparse, but early witnesses imply believers gathered regularly for activities like sharing, teaching, prophesying, attending to the needs of others, eating together, rituals (baptism, the Lord's Supper), singing, and praying. From the outset, church communities engaged in their traditions with faithful adherence and innovation. This informs how church communities today may strive for unity in practice but also bless organic diversity. Among all the activities we may do, simply gathering together for what many today deem "unproductive" activities of worship (praying, listening, receiving God's gifts) are perhaps what matter most for nurturing depth in Christian spirituality.

Chapter 5 ("Bearing Distinctive Witness") reflects on how church communities are received and perceived by outsiders. Both today and in antiquity, church communities share traits with other social groups—a natural and not unwelcome thing. At the same time, there are real differences that distinguish churches from other groups. How do outsiders perceive the church? Whatever reactions there are, they are more polarized than neutral. We can learn from the ways early church communities in the Roman Empire responded to both widespread hostility and, in time, open acceptance. Their example shows us the significance of a persistent, distinctive witness in the face of a culture that reveres alternative lords. How we implement such a distinctive witness today gets after the heart of what it means to "let your light shine" as Jesus called us to.

The conclusion summarizes observations from the book and proposes that the church of the future will look increasingly like the church of the earliest centuries. In view of this, we ought to approach our questions about church and ministry today with a keen awareness of where we come from. While studies of surrounding society are important, a church lacking a clear sense of its core identity and purpose cannot live authentically into Christ's calling in the world today. While we look forward and around ourselves, as a church we must also regularly attend to our roots.

Bringing It Home: Ideas for Conversation and Implementation

1. Respond to the opening question of this introduction ("What comes to your mind when you think of

'church'?") by jotting notes, consulting Google images, or polling others. What do you find and learn?

2. Start a reading group to explore this book together, whether within or outside of your church community. Make notes of the conclusions and reflections as you come together for sharing with others.

3. Plan to read portions of Scripture alongside this book (see the Scripture study portions at the close of each chapter) for a deeper engagement throughout.

4. Ask yourself, "What are the most essential elements of church and what it means to be a church community?" Write down your responses. After reading and engaging this book, revisit your answers and reflect on how your thinking has changed, grown, or stayed the same.

Scripture Study

Read the Acts of the Apostles (New Testament), especially passages like 2:42–47; 4:23–27; 5:1–16; 6:1–7; 11:19–30; and 15:1–35. What do we learn about the early communities of faith?

For Worship

- Jay Beech, "The Church Song," *Rock Hymnal.*
- Samuel J. Stone, "The Church's One Foundation" (*Evangelical Lutheran Worship* [*ELW*] #654).

Questions for Reflection

1. How significant do you think the models and practices of early faith communities in the New Testament should be for Christian communities today? Why?
2. Do you think the church today has more or less in common with the earliest communities of Christ followers? Why?
3. If the Christian church were to go through major changes in the next few decades—*major* changes—what pieces do you hope would remain constant?
4. What do you hope to learn from this book and study of the earliest communities of faith in the New Testament?

Resources for Further Reading

Finger, Rita Halteman. *Roman House Churches for Today: A Practical Guide for Small Groups.* Rev. ed. Grand Rapids: Eerdmans, 2007. Using Paul's letter to the Romans, this book guides small groups in recreating the house churches of first-century Rome. The book's experiential approach allows participants to enter the story by playing various roles and debating with characters of different ethnic and religious backgrounds.

Meeks, Wayne A. *The First Urban Christians: The Social World of the Apostle Paul.* 2nd ed. New Haven: Yale University Press, 2003. First published in 1983. A classic among sociohistorical reconstructions of earliest Christianity, especially the churches of Paul. Meeks wrote the book in response to the many questions he heard from students about the basic history of earliest Christianity and how things played out in the earliest communities.

Thompson, James W. *The Church According to Paul: Rediscovering the Community Conformed to Christ.* Grand Rapids: Baker, 2014. Explores Paul's thinking about the church with an eye to both his letters and contemporary models for church ministry. More focused on theology and ecclesiology than historical reconstruction, the book's goal is not to describe the earliest communities and their experiences as much as what *Paul envisioned* the church's identity and mission were in the sight of God.

1

Sacred Spaces for a Church on the Way

All in all, it would seem that Paul made use of the household in every possible way for spreading the gospel and instructing believers.

—Mark Button and Fika J. Van Rensburg

For many people today, "church" means a building. People say things like "there's the church," or "we are going to church," or "the coffee shop is across from First Methodist Church." Many people even have clear assumptions about what *kind of building* a church is, making statements like "that building does not look like a church." And in all these references, "church" means a physical building or space.

This thinking is hardly unique to Christians. Most available dictionaries today give the same definition ("a building used for

Opening Questions:

1. What significance do physical spaces have for church gatherings?
2. What spaces or settings have hosted some of your most favorable experiences of Christian community or worship?
3. When you imagine an early church community gathering together, where do you picture this taking place?
4. Do you have positive or negative associations with the earliest gatherings? Why?

Christian worship") before listing any others. For further proof, just ask someone on the street, a child, or an acquaintance what "church" is. Chances are high that talk of buildings and spaces will lead off the response. And if these things are not persuasive, do an internet search for images associated with "church." You will be hard pressed to find an image within the first hundred that does *not* simply show a church building.

Maybe physical spaces are simply the most concrete way to define "church," making more abstract definitions (like church as a community) less appealing. Maybe we even *like* to think of church as something that takes place in certain sacred spaces—even if we do not like what that implies for all the other spaces we live in. In fact, maybe as human beings we have a strange fascination with marking certain buildings as "sacred," whether or not these designations truly reflect where we most often experience connection with the divine.

The Blessings and Burdens of Church Buildings and Spaces

For ministry leaders today, the widespread association of "church" with a building may not be a welcome one. For many church communities, it only encourages focus on *the building*—perhaps at the expense of focusing on other things (like the community). Building projects, for instance, have a way of attracting attention and resources in ways that outshine the energy given to most ongoing ministries. While it may be challenging to solicit interest and input for the average new ministry endeavor, getting the same feedback and energy behind a building project typically faces fewer obstacles. People often like projects that are tangible, concrete, and managed by a specific budget and timeline. And since most ministry work is not so easily bottled down to quantifiable data, many people gravitate toward things they can see, touch, build, and finish.

On the positive side, buildings dedicated exclusively to Christian worship and community have a profound opportunity: they can be tailored entirely to these purposes. For this reason, most church buildings turn core faith symbols into architectural centerpieces (baptismal fonts, crosses, a table, a washbasin, etc.). They also often integrate images in various ways (stained glass, wood panels, etchings) that tell stories of Scripture and faith without words—and in ways unrivaled by the spoken word. Historic cathedrals in Europe and elsewhere, for instance, continue to inspire people without any faith commitments at all. In fact, artistic practices such as these started as soon as early

Christians first had the chance to designate spaces and buildings for worship. In some of the earliest church structures (like at Dura-Europos) and gathering spaces (like the catacombs), there are frescoes, carvings, and etchings that portray biblical stories and Christian symbolism.

Church buildings can also be designed to address practical needs of the communities that use them. Worship spaces can be designed for specific numbers of people, oriented toward appropriate points of focus, and made to accommodate various abilities and ages. They can also create atmospheres that deliberately foster things such as reverence, joy, introspection, imagination, community, warmth, solemnity, prayer, contemplation, inspiration, or the like. As spaces entirely dedicated to Christian community and faith, church buildings can be tailor-made for the things Christians gather to do.

However, these same intentional designs can just as easily become burdens, especially for people who inherit them years later. In fact, many church communities in the Western world today find themselves in the situation of being financially tethered to a building originally designed for a community long ago. Historic buildings may offer distinctive charm and atmosphere, but they can also make for maintenance issues and inflexible designs that present major challenges for those now occupying them. For example, a congregation I once served occupies a building nearly two hundred years old, whose external walls are made of hand-chiseled rock. Simply getting property insurance for this antiquated handiwork is remarkably complicated—not to mention a challenge for insurance adjusters asked to evaluate its replacement value! For some church communities today, if an easy path to renovation, rebuilding, or relocation offered itself, it would be taken in a heartbeat.

Even church communities who love their current building face the obligation every homeowner knows very well: maintaining a building (or home) is a lot of work! From repairs to maintenance, from insurance to safety measures, from necessary updates to aesthetic enhancements, buildings require significant, ongoing investments just to be adequate, comfortable, and safe. Some ministry leaders enjoy this task of stewardship. Many others wish they could ignore it or somehow make it go away.

> As spaces entirely dedicated to Christian community and faith, church buildings can be tailor-made for the things Christians gather to do.

Still, amid their blessings and burdens, church buildings can be rich with spiritual significance. Buildings can create sacred space, and some do it remarkably well. The seminary where I teach, for instance, is modeled after the Wartburg castle in Eisenach, Germany. Even though its architecture goes directly against the grain of some modern architectural trends (e.g., allowing extensive natural light), the building still has an aura that many appreciate as distinctive, interesting, and somehow sacred. Distance students, visitors, and people without any connection to the seminary find this castle a spiritually enriching space. And precisely why is a question that defies simple answers.

Reevaluating Sacred Spaces

What makes a space "sacred" for church communities? Is it artistry and beauty or simplicity and openness? Is it the familiar and comfortable or the foreign and strange? Is it the way space allows for expansive imagination, or the way it embraces warmly? Is it the things that are distinctively Christian or things entirely mundane? Is it the way a space resembles a cathedral or the way it feels more like Starbucks? Ask someone you know what makes a space sacred. You may be surprised at what you hear.

Pastor Nadine Ellsworth-Moran shares her own experience of asking various people how they defined sacred space:

> Several noted that sacred space held a special memory or had a personal or corporate history attached to it that was remembered each time they entered that space. Some cited spaces that encouraged a willingness to be awed or to find beauty and imagination at work in their midst. Others recalled spaces that allowed for openness to God's presence—where one might even feel compelled to set a stone marker like the Hebrew tribes after crossing the Jordan and say, "God was here with us, right here at this spot." Yet others equated a profound sense of safety, belonging or peace with sacred space, which might be at the bedside of a dying loved one as much as in any church.[1]

This sampling of responses shows us something significant: space is less sacred in and of itself than we may assume. More often, spaces *become* sacred through *experiences we have* in them—experiences that foster connection with the divine.

For these and other reasons, many ministry leaders and church communities today are reevaluating what makes for sacred space, not so much for churchgoers but for *non*churchgoers. That is, what kinds of spaces might create holy ground for those entirely unfamiliar and unlikely to associate with church buildings?

Many church ministries today are experimenting with gatherings in tap rooms, coffeehouses, and restaurants. Other ministries are hosting gatherings in storefront offices, public buildings, and shopping centers—not just for financial reasons, but for the sake of public presence. Other ministries are experimenting with nontraditional church buildings, choosing instead to build multiuse facilities that lack Christian distinctives in order to share space with community partners. Still other ministries are choosing to use home spaces (vs. traditional church buildings) for both meetings and office space in hopes of being more efficient with time, money, and available spaces. Some deem these practices passing fads, reflective more of cultural trends than enduring mission investments. Others deem them signs of spiritual life and creativity, reflective of a new day of ministry that moves outside "the box" of traditional buildings.

Whether you are a ministry leader, church member, or merely a spiritual person, reevaluating sacred spaces—especially church building spaces—is relevant. How we evaluate sacred space is not merely something for church building and grounds committees. It directly impacts the priorities of church communities, the investments made by people of faith, the architectural footprints we leave behind, and the political policies we endorse regarding "holy lands" across the globe. What precisely constitutes "holy ground" for our time, place, and people?

Especially in societies of the Western world, many church communities find these kinds of questions pressing. Many church leaders today struggle with buildings that feel more like burdens than blessings, church communities more insulated from than engaged with their neighborhoods, and pervasive ideas that "church" is a place we go to instead of an identity we live out. The trends of the twenty-first century context are challenging church communities to recapture a vision of what it means to be a church in motion—or to use biblical language, a church "on the way." Such a vision means being a church open to adaptation, creativity, and innovation, especially in regard to physical spaces. The goal here is not newness for its own sake but to engage people's everyday lives more effectively.

> **Such a vision means being a church open to adaptation, creativity, and innovation, especially in regard to physical spaces.**

For church people today, questions and ideas regarding sacred spaces can benefit from looking at where church communities first began. Many people today seek the uses of space that are somehow biblical, historic, or theologically grounded. Given this, what do the earliest church communities of New Testament times show us about the importance of physical spaces?

Evidence from Paul's Letters: Gatherings in Homes

One summer when I was twenty-four years old, I paid a visit to ancient Corinth. Armed with a rucksack, a Bible, and a Eurail Pass, I was on a personal quest to visit places on the European continent where churches large and small have taken shape, hoping to learn a few things in the process.

Not only was Corinth a major city that hosted Paul for some time and on several occasions, it also hosted several other significant leaders mentioned in the Bible: Apollos, Priscilla and Aquila, Silas, and Timothy, to name a few. Even more, Corinth boasted a Christ-following community for whom Paul was deeply influential and with whom he had sustained ties. The church community received at least four of Paul's letters, including two major NT writings. Together these two writings make up over 10 percent of the New Testament. Even after Paul's time, this community endured and remained in correspondence with other Christian communities.

At the ruins of ancient Corinth, I realized something anew. At the city's museum, I gazed at an ancient synagogue inscription (figure 1.1). Although it dates a few hundred years after Paul, it once marked a spot along the Lechaion Road that may have been where Jews gathered as early as the first century. Pondering

Figure 1.1. Marble capital with Jewish menorahs (below), and above it a marble cornice with the inscription "[Syna]gogue of the Hebr[ews]." Photo by Doug and Rebekah McPherson. Used with permission.

this, I asked out loud, "So where did the early Christians meet?" And then I remembered: they had no such dedicated buildings. Not until centuries later would structures exclusively dedicated to Christian gatherings appear. Like ecologically minded hikers, they came and went without leaving an enduring physical trace.

This is one of many examples of how sparse hard data is regarding physical gathering spaces for the earliest Jesus followers. A great cloud of mystery enshrouds our knowledge of the places, spaces, and buildings they used. What we do know, however, comes from the New Testament—especially the letters attributed to Paul.

Several depictions in Paul's writings give a strong impression that the earliest church gatherings took place in homes. First among these are the references below.

- From Ephesus Paul writes to believers in Corinth that "Aquila and Prisca, along with the church-gathering in their home, send you abundant greetings in the Lord" (1 Cor 16:19).[2]

- From Corinth Paul extends greetings to Aquila and Prisca, who have evidently relocated to Rome: "Give greetings to Prisca and Aquila, my fellow workers in Christ Jesus . . . as well as the church-gathering in their home" (Rom 16:3, 5a).

- From prison Paul writes to his friend Philemon, along with Apphia, Archippus, and "the church-gathering in their home" (Phlm 2).

- The letter to the Colossians portrays Paul as extending greetings from prison to believers in nearby Laodicea, as well as Nympha and "the church-gathering in her home" (Col 4:15).

In all four cases, the same phrase appears: "the church-gathering in [lit. "according to"] their/your/her home" (*hē kat' oikon . . . ekklēsia*). Clearly these gatherings took place regularly under the roofs of private homes.

Paul likely did not start any of these home-based church gatherings. Prisca (Priscilla) and Aquila initiated the church-gathering in Rome without Paul, and they may well have done

---

Defining some terms

Septuagint: a Greek translation of the Hebrew Bible (or Old Testament) widely used among early Christians of the Mediterranean world, especially outside Judea. An ancient tradition credits the translation to seventy translators (*Septuagint* means "seventy"), but its origins are unknown.

Hebrew Bible: a religiously neutral designation for what Christians call the Old Testament.

---

the same in Ephesus. The letter of Colossians implies Paul never established any of the churches in Colossae or Laodicea—including those associated with Philemon and Nympha (Col 2:1). So the practice of home church-gatherings is not Paul's invention, but a practice that preceded his ministry. Whatever significance these home-based gatherings had, they were prominent enough to be mentioned explicitly in four letters attributed to Paul.

Two different Greek words for "home" or "house" appear in the New Testament: *oikia* and *oikos*. Classical Greek distinguished the two: one referred more often to wealth and possessions associated with a physical space (*oikos*), while the other referred more often to people (relatives and servants) associated with the same space (*oikia*). But the NT writings do not preserve this distinction clearly. They treat the words like virtual synonyms, just as the **Septuagint** (the Greek translation of the **Hebrew Bible**) uses both words interchangeably to translate the word *bēyt*, a Hebrew word that itself has many nuances.

All this language comes from the basic concept of a physical structure belonging to people who live there. Floor plans of large houses from the Roman Empire of Paul's day give a glimpse into what some wealthy people used as homes—like the House of the Vettii at Pompeii (figure 1.2) or the villa of Anaploga from ancient Corinth (figure 1.3). At the center stood a large atrium (courtyard) with an impluvium (small pool) at its center. Based on a survey of several wealthy homes from ancient Corinth, Pompeii, Olynthus, and Ephesus, Jerome Murphy-O'Connor estimates that an average atrium size was about 797 square feet (74 square meters).[3] Just off this space was the dining room (triclinium), about half the size of the atrium, where up to nine or so family members and guests could recline on couches around the wall to share in a meal together. For a large gathering, guests might overflow into the atrium area during the meal. Other rooms in the house—including those on an upper level—served as private rooms and offices for the head of the house (the *paterfamilias*), with other sections and rooms for family members and servants. Some houses used rooms along the street as shops, taverns, or lodgings for rent. Figure 1.4 gives a reconstruction of what the Villa at Anaploga may have looked like from the outside.

Of course, these homes belonged to wealthy families. Poorer homes were smaller and simpler. And roughly 85–90 percent of those living in the first-century Roman Empire were among the lower classes: peasants, farmers, slaves, household servants, artisans, and the like. These individuals more likely occupied rented apartments or smaller homes of less lavish materials, with several extended family members together under one roof.

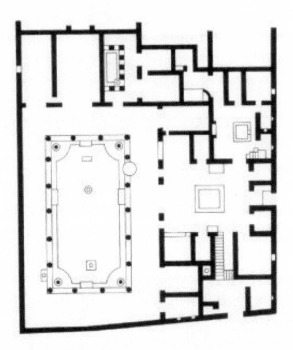

Figure 1.2. House of the Vettii at Pompeii (floor plan). The doorway is the opening in the wall on the right side, which enters into an atrium around the square shape. The large room in the bottom left is a garden area that took up nearly a third of the home's available space. Image by Michael Cole. Used with permission.

Cities in the Mediterranean world were also very crowded. In Rome, for example, it is estimated that about 3 percent of the population lived in one-third of the residential space. Plus, a fair share of urban land was dedicated to public areas, compressing residents all the more into limited housing. In cities like Rome, the population density was very high, perhaps even approaching ratios comparable to industrial slums in modern cities today.[4] The lion's share of city dwellers (the lower classes) lived in rented apartments (*insulae,* see figure 1.5). These apartments frequently were built on top of ground-level shops and factories, with just one or two rooms each and no kitchen or toilet facilities. Residents depended on public places for cooking, water, toilet needs, and places for socialization. Even so, the high cost of rent in urban areas compelled many renters to share these spaces, however small.

Paul's language regarding home church-gatherings does not specify a particular building size, whether large or small. Words like "home" or "house" (*oikos, oikia*) can refer to a large home

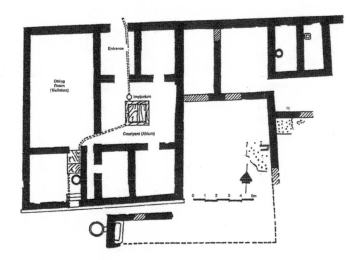

Figure 1.3. Layout of the Villa at Anaploga (outside Corinth), first century CE. From Jerome Murphy-O'Connor, *St. Paul's Corinth: Texts and Archaeology,* 3rd ed. (Collegeville, MN: Liturgical Press, 2002), 179. Used with permission.

(a *domus* or *villa),* an apartment (*insula*), or even a workshop dwelling (*taberna*)—and by extension to those who live in these quarters. In addition, most "households" in antiquity entailed far more than a nuclear family: parents, relatives, grown siblings, temporary residents, and various slaves and servants. Traditionally, the notion of "house churches" in the New Testament has been associated with large homes like the villas displayed in this chapter. But more recent research suggests some gatherings may also have taken place in smaller living quarters like tenement apartments.[5] In short, the language of "house" and "home" for

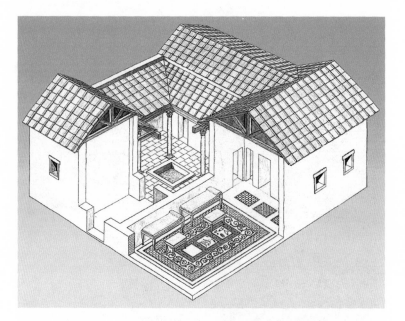

Figure 1.4. Visual reconstruction of the Villa at Anaploga in ancient Corinth based on archaeological evidence. Image copyrighted by Ritmeyer Archaeological Design. Used with permission.

Figure 1.5. *Insulae* (apartments) from Ostia (second century CE), the Domus di Giove e Ganimede (1.4.2). Wikimedia Commons.

early church gatherings is expansive, open to a wide variety of different building spaces.

Evidence from Acts: Home Is Where the Church Is

Paul's letters are not the only NT writings to portray early church gathering in homes. The narrative of Acts depicts similar practices of gathering in homes even more often, more regularly, and with more details for fleshing out how they may have taken shape:

- In Acts 1, Jesus's followers gather in a "room upstairs" (1:13) for prayer and discernment (1:12–26)—evidently the same space where they gathered with Jesus and where they presumably were at Pentecost (1:1–8; 2:1–4).[6]

- After the events of Pentecost, thousands of believers devote themselves to gathering daily in the temple precincts and to breaking bread "in homes" (*kat' oikon*) (Acts 2:46).

- Later the apostles teach and proclaim Jesus as the Messiah "every day in the temple vicinity and at home (*kat' oikon*)" (5:42).

- At Cornelius's house in Caesarea, Peter joins with non-Jewish believers for several days in sharing the message, experiencing the Spirit, and enacting baptisms (10:24–48).

- In Jerusalem, Mary the mother of John (Mark) hosts "many" at her home for prayer for Peter's safety. At his release, Peter goes to her home, implying it was a place of regular gathering for believers (12:12–17).

- After hearing Paul's message, Lydia invites him and his colleagues to stay at her home (16:13–16). After release from prison, Paul and Silas return there to "encourage the believers"—implying an assembly to whom Paul preached (16:39–40; see also 16:25–34).[7]

- In Corinth, after opposition mounts at the synagogue, Paul makes the house of Titius Justus a new base of operations for ministry (18:5–8).

- In Troas, on a Sunday gathering for breaking bread together, Paul holds discussion with believers in "a room upstairs" (20:8). That Eutychus falls from "the third story" implies the room is a tenement flat in an apartment block.

- In Ephesus Paul summarizes his ministry pattern in Acts as proclaiming and teaching "publicly and from house to house" (*kat' oikous*) (20:20).

- In Caesarea, while staying at the house of Philip the evangelist, Paul receives a prophecy from Agabus while gathered with other company—presumably at Philip's home (21:8–14).

- At the end of Acts, Paul lives "two whole years in his own hired house," where he welcomes all (28:30–31). Just beforehand he welcomes Jewish leaders to his lodging for extensive dialogue (28:21–28). In these ways, Acts concludes with a portrait of ministry taking place in the context of a home.

In these passages, the narrative places clear and repeated emphasis on homes as meeting places for church gatherings.

In addition, people hostile to the believers in Acts pursue them in home settings: Saul enters "house after house" (*kata tous oikous*) to haul off "both men and women" (8:3), and a mob in Thessalonica seeks out Paul and Silas at Jason's house (17:5–9). Given the precedent of home assemblies throughout Acts, these two cases imply the persecutors were targeting spaces potentially used for church gatherings. Finally, a few other homes mentioned in Acts may also have served as spaces for church gatherings, although Luke's narrative does not say so specifically: the house of Judas in Damascus (9:11–17), the house of Simon the Tanner in Caesarea (9:43), the house of Aquila and Priscilla in Corinth (18:2–3), the house of Crispus in Corinth (18:8), and the house of Mnason in Jerusalem (21:16).[8]

> "[Paul] remained for two whole years in his own hired house and was welcoming all those coming unto him, proclaiming the kingdom of God and teaching the things concerning the Lord Jesus Christ with every boldness of speech, in an unhindered manner." (Acts 28:30–31)

Altogether, Acts paints a picture of homes regularly serving as spaces for church gatherings, breaking bread together, proclaiming and encouraging, entertaining prophecy, and simply being together. The combined evidence is so pronounced that even Edward Adams—a critic of the conventional idea the earliest church gatherings predominately took place in homes—admits, "The book of Acts offers the clearest and fullest New Testament documentation of the use of houses as Christian meeting places."[9]

Evidence from the Gospels: Homes as Ministry Starting Points

Besides Paul's letters and Acts, the four Gospels also suggest the significance of homes for early believers.

First, the Gospels portray Jesus regularly teaching, gathering, and holding discourse in home settings. For example, in

Mark alone—the earliest of the NT Gospels—some of Jesus's most significant teachings and healings take place in homes:

- At Simon and Andrew's home, Jesus heals Simon's mother-in-law and many others, and casts out many demons (1:29–34).
- At a home in Capernaum, Jesus heals a paralyzed man lowered through the roof (2:1–11).
- At Levi's home, Jesus tells the scribes and Pharisees why he eats with "tax collectors and sinners" (2:15–17).
- At a home in Capernaum, Jesus teaches on Beelzebul and his true kindred (3:19b–35).
- At Jairus's home, Jesus raises a girl from the dead (5:40–43).
- On several occasions, Jesus uses the private setting of a home to instruct his disciples further (7:17–23; 9:28–39; see also 4:10–20).
- At a home in Tyre, Jesus heals a Syro-Phoenician's sick daughter (7:24–30).
- At a home in Capernaum, Jesus teaches on true greatness (9:33–37).
- At a home in a Judean region beyond the Jordan, Jesus instructs disciples about divorce (10:10–12).
- At Simon the Leper's home in Bethany, Jesus is anointed, anticipating his burial (14:3–9).
- In the guest room of a house in Jerusalem, Jesus celebrates the Passover—and institutes the Lord's Supper—over a meal with disciples (14:13–31).

The three other Gospels (Matthew, Luke, John) show Jesus acting similarly in home settings. In some cases, they are stories borrowed from Mark's account (named already above). But in other cases, the Gospels of Luke and John include new, original stories taking place in homes.[10]

All these occasions show Jesus performing some of his most significant miracles and issuing some of his most important teachings to disciples and crowds in the contexts of homes. Since the NT Gospels came into their final forms at least a decade after Paul's undisputed letters, some scholars believe the physical settings (of homes) in these stories may be later enhancements more than authentic history. But the regularity, abundance, and prevalence of references to home settings associated with Jesus's ministry in the Gospels—especially in Mark's Gospel—are not likely all later enhancements. Various economic and social realities surrounding Jewish teachers and synagogues in first-century Galilee make it not only possible and reasonable but *very likely* that major events of Jesus's ministry historically took place in homes.[11]

Even more, the Gospels portray Jesus's disciples as sent out for itinerant ministries that used homes as strategic outposts. According to Mark, Matthew, and Luke, Jesus sent out his followers with authority to proclaim, heal, and cast out evil spirits (Mark 6:6b–13; Matt 10:5–15; Luke 9:1–6; cf. 10:1–12). He also gave some logistics regarding their travel accommodations: "He ordered them to take nothing for the journey except a staff—no bread, no bag, no money in their belts—and to wear sandals but not two tunics. And he said to them, 'Wherever you enter into a house, remain there until you leave from there'" (Mark 6:8–10; see also Matt 10:8, 10b; cf. Luke 10:7–8).

Luke's Gospel includes an additional warning from Jesus, issued to a larger group (seventy) of apostles: they should not "move about from house to house" but instead "remain in the same house, eating and drinking whatever is provided" (10:7). These words imply that early itinerant ministers typically sought out fixed quarters in specific locales; they did not relocate quickly and at random. In short, the apostles were less like overnight street preachers than we may imagine. They likely stayed in communities for sustained time periods, ministering from the contexts of households, extended families, and newly formed relationships. Although the Gospels give no time frames for these stays, the very ethos of many first-century village communities lends itself to the idea that these apostles worked as much as possible from the starting point of fostering lasting relationships, especially for the sake of establishing enduring communities.

Jesus's words about being provided food means more than just sustenance. It means formative table fellowship with hosts. By first-century Jewish cultural standards, eating and drinking together meant welcome and acceptance: it was a sign of authentic bonds between host and guest, and a relationship with lasting significance. Whether a home received these messengers was no light matter: it indicated whether it was worthy of their peace and their Lord, or worse than Sodom and Gomorrah (Matt 10:11–15, 40–42; Luke 10:5–6). The homes that offered hospitality and provision likely became, in Roger Gehring's words, "a starting point, a kind of headquarters, a center and base of operations for the following stage of the mission, reaching the entire town."[12] Patterned after Jesus's ministry, his followers traveled from village to village—and house to house—calling new communities of believers into existence and fostering their well-being as they traveled.

The lion's share of tradition from the Gospels implies homes were vital hubs for teaching, proclaiming, table fellowship, healings, worship, prayer, newfound connections, and spreading the Jesus movement. The Gospels never use the language of "house churches"—and very rarely the language of "church." But regular glimpses from Jesus's earthly ministry collectively paint a picture of homes playing a central role for the earliest gatherings of Jesus followers. Both during Jesus's ministry and in later decades, homes are where most early communities gathered into newly formed associations, based not on family ties but on a shared devotion (Mark 3:31–35).

For Reflection: Homes and Ministry Today

What role do homes play for our ministries and church communities today? As many as ten million Americans—and far more around the globe—are part of church communities based primarily out of homes.[13] Further, many church communities with dedicated facilities use home spaces extensively for gatherings—not just occasional meetings but small groups, regular Bible studies, prayer gatherings, worship, and shared meals. Some ministries even use homes for office spaces, not just out of financial necessity, but as a preferred practice. A friend of mine serves as pastoral staff for a church community that does this. Family-work boundaries can be messy, and quiet space alone is at a premium (he has five kids). But he finds the practice makes meetings more intentional and gatherings more deliberate and relationship-focused. Building on the legacy of home gatherings among New Testament church communities, how might church communities today make use of home spaces in ways that enhance, complement, and build up our ministries?

The question is not limited to church programs and functions. Recent research on youth and family faith formation continues to show faith activities that happen at home are far more influential than most of what happens "at church" (i.e., at a church building). At home people may experience fundamental influences on their notions of identity, self-respect, relationships, conflict resolution, vulnerability, affirmation, ethics, theology, and faith. Any faith practices that are not somehow integrated into home life are not likely to endure long. So not only might we ask how church communities may *make use of* home spaces, we might also ask, How are the faith practices of church communities *integrated* into the daily rituals that take place in our homes?

> Any faith practices that are not somehow integrated into home life are not likely to endure long.

Dedicated church buildings offer distinctive assets for fostering faith. But they also run the risk of leading people to believe that faith formation is best "outsourced" to other spaces—and other people. While most Christian parents today hope for meaningful faith formation for their children, the majority neither initiates nor facilitates formative faith conversations at home. Instead, they hope "the church" will take the lead. Not only does this model fall flat in actual practice, it is basically unbiblical. The earliest church communities were fundamentally a home-based movement. Even before their time, the people of Israel saw faith instruction as something that primarily took place at home (Deut 6:1–9). How we, as church people and communities today, recapture this vision is our question to wrestle with.

Revisiting the Conventional Idea: Were Homes the Only Meeting Places?

In view of the NT evidence named above, the conventional idea is that early Christians met in private homes. As Roger Gehring describes it:

> On one point nearly all NT scholars presently agree: early Christians met almost exclusively in the homes of individual members of the congregation. For nearly three hundred years—until the fourth century, when Constantine began building the first basilicas throughout the Roman Empire—Christians gathered in private houses built initially for domestic use, not in church buildings originally constructed for the sole purpose of public worship.[14]

The earliest believers had no buildings exclusively devoted to worship, and certainly they made use of private homes for gathering. But that alone is not the whole story.

In the New Testament, hard evidence for alternative gathering spaces is sparse. But there are clear insinuations. In Acts, the apostles preach and teach in a variety of public spaces: the temple vicinity in Jerusalem (3:1–4:3), synagogues throughout the Mediterranean (9:20; 13:5, 14–43; 17:1–3, 10, 17; 18:4, 19; 19:8), city gates (14:13–18), riversides (16:13), marketplaces (17:17), spaces for court hearings (17:22–31), and lecture halls (19:9–10).[15] Further, throughout the early chapters of Acts, early believers in Jerusalem devote themselves to gathering not only in homes but also in the temple area (2:46; 5:12, 42). In fact, at various points the narrative emphasizes that believers gathered in *both* public arenas as well as private homes (2:46; 5:42; 20:20). According to Acts, early gatherings of believers in Philippi started at a "place of prayer" along a riverside (16:13, 16).[16] Finally, Paul's ministry in Ephesus—his longest stint of ministry in the narrative (two years)—is based primarily out of the "lecture hall" (*scholē*) of Tyrannus, a building that was probably a guild center or even a site for philosophical instruction (19:9–10).

What these gatherings in public spaces may have looked like is not clear. Did they merely entail public teaching, or were they used equally for mutual encouragement of one another in gathered communities? Did they entail sacred rituals or not? The narrative leaves unspecified precisely what took place in these spaces. Also unclear is the extent to which Acts reflects authentic history on this point, since the narrative appears to have interest in portraying the ministry of the apostles as a public force. Still, it is unlikely that Acts exaggerates entirely in its portrayal of gatherings in public arenas and spaces alongside those in private homes.

The NT Gospels also speak to these questions. All four Gospel accounts portray important events of Jesus's ministry taking place not just in homes but also in synagogues, in the temple vicinity, and in various outside spaces: the Sea of Galilee, the Jordan River, the Mount of Olives, deserted places, and the like. In Mark's Gospel alone, for example, significant events take place in synagogues (1:21–29; 3:1–6; 6:1–2), in the temple vicinity (11:15–19; 11:27–13:1; 13:3; 14:49), on the seashore (2:13–14; 3:9–12; 4:1; 5:1–20), on water (1:16–20; 4:35–41; 8:13–21), at rivers (1:9–11), in fields (2:23–28), on mountains (3:13–19a; 9:9; 13:3), while traveling (8:27; 9:33; 10:32), and in deserted places (1:12–13; 6:32–45; 8:1–10). Although these events are not "church gatherings," they set a precedent within the larger Jesus movement for gathering, teaching, and sacred rituals in outdoor settings. These traditions and their potential influence on the later gatherings of Jesus followers insinuate some real possibilities. Amid the scarcity of historical data regarding where they gathered, the patterns of Jesus's ministry—as recorded in the Gospels—invite imagination about assembly spaces less likely to leave archaeological footprints.

Edward Adams points out, "While there is indeed good evidence for houses as Christian meeting places in the first two centuries, it is not as extensive or exclusive as usually thought." [17] Jewish synagogue communities and voluntary associations

Figure 1.6. River outside the city of Ancient Philippi near the traditional site of Lydia's baptism (author's photo).

in the Roman Empire—groups comparable to early church communities—were prone to use diverse settings for gathering spaces: temples, marketplaces, watersides, rented halls, clubhouses, inns, and restaurants. Jewish gatherings especially used waterside areas for prayer and special occasions. In fact, like early Christian gatherings, Jewish synagogues were once believed to have started in homes—though this theory has more recently come into question.[18]

As for early Christians, certainly in later decades and centuries they used waterside areas for baptisms and burial sites for gathering spaces.[19] It is also possible they used gardens, urban spaces, retail shops, industrial warehouses, and public leisure spaces (bathhouses, rented dining rooms). Although there is no clear evidence that early church communities gathered regularly in such spaces, their availability and size capacity make it likely they were used at least on occasion. Though homes likely served as primary gathering spaces for many early church communities, alternative spaces and public areas were likely also used at various times, by various assemblies, and for various purposes.[20]

For Reflection: The Church in Public Spaces Today

In what ways do our church communities today have presence in public arenas and spaces? Very often in American society, church communities exist in towns and cities without any real awareness on the part of their neighbors. As part of a seminary class, I was once assigned to interview local neighbors of my church community (within a few blocks) and to ask them what they knew about the church. Their answers were shocking. Most neighbors had no significant knowledge of or past interactions with the church. A few did not even realize it existed! Their overwhelming impression was that our church community, whatever it did, largely kept its activities and voice restricted to behind the walls of the building.

My church community's lack of influence among its neighbors is not an isolated experience. Right or wrong, outsiders' impressions of most churches are far more like secretive societies than communities actively engaged with their surrounding neighborhoods. Some of this depends on how deliberate a church community is about engaging local and global issues of justice. But another part is due simply to the spaces we inhabit. As communities that largely worship in church buildings, we are regularly separated from our surroundings by walls. Although this is constructive for community formation, it is terrible for public witness.

For these reasons, some church communities intentionally choose to hold worship services and other events in storefront buildings, rented civic spaces, and outside spaces. Other church communities share space with local organizations, groups, and gatherings, whether by official partnerships or by more informal practices of space stewardship. Although these routes have their challenges, church communities that choose them find many unanticipated in-roads to people they otherwise might never engage. And right or wrong, outsiders often regard these churches more favorably as groups tangibly invested in their local communities.

What if our church communities made an effort to enter more deliberately into public spaces, physically and otherwise? What keeps our church communities from doing this now? The narrative of Acts portrays early believers and apostles proclaiming and gathering in public areas as well as in homes. How might our own church communities foster this kind of public presence and witness today in our own local contexts?

From Sojourners to Settlers:
The Move to Church Buildings

In a few centuries' time, homes and public areas would not continue to be the prevailing spaces for gatherings of believers. As early church communities grew into greater numbers, more economic resources, more developed leadership stability, and received imperial sanctioning, they entered possibilities for building and owning dedicated spaces and structures.

What if our church communities made an effort to enter more deliberately into public spaces, physically and otherwise?

The earliest known instance of a Christian building is at Dura-Europos (figures 1.7–9). Originally a private house built around 232 CE, the building was renovated and dedicated sometime before 256 CE as a Christian gathering and worship space, complete with a baptistery, biblical frescoes, and an assembly hall that may have accommodated as many as seventy-five people.[21] In fact, the way this renovation transformed a domestic space into a church building reflects the larger historic progression from homes to professional buildings. Church communities in time followed this pattern, increasingly shifting from homes over to designated buildings for gathering and worship.

Archaeological evidence attests to about twenty other dedicated Christian buildings that originated in the third and fourth centuries throughout the Mediterranean.[22] Not coincidentally, that same time period saw the end of imperial persecution of Christianity (the Edict of Milan, 313 CE) and its embrace by Emperor Constantine. In that new age of imperial acceptance and endorsement, church buildings appeared that were more elaborate, expansive, and stately than any Jesus followers had known before. And with these changes came distinctive blessings and challenges for emerging Christianity: holy sites became prime real estate, imperial protocol influenced worship

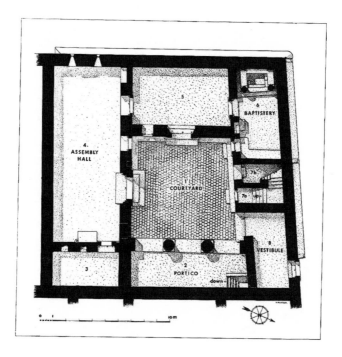

Figure 1.7. Reconstructed Plan of the Christian Building at Dura-Europos, the earliest example of a house later dedicated to Christian gathering space. Public domain, made available by the Yale University Art Gallery.

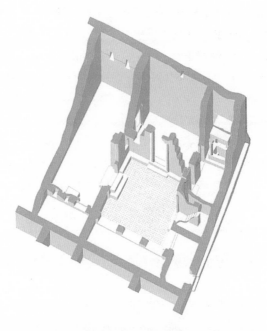

Figure 1.8. Isometric reconstruction of the Christian building at Dura-Europos (ca. 245 CE). Public Doman, Wikimedia, based on Carl H. Kraeling, *The Christian Building (Excavations at Dura-Europos. Final Report 8.2)* (New Haven: Dura-Europos, 1967).

practices (incense, garments, etc.), and sacramental rituals suddenly had to accommodate large numbers of people. Inevitably, the intimacy and active participation of gathered believers in worship diminished. Christianity effectively exited their homes and catacombs and entered en masse into cathedrals. These changes brought security, safety, and stability to a once-persecuted group of sojourners. But this also changed how they gathered as they transitioned to settlers who owned and maintained property.

Figure 1.9. Dura-Europos Church, public domain, Wikimedia Commons.

For Reflection: How Spaces Shape Us

As church communities, how do the spaces we inhabit influence what we do, how we practice faith, and the kind of people we are? All buildings and spaces have auras. All architectural designs send messages. Even seating arrangements say things. What messages do our worship and gathering spaces send—whether we realize these things or not?

A church community I know once began in space rented from a school. After growing sufficiently and raising funds, they built their own building and moved out. What they did not expect was how the move shifted their sense of identity. When in the school, they maintained a strong focus on worship, education, and congregational participation. When they moved into their own space, things shifted. Although worship thrived, education dwindled because they had no dedicated space for it. Congregational participation also lessened; gone was the need of weekly setup and teardown. But at the same time many new people from the neighborhood joined. Not all these changes were bad. But clearly, the move shifted how the community saw itself.

Our spaces and buildings influence how we perceive God, our faith, our leaders, and each other in a community. They also influence the spiritual practices we emphasize, the opportunities we can embrace, and the ways in which we engage our surrounding world. The spaces we inhabit as gathered church communities are neither bad nor good in and of themselves. But they are profoundly influential to who we are.

Meaningful Metaphor: The Church as Household

Many twenty-first-century people hear the word *church* and think of a building. But as this chapter has shown, the notion of "church" for early believers was more associated with *homes* than any other space.

Most Christians today have positive associations with the idea that earliest Christianity started largely in homes. To the modern mindset, it characterizes the earliest stages of the Jesus movement as humble, organic, and truly "homegrown." Many Christians today also believe church-gatherings were at their best at this early stage: community oriented, genuine, and lacking the hierarchy, bureaucracy, and rules of later centuries. As chapter 3 later discusses, this line of thinking often idealizes the social dynamics of early church communities a bit too much. Regardless, many church groups and individuals today regard house church Christianity as the only model that truly reflects the spiritual roots and vitality of the earliest Jesus movement.[23]

Attractive as some things may be about home gatherings, the model is no guarantee of authentic, Spirit-led community. No model is immune to harmful social dynamics such as manipulation, divisiveness, inappropriate conduct, and unchecked egos. More important than specific models are the mindset and ethos of early Jesus followers, who envisioned participants as members of an extended household.

On the one hand, the locations of early gatherings probably depended heavily on contextual circumstances. Some church communities may have had more access to public spaces than others. Some communities had more willing hosts with available homes. And some periods of time in the Roman Empire were safer for Jesus followers to use public spaces than others. A variety of factors likely determined the spaces most often used, including availability, size, adequacy, safety, and flexibility, to name a few.

On the other hand, early believers probably used homes not purely out of necessity but because of their desirability. Private homes not only offered availability, privacy, and resources for food preparation. They were also tailored well to reorienting people to a new vision of community centered around the concept of family. For many early church communities, houses and homes were not simply gathering spaces; the ideals of "home" came to characterize much of the ethos of early Christian community according to the New Testament.

In Paul's letters alone, for example, the frequency of family and household language for church communities is striking.

- His most common designation for believers is "brothers and sisters" (*adelphoi*).

- He portrays himself as a father to the communities he started and to individuals he mentored (1 Thess 2:11; 1 Cor 4:14–15; Phil 2:22; Phlm 10).

- He depicts himself to church communities as a nursing mother (1 Thess 2:7) and a mother in childbirth (Gal 4:19).

- When Paul describes his care and nurture of church communities, he uses language derived from the idea of a home or household (*oikos*).

- He characterizes the work of nurturing faith communities as "building up" (*oikodomeō, oikodomē*) the church (1 Thess 5:11; 1 Cor 8:1, 10; 10:23; 14:3–5, 12, 17, 26; 2 Cor 10:8; 12:19; 13:10; Rom 14:19; 15:2; 15:20; see also Eph 2:21; 4:12, 16, 29).

- He calls himself a wise "architect" (*architektōn*) of the church (1 Cor 3:10).

- He calls apostles "household stewards" (*oikonomoi*) of God's mysteries (1 Cor 3:10; 4:1–2).

- He identifies believers as "members of the household" (*oikeioi*) of faith (Gal 6:10).

All these word choices reflect an overarching metaphor for the church: that of a household, with its founders as builders and its community members as family. In short, Paul clearly envisioned the communities he served as members of a household or family. But it is not just Paul. Nearly every writing of the New Testament uses the language of brothers and sisters to refer to members of their communities.[24] Hebrews even describes the exalted Jesus as a "brother" to believers, further emphasizing their shared connections as that of a family ("he is not ashamed to call them brothers and sisters," 2:11). In the same way, references to God as "Father" abound across the New Testament, with Jesus being the most significant proponent of its use. In John's Gospel alone, Jesus calls God "Father" well over one hundred times.[25] In the first-century Mediterranean world, households normally operated under the authority of a father or designated male, so emphasizing God as "Father" and believers as "children" was a natural outgrowth of the familial vision of early Christianity.

Further, several NT passages make use of the household metaphor as they issue ethical charges to designated groups, patterned after household codes familiar to first-century readers.[26] Even more, several NT voices unite in characterizing the church as the family or household of God (all italics are my own):

- "So then you are no longer foreigners and aliens, but you are citizens with the saints and *members of the household of God*, built upon the foundation of the apostles and prophets, with Christ Jesus himself as the cornerstone" (Eph 2:19–20).
- "If I delay, you may know how to live within *the household of God*, which is the church of the living God, the pillar and mainstay of the truth" (1 Tim 3:15).

- "But Christ was a Son over [God's] house; *and we are this house*, if we hold firm the boldness and confidence characteristic of hope" (Heb 3:6; see also 10:21; 1 Pet 4:17).

A number of NT passages describe this "household" as being "built up" (*oikodomeō*)—using architectural language—by God's power, the message of God's grace, or Christ himself (Acts 20:32; Matt 16:18; 1 Pet 2:5). In all these instances, the work of nurturing the faith community leads to its formation into a "spiritual house," a "holy temple," a "dwelling place for God," or the "temple of God" (Eph 2:21–22; 1 Pet 2:5; 1 Cor 3:16–17). These passages do not speak of actual buildings or biological families but church communities. And they give participants in church communities a sacred significance: they are God's own famly.

> "So then you are no longer foreigners and aliens, but you are citizens with the saints and members of the household of God, built upon the foundation of the apostles and prophets, with Christ Jesus himself as the cornerstone" (Eph 2:19–20).

As these references show, family and household language was not a matter of mere words for the early church communities. Nor was it a metaphor borrowed from culture or tradition without critical reflection. The vision of church community as the family or household of God permeates the NT writings, reflecting one of the earliest ways communities of Jesus followers defined themselves. Like ideals of families and households in the first-century Mediterranean world, the earliest believers valued church communities as groups marked by intimacy, binding ties, community sharing, and mutual love and affection. Although not the only metaphor, the notion of Christian community as a family prevails across the New Testament writings.

Whether or not a church community today ever gathers in home settings, the metaphor of a household or family is still instructive. It conveys core NT values for community in Christ. For the earliest believers, their community was a "family of faith" (Gal 6:10 NRSV). And although there are real differences between first-century and twenty-first-century notions of family, the commonalities of kinship, commitment, and love give the metaphor enduring value.

The question is rightly posed to church communities today: Do we actively embody the legacy of being God's "family" in meaningful ways in our own respective contexts?

Conclusion: Being a Church on the Way

The church is not a building. The thought of church as a building never even occurred to early believers until centuries after Jesus's ministry. According to the earliest sources and our best historical reconstructions, the earliest church gatherings often took place in homes, both large and small. They may well have taken place in other locations as well: public spaces, rented halls, temples, and outdoor areas. But the lion's share of the evidence implies that domestic spaces proved to be the most regular, reliable, and available sites for early believers across the Mediterranean world. In view of this, early Christ-following communities quickly adopted the metaphor of being the "household" of God, with individual believers as sisters and brothers to one another.

> Early Christ-following communities quickly adopted the metaphor of being the "household" of God.

Despite the way modern Christians frequently associate "church" language with buildings, the New Testament authors understand "church" less as a noun and more as a verb. "Church" was less a stationary object than it was a gathering of community—wherever it happened, no matter the spaces. Where believers in Jesus the Messiah gathered together in Jesus's name, "church" happened in the most authentic sense.

If a single word best characterizes the earliest church communities' relationship to physical spaces, it is *adaptable*. These believers used various spaces that were available and serviceable, without binding themselves to any specific space as necessary. Nowhere among early Christian voices are particular spaces deemed essential for church gatherings to happen. In all honesty, surviving references and allusions to early gathering spaces are frustratingly vague and unspecific—proving all the more that the physical spaces they used simply did not matter that much. For the earliest followers of Jesus, physical spaces were evidently nothing more than a means to a greater end: gathering together as the community of Christ followers.

Adaptable is not a word that many people today readily associate with churches and their relationships to physical spaces, at least in many parts of the Western world. Many church communities today are better characterized by words like "maintenance," "preservationist," or perhaps even "inflexible." Some of this may stem from the ethos of a particular community, but often it is at least partially influenced by that community's relationship to a building. Building spaces entail both great assets and great responsibilities. But at the end of the day, physical spaces tend to "ground" church communities in ways that can both enhance ministry and drain energies, can both plant people in community and segregate people from it, and can both set apart space for worship and separate worship from people's daily lives.

At the conclusion to his book *The House Church in the Writings of Paul*, Vincent Branick points out a widespread tendency among human beings: "Something in the human heart calls for sacred space. We want to point to a spot as the place of God's presence, just as the Israelites could point to their Holy of Holies as the place of God's glory. We want a place where we can shift religious gears and somehow put behind us the perception of divine absence."[27] Yet, aside from occasional use of the temple in Jerusalem—a site of regular conflict for Jesus according to the Gospels—the earliest Jesus-following communities largely took shape without dedicated sacred spaces. In this environment, they emphasized not physical buildings but the community itself as holy and sacred. They rebranded their community as God's holy temple and their daily lives as living acts of worship (1 Cor 3:16–17; Rom 12:1–2). And by most historical evaluations, they thrived.

This chapter reminds us today that church communities have not always been so wedded to sacred spaces—and the ways of doing "church" associated with them. The earliest Jesus followers distinguished their identities more clearly from the physical spaces they inhabited. They fostered an identity that placed greater value on mobility and transferability, preferring self-designations like "the Way" (or "the Journey"), "aliens and exiles," and a people with "no lasting city" (Acts 9:2; 18:25; 19:9, 23; 22:4; 24:14, 22; 1 Pet 2:11; Heb 13:14). This undoubtedly assisted the spread of the movement across geography and cultural boundaries. Even more, communities of Jesus followers saw *themselves* more readily as God's sacred "space," wherever they happened to gather.

Based on current trends in the twenty-first century, many church communities in the Western world will increasingly need to recapture a vision of being a church "on the way" that is adaptable to new circumstances, open to new ways of using physical structures, and seeking to be relevant to people's everyday faith in daily life. One piece of this is reevaluating the building spaces owned and used by church communities. They must ask, Does our faith community's building space serve largely to foster its God-given mission? Or does our mission exist largely to serve and take care of the building?

But recapturing a vision of mobility and adaptability entails more than simply evaluating physical spaces. It entails a shift of a cultural mindset from one of stability, tradition, and preservation to one of creativity, mobility, and imagination. It entails recapturing a vision of what it means to be a sojourning people whose treasure is found ultimately not in institutional legacies but in lasting change on spiritual and ethical planes. It entails a shift from seeing church as a building to striving to *be* the church where it is most needed in the world. In a context where church resources are rapidly changing (if not diminishing), these matters do not raise questions about buildings per se as much as they raise questions about *faithfulness*. How might church communities adapt appropriately so as to address and engage the world around them most faithfully?

Whatever relationship church communities have to physical spaces, at their best, physical spaces enhance opportunities to hear and respond to the call of the Holy Spirit and the needs of the world around them. Physical spaces do not define a church community. At their best, they assist a community in discerning and fully living out a calling to be God's "household" for isolated wayfarers still struggling to find the way.

Bring It Home: Ideas and Conversations for Implementation

1. Engage a small group of leaders within your church community about some of the ideas raised by this chapter. Consider together some of the reflection questions named below, either as a group or with other participants and leaders in the community.

2. Move a regular church activity (worship, faith formation events, staff meetings, leadership gatherings) to an alternative space—whether off-site or closer to home

base. Invite reflections on the experience as a source of learning.

3. Get access to a church budget and pay attention to how much of the community's funds go toward caring for its building space. Compare that with funds dedicated toward children's faith formation or youth ministry or adult faith formation. What do you learn?

4. Develop worship materials that could be used by families at home on weekdays and alternative times. Invest in creative ways that elements of gathered worship (confession and forgiveness, sharing the peace, singing) could be used and implemented in homes.

5. Invite outsiders to tour your church community's building (if it owns one). Ask for their impressions, reactions, likes (and dislikes), and suggestions for hospitality toward visitors.

6. Start a Bible study around selected Scripture passages from Acts, Mark's Gospel, or others named in the "Scripture Study" portion below. Meet in a home or public space (not a church building) if possible.

Scripture Study

- The Acts of the Apostles (selected portions). Consider giving special attention to passages that feature the growth and spread of early church communities (Acts 2:41–47; 8:1–25, 26–40; 10:1–11:18; 16:6–40; 28:16–31), or ways the narrative calls the early community "the Way" (9:2; 18:25; 19:9, 23; 22:4; 24:14, 22).

■ Mark 1–8. Consider paying close attention to how many events of Jesus's ministry take place in homes and how that might have shaped the earliest followers of Jesus during his earthly ministry.

■ Study Ephesians 2:19–20 and other NT passages that use the metaphor of the church community as God's "household" (1 Tim 3:15; Heb 3:6; 10:21; 1 Pet 4:17).

For Worship

■ Marty Haugen, "All Are Welcome" (*ELW* #641).

Questions for Reflection

1. How has this chapter changed or challenged your imagination of where the earliest church communities gathered?

2. Physical spaces matter for church communities and groups of all kinds. How do you think physical space and location influence the ethos of a Christ-following community—in both the first century and today—in good ways and bad ways?

3. Homes certainly played a vital role for many of the earliest Christ-following community gatherings. And yet, for many today the language of "church" implies a sacred

building very different from "home." Where and how might the faith fostered by church communities better take root in everyday home life of individual believers? Where might overlap between "church" and "home" best happen today?

4. If you associate with a church community, what significance does your meeting space have? Do your building spaces serve your God-given mission, or is your mission largely oriented around your building spaces?

5. What if the building space your church community inhabits were to burn down overnight? What would change?

6. In an ideal world, what would characterize a church community's relationship to physical meeting spaces? Think big. What do we learn from this?

7. Where do you see church communities and their activities today most characterized by adaptability, responsiveness to community needs, and creative imagination?

Online Resources for Further Exploration

- AncientVine, "Virtual Roman House," https://tinyurl .com/hhmg3t3. A virtual tour of an ancient Roman house.
- Jeffrey A. Becker, "Roman Domestic Architecture" (on the Roman Domus, Insula, and Vila), Khan Academy, https://tinyurl.com/q5jvpon.

- Ian Lockey, "Roman Housing," in *Heilbrunn Timeline of Art History* (New York: The Metropolitan Museum of Art, 2009), https://tinyurl.com/y55mf75e.
- Yale University Art Gallery, "Dura-Europos: Excavating Antiquity," https://tinyurl.com/yxb8wmbl. Offers maps, diagrams, photos, and a virtual tour of the archaeological site of Dura-Europos (in modern-day Syria) as it was in the third century CE. Special features are a shrine to Mithras, a synagogue with a host of painted biblical scenes, and one of the earliest buildings dedicated to Christian worship to date.

Resources for Further Reading

Adams, Edward. *The Earliest Christian Meeting Places: Almost Exclusively Houses?* London: T&T Clark, 2013. Adams offers a robust challenge to the working consensus reflected in Gehring's work, addressing questions and loopholes in systematic fashion. Whether or not Adams overturns mainstream consensus, his book contributes substantially to the ongoing conversation by broadening its scope to alternative venues for first-century Christ-following assemblies.

Gehring, Roger W. *House Church and Mission: The Importance of Household Structures in Early Christianity.* Peabody, MA: Hendrickson, 2004. Gehring's book is an extensive and thorough study into the notion and historical evidence of houses as critical bases for early Christian community, including numerous floor plans (appended) and a robust bibliography. Originally written as a dissertation, it dialogues regularly with NT scholarship engaged in questions about early house churches.

Johnson, Luke Timothy. *Prophetic Jesus, Prophetic Church: The Challenge of Luke-Acts to Contemporary Christians.* Grand Rapids: Eerdmans, 2011. An engaging study of dynamics at work in the ministries of Jesus and of the church in Luke-Acts, with application to particular challenges for church communities to consider today. Chapter 6 includes a prophetic reflection on the call of these narratives to ministries that are itinerant by nature (not anchored to specific spaces).

2

Being True Siblings in a Divided World

Clearly, the newborn church caught Jesus's habit of bringing people together across difference for a larger, common good. . . . And when that happens, the world notices.

—Allen Hilton

For many people today, experiences of church are associated more with divisions than with signs of unity. Many church communities are divided by worship preferences. Some congregations have "worship wars" between those who prefer historic or liturgical practices and those who prefer modern or "contemporary" practices. These disagreements are about far more than music. They often relate to whether a church

Opening Questions

1. What people come to your mind when you think of "church"?
2. What kinds of people are missing from your experiences of church?
3. In your experience, do church communities tend to be places of unity or of division? Why so?

community has and uses all kinds of things—like hymnals, projection screens, pews, chairs, an altar, an organ, a piano, a band, microphones, robes, liturgical banners, bulletins, call-and-response participation, offering envelopes, a website, online streaming, and informational video clips, to name a few. In fact, disagreements about these kinds of things inevitably tap into key questions about the extent to which a faith community's practices should reflect its historic roots or focus instead on engagement with the surrounding world. At a congregation I once served, there were stark divisions between "traditional" worshipers and "contemporary" worshipers. Most people from each group did not know who made up the other. In practice, they functioned like separate church communities that met in the same building.

Many church communities are divided along age lines. In the late twentieth century, when developmental psychology showed how various ages learn differently, most American congregations invested in faith formation classes divided by ages and

Figure 2.1. Ecumenism Symbol, from a plaque in St. Anne's Church, Augsburg (Germany). Wikimedia Commons.

developmental stages. There are strengths to this model. But the immediate downside is segregating families and ages into separate groups, taking away opportunities for fostering relationships across generations. Current research shows intergenerational faith experiences have profound potential for enhancing people's faith, but many congregations still operate with "age-and-stage" models, grouping people into developmental categories (infants, kids, youth, young adults, middle-aged adults, seniors). It's no surprise, then, how many people have limited meaningful relationships with church people younger or older than themselves.

On a given Sunday morning or Wednesday evening, they may well never enter the same space at the same time.

Many church people are also divided along economic lines or social classes. Most church communities never set out deliberately to attract certain classes of people. But many church communities have significant socioeconomic distinctions—and they inevitably determine who feels comfortable there. At a congregation I served, a member once invited a friend to worship. She responded, "I don't think I have clothes nice enough to go to your church." Her comment shocked him, but it had some basis. At another congregation I served, many proudly identified their church community as "blue collar." At yet another congregation, a pastor friend of mine was pulled aside early into his ministry there and told, "Pastor, you *need* to dress better to be effective here." All these comments betray social and economic divisions that matter to some people. They are not unique to church communities, but are they less influential in our churches? In general, human beings gravitate toward those with similar incomes, occupations, and social backgrounds. And in these regards, many church communities tend not to be radically different.

Many church people are divided along racial and ethnic lines. In an interview with NBC's *Meet the Press* in 1960, Martin Luther King Jr. famously observed that "eleven o'clock on Sunday morning is one of the most segregated hours, if not *the* most segregated hour, in Christian America."[1] Not much has changed since King's day. No matter the denomination, congregations across the board tend to be composed of one racial group or another. Those that are racially mixed (where no one group makes up 80 percent or more of the membership) are less than 3 percent of congregations in the United States.[2] As a member myself of one of the least racially diverse church denominations (the ELCA)—despite efforts in recent decades to diversify and confront racism—I know this reality firsthand.[3] And these divisions are not merely ethnic. They often come with entirely different understandings of Christian heritage, faith practices, community bonds, and ethics in ways that reflect distinctive experiences of groups across time.

No matter the denomination, congregations across the board tend to be composed of one racial group or another.

Many church communities are divided along political lines. Few church communities strive deliberately to be "conservative" or "liberal" politically, but most communities are more homogenously so than mixed. A friend of mine, newly hired at a congregation, shrewdly decided to identify its primary demographic—in this case, conservative Republican. In view of that, he advertised in a local newspaper whose target audience was the same. And two new families joined within weeks—instantly doubling the church's new membership from the past three years. Acknowledged or not, a core value of the congregation was being politically conservative. Indeed, for many people, religious faith and politics interweave inseparably, making the political persuasions of their faith community (often unspoken) very important. A 2014 US Religious Landscape study shows percentages of membership in major Christian denominations that affiliate with one political party or another.[4] Two of the groups nearest to each far end of the spectrum are both Baptist: the Southern Baptist Convention (64 percent Republican) and the National Baptist Convention (87 percent Democrat). This only further suggests the limited influence heritage and doctrine have upon the social distinctions that often divide.

Many church people are divided by denominations—not just organizationally but in daily practice. This is truer in some parts of the world more than others. A visiting Anglican pastor at my seminary recently pointed out, "You Americans have so many church denominations—and you know absolutely nothing about each other, much less what each other is doing!" I once served a congregation in a community that had well over three dozen different faith communities. But during my five years there, never once did I meet a leader from the majority of those communities. It's not because I—or they—were unwilling. It's because we did not *need* to. Our church communities were large enough to sustain themselves, and it was work to build new ties across denominational lines (sad to say). Depending on how one defines "denomination," there are anywhere from hundreds to tens of thousands of Christian denominations across the globe. And despite the unity we Christians share in Christ, we know remarkably little about each other. It is no wonder that many today refer to Christian denominations as different "religions." For all practical purposes, they are.

Jesus once said, "A house divided against itself cannot stand" (Mark 3:25). Yet the global church community is marked by real divisions. Are these divisions natural and normal, or signs of corrosive unhealth?

The Church and Its People

There is a difference, however, between divisions and differences (or distinctions). Divisions divide, whereas differences just differentiate and distinguish. Although social divisions often start from entrenched differences, differences are neither inherently divisive nor obstacles to unity. Sometimes differences are precisely what prod different groups of people to discern and discover what truly unites them. In fact, sometimes differences make a shared unity more profound, more enriching, and stronger.

Church communities are defined less by their physical spaces and denominational ties than by different kinds of people who make up those communities. Churches are not merely businesses or institutions or organizations—they are *people*. And no two people are precisely the same. So, as long as church communities are made up of people, there will always be significant differences from one community to the next.

In fact, the global church of Jesus followers has been this way from the very start. Like their modern counterparts, first-century church communities were defined not by physical spaces as much as by the people who gathered. As Paul told believers in Corinth, "You are the body of Christ and individually members of it" (1 Cor 12:27). Both then and today, church communities were and are assemblies of diverse personalities and individuals: people like us and unlike us, those with social standing and those without, parents, children, families, and those without any connection to one another at all.

Still, however natural our differences may be, they raise a very basic question for church people today: Do we foster and display genuine unity across our differences and divisions? If so, on what grounds? What unites us amid our differences? Some of us may assume church communities across distance and time look more alike than different. Maybe so, maybe not. The question still stands: What does unity look like for the Christian church in today's world?

Questions such as these need to explore where our churches first began. Who made up the earliest church communities? What kinds of people were they? And on what grounds did they identify together as a shared community? Finally, what can we learn from their experiences, both their successes and failures?

Simply from the New Testament, we know about quite a few early believers as well as the church communities associated with them. We also know things about the cities where these church communities took shape—things that influenced the lives and livelihoods of those who professed the faith of Jesus there. In fact, to gain a sense of the earliest church gatherings, it's best to zero in on a few specific church communities for which we have the most information: Corinth and Rome. Stepping into these communities gives us a feel for what some first-century believers were like as we sit with questions that linger for church communities today.

Early Church Community 1: Corinth

Ancient Corinth was founded in the sixth century BCE, destroyed in 146 BCE, then reestablished in 44 BCE by Julius Caesar. By the first century CE, the city was still relatively young. And it was experiencing a surge in prosperity. Jerome Murphy-O'Connor characterizes Corinth in Paul's day as "a wide-open boomtown," comparable to "San Francisco in the day of the gold rush."[5] With a population between fifty-six thousand and eighty thousand,[6] Corinth hosted the Isthmian games, the largest Greek national festival besides the Olympian games. Ancient evidence suggests the city featured active devotions to Poseidon, Apollo, Hermes,

Figure 2.2. Corinto Scavi Strada. Public domain, Wikimedia Commons.

Aphrodite, Asclepius, Dionysus, Demeter, Artemis of Ephesus, Roma, the Emperor, and the God of Israel—in addition to Jesus the Messiah.

In earlier generations, NT interpreters characterized Corinth as a kind of "Sin City." This was based on a few comments by a handful of ancient voices: Aristophanes used the verb "Corinthianize" (*korinthiazesthai*) to refer to sexual immorality (Frag. 354), Plato used the phrase "Corinthian girl" to refer to a mistress or prostitute (*Rep.* 404D), and Strabo alleged Corinth had over a thousand temple prostitutes, calling it "the seat of sacred

Figure 2.3. Poseidon as the lord of the Isthmian Games (Kunsthistorisches Museum, Vienna). Wikimedia Commons.

prostitution in the service of Aphrodite" (*Geogr.* 8.6.20). Today interpreters believe these comments reflect Athenian stereotypes more than reality, as well as a Corinth more than four centuries before Paul's day.[7] The Corinth he saw was economically prosperous, religiously diverse, a port city, and a place ripe for social mobility. But it was not "Sin City" of the Roman Empire any more than another port city in economic prosperity.

Who made up the church community at Corinth? The New Testament names over a dozen participants and infers there were many others. Paul's letters name the following individuals.

- Chloe, whose "people" (family members, slaves, or business associates) once informed Paul of the community's well-being (1 Cor 1:11).
- Stephanas, who later came to Paul in Ephesus. Stephanas and his household were baptized by Paul and became the "first converts in Achaia." Their devotion to "the service of the saints" was likely a ministry of hospitality (1 Cor 1:16; 16:15–16).
- Gaius, who was baptized by Paul and became host to him and "to the whole church" of Corinth (1 Cor 1:14; Rom 16:23).
- Crispus, who was baptized by Paul (1 Cor 1:14). Acts identifies Crispus (likely the same individual) as "the official of the synagogue," whose household became believers (18:8).
- Achaicus and Fortunatus, who came to Paul in Ephesus (1 Cor 16:17–18).

- Phoebe, a deacon of the church at Cenchreae (just outside Corinth). She is the esteemed deliverer and interpreter of Paul's letter to the Romans (Rom 16:1–2).
- Erastus, the "city treasurer" of Corinth (Rom 16:23). City treasurers, like modern city managers, handled a city's revenue, streets, and public buildings. Each city generally had two treasurers at a time. See figure 2.4 (also Acts 19:22; 2 Tim 4:20).
- Quartus, a believer who likely lived in Corinth (Rom 16:23).
- Apollos, a teacher who attained significant influence in the community at Corinth (1 Cor 1:12; 3:4–6, 22; 4:6; 16:12; Acts 18:24–19:1).

In addition, Acts names three others.

- Prisca (Priscilla) and Aquila, who worked alongside Paul and hosted church gatherings in Ephesus and Rome. Acts implies it was at Corinth where Paul met them, stayed with them, and began working with them as tentmakers (1 Cor 16:19; Rom 16:3–5; Acts 18:1–4).
- Titius Justus, a "worshiper of God" whose house (next to the synagogue) hosted Paul and may have been his base for operations in Corinth (Acts 18:7).

Among these individuals, two have households that became believers (Stephanas, Crispus), some of whom "devoted themselves to the service of the saints" (1 Cor 16:15). Chloe's "people" may have done the same. And the active hospitality ministries of

Figure 2.4. Erastus Pavement Inscription at ancient Corinth from the middle of the first century CE: "Erastus for the cause of being an *aedile* [city treasurer] laid [this pavement] at his own expense" (*Erastus pro aedit[at] e s[ua] p[ecunia] stravit*). Cf. Romans 16:23: "Erastus the city treasurer (*oikonomos*), greets you." The two references may well refer to the same individual, since neither city overseers nor the name "Erastus" were terribly common at the time. Photograph by author.

both Gaius and Titius Justus imply their households were equal participants in these ministries.

As their names show, most participants in the Corinthian church community were not Jewish. Certainly, some may have been, and many were familiar with Israel's scriptural traditions.[8] But the community's fundamental identity—in Paul's mind—was non-Jewish, so that he referred openly to their past identities as "pagans" (1 Cor 12:2).

How big was the church at Corinth? Estimates vary from as low as ten participants to as high as several hundred.[9] In recent years, scholars have estimated lower numbers, based on the limited space of ancient dining rooms and some surviving membership lists from voluntary associations in the Roman Empire (averaging ten to twenty-five members).[10] But private homes were not the only spaces for church gatherings (see chap. 1), and many voluntary associations were more socially homogeneous than church communities, which included women, slaves, and children.[11] Many family systems in the Roman world were large and complex, often including extended family, household servants, and freed slaves. Given this, the more expansive language of "participation" is more helpful than "membership" for early church communities. Based on these factors, the church at Corinth likely entailed at least forty to fifty participants. Although by today's standards that may be a relatively small congregation, in the first century it was a sizeable and significant community.

Were the Early Believers All Poor and Lower Class?

Not long ago, the conventional idea was that the early Christians were generally poor, uneducated, and lower class. This idea has a long history, first voiced by early critics of Christianity like Celsus. He argued the movement drew primarily from "the foolish, the lowly, and the senseless, along with slaves, women, and children," as well as "the most uneducated and most uncultivated people" (Origen, *Against Celsus* 3.44, 55). Celsus was not the only one circulating these stereotypes.[12] The fact that Christianity came from Judea and centered on a peasant executed by Rome only fueled these prejudices. However, we now realize the earliest churches were more often cross-sections of society than gatherings of the disenfranchised. The church at Corinth reflects this very well.

> We now realize the earliest churches were more often cross-sections of society than gatherings of the disenfranchised.

On the one hand, Paul characterizes many in the community as neither socially powerful nor influential: "Not many of you were wise by human standards, not many were powerful, not many were of noble birth" (1 Cor 1:26). On the other hand, the community was far from economically impoverished. Among its most active participants were these individuals:

- Erastus, the "city treasurer" of Corinth (Rom 16:23).
- Gaius, the "host to [Paul] and to the whole church" of Corinth (Rom 16:23).
- Stephanas, whose household had the means to extend hospitality (1 Cor 16:16).
- Crispus, a synagogue official (according to Acts 18:8).

These individuals likely had means, influence, and social credentials—and not just within the church community. Three of these individuals are the only Corinthians Paul claims to have baptized: Crispus, Gaius, and Stephanas's household

(1 Cor 1:14–16). Gerd Theissen points out, "If Paul makes it quite clear that the majority of Corinthian Christians come from the lower strata, it is all the more noteworthy that all of those baptized by him belonged to the upper strata: Crispus, Gaius, and Stephanas. They must have been especially important for the Pauline mission."[13] So, although "many" in the community lacked means and social distinctions, several did not—and these individuals did not escape Paul's eye.

Further, this church community was able to set money aside on a weekly basis for Paul's collection (1 Cor 16:1–4). He even characterizes their economic resources as "abundance," although largely to inspire generosity (2 Cor 8:14). Some believers at Corinth may have been offended at Paul's refusal of their monetary support—a support they may have given his opponents (1 Cor 9:12–15; 2 Cor 11:7–12; 12:13, 20–21). These various glimpses give the impression this church community embraced both the poor and the wealthy, the socially insignificant as well as the influential. Bringing together people of such different social standings, Paul would find, came with related challenges for building community across social divisions.

The church community at Corinth was more a cross-section of surrounding society than a lopsided group of the lower class. Other church communities that Paul began or influenced had similar traits. Early church communities like these were neither elite country clubs nor assemblies of society's dregs. By and large, they were representative slices of their surroundings, reflecting the contexts in which they first took root.[14]

For Reflection: Churches as Cross-Sections Today

Does your church community reflect the various people of its surrounding society and context? If not, what groups are most represented by your church community? What groups make up the surrounding context?

For most church communities today, these questions are challenging. After all, a great deal of church communities in Western society are marked less by variety and diversity than by uniformity and similarity. Even among Christians, birds of a feather tend to flock together. In addition, areas that experience major demographic shifts generally find existing church communities are far slower to reflect any comparable shifts—if ever.

But this reality is not purely the church's failure. People join church communities to find relationships with others. And for most people, it is easier and simpler to connect with the like-minded than with those who differ—whether culturally, ethnically, linguistically, economically, socially, theologically, politically, professionally, educationally, or morally. Related to this, many ethnic minority people find church communities made up largely of their cultural demographic to be especially valuable—not to exclude others, but for solidarity among those with distinctive, shared experiences. Many nonminority churches in the United States today once started as ethnic communities (e.g., German, Irish, Hungarian) for the same reasons. At the end of the day, human beings crave community—and they understandably gravitate toward finding it in the places that require the least effort and hard work.

But none of this diminishes the value of the vision set by Paul's church at Corinth: a community reflective of the broader diversity of surrounding society. To be fair, what we know of Paul's mission strategy suggests he was more opportunistic and pragmatic than exclusivist in whom he engaged. In each region, he largely responded to the doors that opened and to the people who listened, whether in workshops, public places, synagogues, or private homes. At the same time, Paul was strategic about the areas he targeted. The places in which he invested were not arbitrary stops on a meandering journey but strategic outposts across the Mediterranean, enabling him later to boast that "from Jerusalem as far around as Illyricum I have fully proclaimed the gospel of Christ" (Rom 15:19–20). What Paul did prioritize were places and people unfamiliar with the gospel and the resources (including people) that would nurture a church community to endure after he left. Paul's mission strategy did not aim rigidly to recruit a specific social demographic but to foster a community that authentically came from surrounding society. What resulted was a relative cross-section, even if not a perfect one.

How do our church communities today authentically engage those around us? In many cases, church communities are more at risk of *under*engaging their neighbors. In other cases, a specific vision of community—often no different from the present reality, but with specific token people inserted—can itself become an obstacle to more collaborative and transformative ways of connecting with others. As we discern how to engage our neighbors faithfully, we must also consider how the social distinctions that divide us in society do not go away in a church community.

Christians are not people in the abstract but embodiments of particular experiences, cultural contexts, socioeconomic backgrounds, and the like. What most of us yearn for is a church community that does not deny our particular, lived experiences but takes them seriously—and connects us to others who share the faith of Jesus Christ.

One more consideration. Even though we now realize Paul's churches were not simply poor people, that does not change the fact *many* of the poorer and humbler of society were attracted to this new movement. They heard in the gospel a message of affirmation, equality, and justice that they did not experience elsewhere. Would they have the same experience in our church communities today? At a congregation I once served, I noticed how most of the

Figure 2.5. Roman Colosseum, constructed within two decades after Paul's imprisonment. Photo by Bengt Nyman, Wikimedia Commons.

people we assisted financially (with various needs) never came to worship. It's not that they were not invited. Somehow, they simply did not feel comfortable. I ponder that still. Jesus prioritized the poor and disenfranchised throughout his earthly ministry, pressing the question to us today: How will our church communities continue his ministry to the same kinds of people?

Early Church Community 2: Rome

Another early church community worth considering is that at Rome. As the capital of the empire, the city of Rome was the center of the Mediterranean world. Founded as a shepherd's village centuries beforehand (trad. 753 BCE), by Paul's time it was nearly a half million strong.[15] Due to its size, centrality, and resources, the city attracted people from surrounding provinces like a magnet. This included many Jews.

Since at least the middle of the second century BCE, a major Jewish presence lived at Rome. Once Rome gained control of Judea (63 BCE), exchanges between Judea and Rome increased. In Paul's day, Jews in Rome numbered forty to fifty thousand, with synagogues in several quarters of the city.[16] Although the origins of the church at Rome are uncertain, it very likely began among these Jewish citizens.

Paul did not start the church at Rome. Even though an old tradition credits Peter as the founder, the earliest Christian writings from Rome never name Peter as founder or first overseer. By the time Paul wrote the book of Romans (late 50s), the church's presence in Rome was well-established. Right after his letter's introduction, Paul claims the community's "faith is proclaimed throughout the world" (1:8). Though perhaps overstated to earn their good will, his words suggest the church's reputation—if not size—were widely known. Paul also says he has long wanted to visit the church at Rome (1:9–15; 15:22–24), suggesting it began well before the writing of Romans. In view of this, most scholars believe the church started sometime in the 40s by Jesus followers who brought the faith from Judea—whether as transplants to Rome or as visitors to Judea such as those named at Pentecost in Acts: "visitors from Rome, both Jews and proselytes" (2:10–11).

Who made up the church community at Rome? At the close of his letter to them, Paul greets well over two dozen people associated with the community.

- Prisca and Aquila, named earlier in association with Corinth. By this point they had evidently relocated to Rome and now hosted a church-gathering in their home. Acts explains that they originally came to Corinth (by the early 50s) due to an expulsion of Jews from Rome (Rom 16:3–5; 1 Cor 16:19; Acts 18:1–4).

- Epaenetus, named the first convert from Asia (western modern-day Turkey). He may have encountered Paul at Ephesus and later resettled to Rome (Rom 16:5; 1 Cor 16:8–9).

- Mary, who "has worked very hard among you" (Rom 16:6).

- Andronicus, Junia, and Herodion, all Jewish compatriots.[17] Andronicus and Junia preceded Paul in the faith, were imprisoned with him, and were "outstanding among the apostles" (16:7, 11).

- Ampliatus and Stachys, affectionately called "beloved" along with Epaenetus and Persis (16:8–9; cf. vv. 5, 12).
- Urbanus, a coworker of Paul and his colleagues (v. 9).
- Apelles, an individual "approved" or "tested" in Christ (v. 10).
- The households of Aristobulus and of Narcissus (vv. 10, 11).
- Tryphaena, Tryphosa, and Persis, who had all "labored in the Lord" (v. 12).
- Rufus and his mother. The latter became a mother also to Paul (v. 13).
- Asyncritus, Phlegon, Hermes, Patrobas, Hermas, Philologus, Julia, Nereus, his sister, Olympas—and all the believers associated with them (vv. 14–15).

This is an impressive list of people for Paul to name, especially since he had never visited the church in Rome! It was strategic for him to name as many as he knew personally, since he was interested in partnering with the community (1:8–15; 15:22–33). For our purposes, Paul's "name dropping" is helpful: no other NT writing names so many individuals associated with a specific church community.

Paul's list of names implies some important things about this church community. First, it was not small, by mid-first-century standards. The number of those named by Paul is far more than are named in association with any other NT community. This, along with his remarks about the church's reputation, suggests it was large. Further supporting this is the fact several later Christian authors and their writings are associated with Rome.[18]

> ## Defining some terms
>
> **Gentile:** Non-Jewish. The words used in the New Testament (*ethnē*) may equally be translated "nations," referring to all peoples outside of Judea and the people of historic Israel.

Second, many of these individuals were either transplants or at least well-traveled. This must be the case if Paul has had opportunity to befriend so many of them—at the very least, Prisca, Aquila, Epaenetus, Andronicus, Junia, Urbanus, and Rufus's mother.

Third, very few of the names are recognizably Jewish. This is surprising, since we think the Roman church started among Jews. Among the twenty-five names Paul gives, just three are singled out as Jewish "compatriots" or "kin." And no more than five others have names attested elsewhere among Jews at this time.[19] Whatever its origins, by the time Paul writes Romans, the church at Rome had gained a marked number of gentile participants.[20]

The Church or Churches? What Paul's Vision Has to Say

Many people today think of the earliest church like a collection of independent house churches. In this vision, individual homes each hosted a particular "church," with each a building block for the larger believing community. Only occasionally did these "churches" gather together. This vision makes sense to modern Westerners, who live in a world where several "churches" coexist even in small towns, with each functioning largely independently. But the idea is more modern than ancient, and it overemphasizes the significance of individual homes for Paul's vision of the church.

Most often, Paul uses "church" to refer to the larger community of believers in a specific place. Though he names individuals associated with the community in the plural (e.g., "to all the saints . . . in Philippi," Phil 1:1), he generally uses the singular "church" to address the entire local community. For example, when he addresses believers in Corinth—a community marked by divisions, who may have met sometimes in separate homes—he calls them "the church of God that is in Corinth" (1 Cor 1:2; 2 Cor 1:1). He does the same with believing communities at Thessalonica, Philippi, and Cenchreae. Paul only uses the plural "churches" to refer to communities spread out geographically across regions, such as Galatia and Macedonia (Gal 1:2; 1 Cor 16:1). When he addresses believers in a city, he always refers to them in the singular ("church").[21]

Whether all believers in a city gathered commonly or rarely together at one place is debated. Corinth is a case in point. Based on the size of ancient homes, Jerome Murphy-O'Connor believes such meetings were rare: "It would simply have been too awkward."[22] But twice in 1 Corinthians Paul refers to "the whole church" gathering together "in one place" at Corinth (1 Cor 11:20; 14:23). Elsewhere he names Gaius, a host to "the whole church" there (Rom 16:23). These instances suggest

Paul experienced gatherings of *all* believers in Corinth in one place, very possibly at Gaius's home. And in addressing worship matters at Corinth (1 Corinthians 11–14), Paul nowhere mentions separate home gatherings—just gatherings of "the whole church." This suggests larger gatherings were more a norm than an exception.

But what about Rome—a city of half a million, with a church community more sizeable than most? Among all church communities associated with Paul, the one at Rome is most frequently assumed to be a loose collection of independent house gatherings. Those of this mindset typically point to the lack of "church" language in Paul's address (Rom 1:7), the arrangement of names

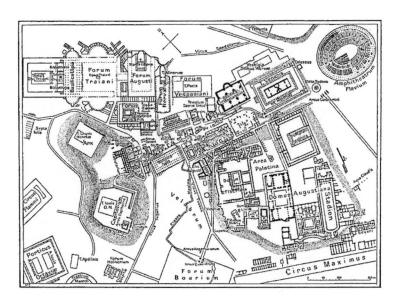

Figure 6. Map of downtown Rome during the Roman Empire. Wikimedia Commons.

in Romans 16 (perhaps signifying different groups), and a lack of evidence for unified organization among synagogues in Rome— a model possibly mimicked by early Christians.[23]

But there is no clear reason to think Paul saw the Roman church community differently. The absence of "church" (singular) language does not mean the community was not one: Paul addresses believers in Philippi the same way but later implies they are a church (Phil 1:1; 4:15). Second, the arrangement of names in Romans 16 does not necessitate separate groups. Besides the church-gathering at Prisca and Aquila's home (v. 5), other references to "households" (vv. 10, 11) and associations (vv. 14, 15) aim to acknowledge existing relationships but do not necessarily clearly imply separate gatherings. Third, while Roman synagogue communities may have been loosely connected, the church community need not have followed the same script. The church was much smaller, and conflict soon after its start catalyzed a separation from the Jewish community in ways that were visible to outsiders by the mid-60s (Suetonius, *Claudius* 25.4; Tacitus, *Annals* 15.44).

After all, if Rome had no unified "church," then to whom did Phoebe bring Paul's letter (Rom 16:1–2)? And why does Paul give no instructions for gathering distinctive communities? Paul's earliest letter asks that it be read to "all" church community members (1 Thess 5:27). And the letter to the Colossians gives explicit instructions for circulation across separate communities: "When this letter is read among you, have it read also in the church of the Laodiceans; and see that you read also the letter from Laodicea" (4:16). Why are there no such instructions for the Romans? Finally, no surviving Christian voice from the first and second centuries calls believers in Rome anything but "the church at Rome," treating them as a singular community.[24] Despite the size of Rome and its church community, Paul and other early Christian writers saw believers in Rome as fundamentally a united church community.

> "Now may the God of patient endurance and of consolation grant that you all may live in harmony with one another according to Christ Jesus, so that together with one voice you may glorify God the Father of our Lord Jesus Christ." (Rom 15:5–6)

Paul's view of both church communities at Corinth and Rome says something important about his vision of church: whether believers met in separate homes, home gatherings were not independent "churches" but extensions of the united community. The true church was the entire community of gathered believers. Paul saw and emphasized unity among Jesus followers, even across the scattered corners of the most expansive cities, even among those whom Paul had not met. He saw an authentic unity in Christ rooted in baptism (Rom 6:3–6), and his prayer was that believers "live in harmony with one another" so that they glorify God "with one voice" (15:5–6). For Paul, early church gatherings in homes were not independent congregations ("Prisca and Aquila's church") but more like small groups or extended activities of a larger church community in that locale. The smaller gatherings derived their core identity from the united community—not vice versa. For Paul, unity was a core value of the body of Christ, and he reflected it in the language he used.[25]

For Reflection: Unity and Individualism

Paul's core value of church unity may feel like an elusive vision for some church people today. Why so?

There are some modern realities we face that Paul did not. First is the cultural value of individualism. For many people in areas of the Western world, the Christian faith is primarily an individual quest. Church communities offer resources for this quest, but what ultimately matters is how well they foster an individual's connection with God. As a result, a strong sense of the church as community suffers. Individuals come to worship without any intentions of interacting with others. In fact, many seek out large church communities in order to be as anonymous as possible. Once there, they evaluate church communities like public services and entertainment offerings, regularly asking, "How well does this fulfill my personal needs?" And if clear answers are not readily available, they move on to the next church community.

Paul had no concept of differentiating faith in Christ from full participation in church community. For Paul, if you profess the faith of Christ, you are automatically part of the local church community. The latter was not an optional activity—it was core to what it meant to be "in Christ." Modern statements like "I believe in God, but I don't need the church" would not have made sense to Paul. For him, faith was a communal activity. We would do well to contemplate this for our own time. Certainly, some church communities and institutions have caused people damage and pain, for which justice, reconciliation, and healing are sorely needed. Still, the roots of NT faith inspire us to recover a fuller sense of how it took shape among the earliest believers: in community, as the body of Christ.

A second challenge today is the heritage some church traditions have of breaking away and separating. Although exaggerated, a comment from a European friend of mine sticks with me: "You Americans have so many churches. And when you decide one day you don't like your church, then you go start a new one!" Certainly, some streams of Christianity have breakaway tendencies at the core of their heritage, making it part of their DNA. Protestantism, for example, despite its ultimate goals of reform, catalyzed a separatist movement. And this trajectory of breaking away hardly ceased after the sixteenth-century Reformation. Today new church groups, subgroups, and "nondenominational" or independent groups abound. In the US alone, there are well over forty Lutheran denominations. Across the globe today, there are tens of thousands of Protestant church denominations.

> Paul had no concept of differentiating faith in Christ from full participation in church community.

Paul was not a fan of divisions among church communities, especially when they centered on different leaders, ethnic differences, or socioeconomic distinctions, or focused on

"Paul, called as an Apostle of Christ Jesus by the will of God, and Sosthenes the brother: to the church of God that is in Corinth, sanctified in Christ Jesus, called as saints, together with all those who in every place call on the name of our Lord Jesus Christ, both their Lord and ours." (1 Cor 1:1–2)

disagreements regarding worship and social practices. Like other NT writers, Paul saw a time and a place for excluding certain individuals or groups, but only to secure repentance and solidarity (1 Cor 5:1–8; cf. 2 Cor 2:5–11). What mattered most to Paul among church communities were the things that made for peace, mutual upbuilding, and united voices in harmony (Rom 14:19; 15:5–6). In fact, the two church communities that likely were the largest Paul addressed in his letters—Rome and Corinth—are the same ones he encouraged most to work toward unity (1 Cor 1:10–17; Rom 14:1–15:13). Other NT writings further show that internal divisions and incidents of separation are not new to our day and time.[26] Still, Paul was an advocate for unity over division. Rugged individualism was not a virtue in his ecclesiology. Throughout his ministry, he emphasized the importance of maintaining a sense of unity "together with all those who in every place call on the name of our Lord Jesus Christ, both their Lord and ours" (1 Cor 1:2).

Other factors also make for unique challenges to fostering church unity in our contexts today: geographical distance, physical (architectural) barriers, busy schedules, language barriers, and more. Whatever the factors, these reflections confront us with the question: Do our church communities reflect an ethos of community and commitment to the whole, or one of independent individuals who occasionally come together? Despite the new and distinctive challenges we face today, the call to authentic Christian community remains.

Significant Groups of People in the NT Church Communities

What kinds of people participated in the earliest church communities? In addition to the specific experiences of believers at Corinth and Rome, are there commonalities we see across many early church communities—at Ephesus, Philippi, Colossae, Galatia, Antioch, Jerusalem, and other places? At the risk of generalizing, here are some of the most represented and significant groups of people we find across church communities of the first century and later.

Men and Women

Undoubtedly, men participated in the earliest church communities.[27] Among the individuals Paul names in his seven undisputed letters, about 70 percent are men (thirty out of forty-three). Men like Gaius and their households served as hosts for entire church communities (Rom 16:23). By exhibiting such generosity, they extended hospitality not only to Paul but to many other believers. Like with Philemon, "the hearts of the saints have been refreshed" through their ministries (Phlm 22; see also 1

Cor 16:15–16; Acts 18:7). Based just on Paul's words alone, male individuals worked alongside him, carried letters for him, spent time with him in prison, preceded him in faith, and were dearly beloved to him.[28]

The narrative of Acts names over fifty male individuals as apostles to, participants in, and supporters of specific church communities. According to Acts, individual men served as proclaimers and apostles (2:14–36; 13:1–3), evangelists (8:26–40; 18:28; 21:8–11), prophets and teachers (11:27–28; 13:1; 18:28), hosts (16:25–34; 17:5–7; 18:7; 21:8–15, 16), and leaders in church communities (11:1–18; 15:6–21; cf. 14:23; 20:17–35). These men were both lower and upper class, both wealthy and nonwealthy, both Jewish and gentile, both itinerant and stationary, both resettled and homegrown, and both conservative and progressive regarding fidelity to traditional Jewish practices.

In the patriarchal society of the Roman Empire, men had great access to social mobility and influence. In this context, men put their social standing and honor at risk by joining a new religious movement that was neither widely understood nor respected. When men of means professed certain religious loyalties, many of their household members often followed suit. As early adopters of the Jesus movement, men like those named in the New Testament were significant movers and shakers in early church communities.

More surprising, however, are the women participants in early church communities. Although they are a minority of the believers named in Paul's undisputed letters (30 percent) and in Acts (23 percent),[29] these percentages do not tell the whole story. For example, in Romans 16 Paul names just eight women in comparison to eighteen men, but the balance shifts when we notice those he singles out as most active. Of those who have "labored" in that community, all four are women (Mary, Tryphaena, Tryphosa, Persis). This "labor" was neither mundane nor trivial: Paul uses the word (*kopiazō*) elsewhere to describe his core work of apostolic mission (Gal 4:11; 1 Cor 15:10), implying these women's work was no less important. Among those highly praised in Romans 16 for risking their lives and standing out among the apostles, women number as many as men (Prisca and Junia vs. Aquila and Andronicus). And among those singled out for special service, women outnumber men six to three.[30] Few as they may have been, women were significant players in the early Roman church.

The church at Philippi is another example. We know far less about this church community than those at Corinth and Rome, but the little we know gives significant attention to women. Among the three individuals Paul's letter to the church names, two are women (Euodia and Syntyche, 4:2). These two "have struggled beside (*synēthlēsan*) me in the work of the gospel," activity he elsewhere hopes will be emulated by the entire church (1:27). In fact, Paul asks the letter's unnamed recipient ("my loyal companion," 4:3) to assist these women, suggesting they were leaders in the community. Further, the narrative of Acts spotlights Lydia, a cloth dealer from Thyatira, as not only the first convert but also the first host of Paul's mission work at Philippi (Acts 16:11–15, 40). Finally, Paul's letter to Philippi is his only undisputed letter that names specific leadership roles in the greeting ("bishops and deacons," 1:1), some of which may have been occupied by women.

Two specific women are worthy of mention all on their own. The first is Priscilla (Prisca). The couple Prisca and Aquila earn more words of praise from Paul than most individuals in his letters (Rom 16:3–5; 1 Cor 16:19; see also Acts 18:2–3, 18, 26). More interesting is how various NT writings often name Priscilla first and her husband second (Rom 16:3; Acts 18:18, 26; cf. 1

Figure 2.7. Sappho Fresco, of a woman in the mid-first century CE with wax tablets and a stylus, Pompeii. Naples National Archaeological Museum item 9084. Photo anonymous, public domain, Wikimedia Commons.

Cor 16:19; Acts 18:2–3). This unconventional practice suggests either that she held a higher social status or that she played a more prominent role in church communities. Either way, she was an outstanding figure in the early church.

The second woman is Phoebe. Not only was she a deacon of the church at Cenchreae—a port town just a few miles outside Corinth— she was the carrier of Paul's longest and most theologically significant

> Women participated integrally in early church communities.

NT writing: the letter to the Romans (16:1–2). As the carrier, she was more than a package deliverer. She served as Paul's chief representative to a community with which he sorely wished to forge ties (1:8–15; 15:22–29). As letter bearer, she served as its first reader and chief interpreter for the community gathered to hear it. In a largely illiterate society, letters were not simply delivered: they were *read,* even *performed*—typically at a public gathering, very possibly followed (or interrupted) by questions.[31] One of the greatest writings of the NT—and of historic Christianity—was entrusted first to Phoebe to deliver, present, and interpret. That Paul trusted her so highly says a great deal.

Women participated integrally in early church communities. They hosted Paul, other apostles, and gatherings in their homes. They worked hard for the cause of the gospel. They kept Paul informed about his churches' well-being and served as couriers and interpreters of his letters. These women supported Paul in his ministry endeavors, sat in prison with him, and risked their lives for his sake. They served in the earliest church communities as prophets, disciples, apostles, and deacons—if not more. Although not always clearly acknowledged and affirmed, women participated significantly in Paul's mission work and many of the earliest church communities.

Free Born, Slaves, and Freed Persons

Many of the individuals already named were freeborn people, if not Roman citizens, who had opportunities to travel, relocate, and assist Paul. But slaves were no less a part of early church communities. Slaves made up about a third of the empire, making it an entrenched and assumed reality of Roman society. Some slaves could own property, save money, become educated, hold positions, and participate in associations and assemblies. Many also had opportunities to earn their freedom. In general, urban slaves (*urbani*) fared better than rural ones (*rustici*). Some people voluntarily became slaves to pay off debts, showing that some forms of slavery were preferred over impoverishment.

That said, slaves were owned—like animals or objects—and so were entirely subject to the whims of their masters, whether kind or cruel. Masters could punish slaves brutally for minor infractions. Physical and sexual abuse of slaves, especially female and young slaves, was likely more common than surviving writings from antiquity admit. Some slaves worked in harsh conditions at backbreaking manual labor, while others served highly skilled roles such as tutoring and overseeing estates. As these discrepancies show, a wide range of circumstances played into whether a slave experienced life comfortably, miserably, or somewhere in between.[32]

Slaves participated in church communities both as members of believing households and as individuals. The most prominent slave in the NT is Onesimus, for whose sake Paul wrote a letter to Philemon, the slave's master. Onesimus had been alienated from or demoted by Philemon, whether due to circumstances or wrongdoing. Onesimus later befriended and was mentored by the imprisoned Paul, which prompted Paul to write and ask Philemon to welcome Onesimus back "no longer as a slave but more than a slave, a beloved brother—especially to me but how much more to you, both in the flesh and in the Lord" (16). Paul here used his social influence to go to bat for a slave: "If you consider me your partner, welcome him as you would welcome me. If he has wronged you in any way, or owes you anything, charge that to my account. . . . I say nothing about your owing me even your own self" (17–19). Such advocacy was an effective strategy in the Roman world.[33] Paul's actions not only show that he valued a slave's well-being, more importantly they show that, for believers, the ties they share within church communities trump the significance of conventional class distinctions (see Gal 3:27– 28; 1 Cor 12:13; also Col 3:11). Paul did not advocate directly for slavery's abolition in his day. But allusions throughout his letters imply the presence and active participation of slaves and household servants in his church communities.

Besides slaves and the freeborn, there was a third group: freed persons (*liberti*). Though free, they honored their former masters as patrons (often continuing to bear their name) and in practice held a social status below the freeborn. Freed persons likely participated significantly in early church communities. For example, based on a comparison of Romans 16 with ancient sources, Peter Lampe suggests that over a third of those named in the Roman church likely came from slave origins—in a city that itself boasted a high number of slaves.[34] According to Acts 6:9, a synagogue of "freedmen" existed in Jerusalem. Finally, Paul's use of slave/free metaphors throughout his letters imply his hearers' familiarity with the concepts, very possibly from their own experiences (1 Cor 6:20; 7:22–23; Rom 6:6–7:6; 8:15; Gal 4:7).

The Young and Old

Different than some societies today, the Roman world conventionally revered the aged. Conversely, it valued children primarily for their potential to become contributing adults. Children were viewed as irrational beings, needing discipline, and ready for work and apprenticeship by five to seven years old. Child mortality rates were high: up to 50 percent by age ten. Physical beatings of children were commonplace, as was their exposure to neglect, violence, and forms of abuse. Vast disparities between wealth and poverty made for widely different experiences of childhood. Family systems were large and complex, with servants and extended family often playing key roles in childrearing. Still, devoted parents loved and cared for their children as sources of joy and happiness.

There is no explicit evidence that children participated fully in all aspects of early church communities. But silence regarding child/adult distinctions may suggest children's involvement more than their exclusion. Several NT writings depict entire households being baptized, without drawing any age distinctions.[35] Both Jesus and Paul taught with young people present (Mark 9:35–37; Acts 20:7–12). And at several gatherings of Jesus followers, children appear and are named (Matt 14:21; Acts 21:5). Early Christians expected all ages to hear and know Christian teaching, including children (Col 3:18–4:1; Eph 5:21–6:9; also 1 John 2:12, 14). Likewise, some Christian writings saw the care of orphans (and widows) as "pure and undefiled" religion at its best (Jas 1:27). The Gospels portray Jesus's ministry as setting a strong precedent for the inclusion of children. He frequently healed children (Mark 5:22–43; 9:14–29; Luke 7:11–17) and, more importantly, welcomed them as full participants in the reign of God (Mark 10:13–16; also 9:36–37).

All told, scholars such as O. M. Bakke suggest children were more involved in early church communities than not. By the mid-third century in many church communities, children are attested as receiving baptism and the Eucharist—practices that may have origins as early as NT times. These considerations suggest that children ultimately, if not early on, were regarded as subjects (vs. objects), capable of genuine spirituality and "full members of the community."[36] In the absence of clear evidence that children were excluded from early church participation, we speculate that, at least in some communities, they were welcomed and included just as they were in later centuries.

Along with children, early church communities revered, respected, and cared for the aged. The realities of disease, famine, malnutrition, unsanitary water, inadequate sewage treatment, and ineffective medical practices made life expectancies lower (thirty to forty years for peasants)—and likewise aged individuals rarer—than in parts of today's world. In antiquity, age itself was a credential for leadership and instructing others—a dynamic named in several NT writings (Phlm 9; 2 John 1; 3 John 1; cf. 1 Tim 4:12). In this context, treating elders harshly or disrespectfully was inappropriate (see 1 Tim 5:1–22). Meanwhile, care for widows (and orphans) "in their distress" was a priority of several early church communities (Jas 1:27; 1 Tim 5:9–16)—a practice with roots in traditions of the Hebrew Bible.[37]

Despite the relative silence of NT writings about participation and involvement of the young and the old, the information we have suggests—and perhaps assumes—their presence more than denies it. In ways that both resonated with and deviated from conventional practices, early church communities included both ends of the age spectrum as acting participants.

For Reflection: Membership or Participation?

Many church communities today use "membership" to designate those affiliated with them. In these cases, membership marks an official status with certain privileges and likely some basic expectations of participation. Many church communities who use this concept also struggle with the boundaries drawn around membership (e.g., basic instruction, giving, worship attendance, profession of faith). Further, it seems that increasingly today in the US people wish to join the spiritual practices of a community without becoming members in the conventional sense. Finally, as many ministry leaders know, membership can be a misleading concept, since it may not correspond with active participation. In a congregation I served, one of the most active young men in the congregation was deliberately not a member (motivated by his extended family's Roman Catholic heritage), while several "members" on our roster never came to worship once in my five years there.

Membership language does not appear in reference to church communities in the NT writings.[38] This suggests it is a dispensable idea if it is not constructive to building up communities of faith today. Paul did not worry about who were "members" of specific church communities; rather, he focused on *who were there* at gatherings and *who invested themselves* in serving the community of Christ. In this sense, his criteria were more functional than static, prioritizing how people showed up and actively engaged more than what status they attained. To be fair, even Paul seems to have had assumptions about the lion's share of gathered believers: most were baptized, participated in Eucharist, and joined variously in worship activities (Gal 3:27–19; 1 Cor 11:17–34; 14:26–40). Still, his focus was more on how worshipers treated one another and lived out their shared identity as sisters and brothers in Christ than on designated benchmarks.

> How people invest time and energy into building up a community, after all, matters more than official affiliations.

Maybe we do well to act similarly today: focusing less on static roles than on signs of active participation. In lieu of "members," perhaps we should think more in terms of "worshipers" or "participants." How people invest time and energy into building up a community, after all, matters more than official affiliations. The notion of membership has potential benefits, but it can also put emphasis on the wrong syllable. Following the examples of Paul and other NT authors, perhaps it is simply unimportant to concern ourselves with determining officially whether someone is "one of us" or not. The ways in which people participate in a community will speak for themselves, regardless of official designations.

Guiding Metaphor: A Gathering of Siblings

Whether at Corinth, Rome, Philippi, or elsewhere, the church communities Paul knew embraced people from many statuses and backgrounds. In these gatherings, patrons and hosts joined in community with peasants, and freed men and women joined together with slaveowners. Gatherings brought together women and men, the young and the elderly, the educated and the uneducated, the wealthy and the impoverished. Sometimes the differences of status, means, skills, and opportunities made for significant challenges for practicing community. And like modern-day countertypes, some of these church communities excelled at authentic community better than others.

But the vision of Paul—and virtually the entire New Testament—is of a church fundamentally made up of siblings. In his seven undisputed letters alone, Paul calls fellow believers "brother" (*adelphos*) and "sister" (*adelphē*) well over one hundred times, making sibling language his undeniably preferred language for them.[39] Paul was well aware of alternative metaphors, as were those in his church communities. So when he chose language that undermined the social divisions and distinctions with which they lived (race, status, gender), it did not fall on deaf ears.

And it's not just Paul. Virtually every writing in the New Testament uses sibling language—some of them quite prevalently— for people in church communities.[40] Sibling language is not unique to early Christianity. It has roots in the Hebrew Bible, and it occurred some among Roman clubs and associations.[41] But by comparison, the practice is distinctively widespread among New Testament church communities.

Language like this served to redefine identity and status in church communities. Whatever roles were occupied in societal spheres elsewhere, gathering in the name of Jesus resulted in a new, shared identity as children of God and siblings united in Christ. As Paul writes, "As many of you as were baptized into Christ have clothed yourselves with Christ" (Gal 3:27). In becoming Christ's, believers joined a new family, received new identities, and entered new relationships that surpassed the significance of those that normally governed life. As Carolyn Osiek puts it, "Those of unequal social status were to treat each other as brothers and sister in the Lord. When husband and wife, master and slave, patron and client belonged to the same house church, they were to express their unity in Christ by sharing the same table and dealing with one another with equal consideration."[42]

We wish we knew more how this new identity in Christ influenced believers' lives outside the sacred times and spaces of gathering as church community. Undoubtedly, early believers navigated conflicting identities between society and their convictions with varying successes and failures in honoring their unity in Christ—as seen in Paul's relationship with believers at Corinth (1 Cor 1:10–17; 6:1–8; 11:17–22). Still, Paul nonetheless identified these believers as "the church of God that is in Corinth . . . sanctified in Christ Jesus, called to be saints, together with all those who in every place call on the name of our Lord Jesus Christ" (1:2). Whatever honor or shame individual members lived with every day in society, in gathering they became something entirely new.

> "I ask not only for these followers, but also for those who by their word will believe in me: that all may be one, just as you, Father, are in me and I in you, that they also may be in us, so that the world may believe that you sent me" (John 17:20–21).

Conclusion: On Being a House United

In John 17, Jesus prays for unity for his followers. Would he give thanks for how this prayer is finding fulfillment today—or lament and weep?

By most estimates, many societies today have grown increasingly divided along political, racial, and religious lines. Many factors influence this, from rising global population to increased awareness of those different from us, from social media to changes in how and where community is fostered. For some people, the more awareness we have of our global challenges, the more overwhelming these challenges appear. For others, greater awareness leads to action and initiative, with new resources now available for connecting with others in the fight.

Whether motivated by fear or activism, many of these same people gravitate toward others with like-minded views, generating more entrenched divisions of distinctive viewpoints. Certainly in the United States, this sorting among people into social, political, and religious camps has taken deeper root in recent decades.[43] Jesus once said a house divided against itself cannot stand. Over 1,800 years later, Abraham Lincoln said the same in reflecting on the plight of the United States, in the context of increasing division over slavery and its affiliated concerns.[44] Many today find increasing societal divisions a mounting problem without a solution, wondering fearfully where this situation will take us down the road.

In some contexts, Christians and church communities fare no better. Some church leaders and people excel more at declaring what they are against than what they are for, differentiating themselves from "those people" (Christians or not) rather than building bridges toward a sense of shared humanity. Many Christians find it easier, more convenient, and more comfortable to be church together with others who are more like themselves. And many of the same people find it easier to identify who they are by first identifying what (or who) they are *not*.

Yet in the earliest church communities, we see glimpses of a different vision. We see gatherings that reflected cross-sections of surrounding society more than homogeneity. Even if our limited data does not attest to the most extreme top and bottom of Greco-Roman society in church gatherings, still a wide variety of its segments are represented well. Those who participated in early church communities were as mixed, assorted, and different from one another as dishes at a potluck. Their gatherings were expressions of variety, difference, and diversity. And although these emerging realities had their share of growing pains, flaws, and failures, they featured a distinctive beauty that testified to a new creation.

Judging from Paul's letters, what most guided the earliest church gatherings toward unity was not a targeted mission strategy on diversity for its own sake but a strong sense of shared unity in Christ. Throughout his letters, Paul emphasized a unity that transcended political divisions, ethnic differences, gender divides, and social statuses. Not all church communities embraced this vision heartily. Not all church communities put the theoretical concept of unity into actual practice in their dealings with one another. But Paul nonetheless cast the vision, and the Scriptures have testified to its significance ever since.

Our church communities today need to recapture the significance of this vision—not just for our sake, but for the sake of the world. Our Earth now boasts nearly eight billion people, along with possibilities for connecting with one another in unprecedented ways. At the same time, studies show that many individuals increasingly feel lonelier and more disconnected, with stratified sectors of society further entrenched in their thinking. As a human race, we are more aware than ever before of each other's presence, but in many ways we are no less segregated than we were decades—or centuries—ago.

Working to foster authentic unity is hard work. Many things divide us, from the philosophical to the practical, from the sacred to the mundane, from space and time to the tyranny of our schedules. People today, it seems, have remarkably limited resources for bringing others together in the name of the unity for which Jesus prayed.

Two things are essential to an effective start. First, we must let the main thing (the gospel) be the main thing. Most ministry leaders and Christians today are passionate about specific remedies to societal problems, even to the extent of dishonoring all others who see things differently. We must take care not to let our passionate convictions overshadow and squelch the unity of the gospel. For Paul, the good news of Jesus was the fun-

> For Paul, the good news of Jesus was the fundamental source of unity for Christians across time and space.

damental source of unity for Christians across time and space. Have we reason to think things are different today?

Second, we must treat our neighbors with love—including their convictions—in the very way we believe God loves us. As Jesus's parable of the good Samaritan shows, neither race nor culture nor religious convictions matter as much as concrete acts of decency toward the stranger before us. These are the kinds of things that build community, no matter how entrenched the divisions.

Amid the challenges we face, we would do well to remember that Christian community is not, in Dietrich Bonhoeffer's words, "an ideal which we must realize" but instead "a reality created by God in Christ in which we may participate."[45] What unity in Christ looks like today is not prescribed from on high as much as it is grown from seeds of faith and the Spirit's work. This unity depends less on our energized efforts than on our willingness to be open and vulnerable to the things God is doing among us. As a reality birthed from our connection to Christ, ultimately it is Christ's work and not ours.

Signs of hope are taking place among church communities today, most often during situations of crisis and need. When Hurricane Harvey struck the southern United States in 2017, Christians from across the country instinctively dropped what they were doing and came to help. In that context, theological and social differences were inconsequential. What mattered simply was that the gospel called believers to show up and help.

Our world needs church communities to show a similar unity apart from natural disasters and crises. By some standards, the first-century Roman Empire was a society more stratified—and divided—than many societies today. Yet, amid these differences, early church communities professed and embodied a distinctive message of unity. This message is no less profound today. Nor is the desire to hear it today any less present. In their earliest stages, church gatherings were deliberate about being sacred spaces for unity in the name of Christ across harmful stratifications and divisions. We today are no less called to bear witness to a Christ who gathers divided people into a new creation, where unity attests to the beauty of the gospel.

Bringing It Home: Ideas and Conversations for Implementation

1. Consider how well the various groups named in this chapter (men and women, the old and young, etc.) are reflected and honored in your own church community. Which groups are underprioritized?

2. Conduct a poll among your church community or a group of Christians regarding the sense of unity they experience among Christians, church communities, and larger society. Give opportunity for people to voice their fears, hopes, and greatest concerns around this issue.

3. Work toward facilitating a shared new venture with some neighboring faith communities (worship service, Scripture study, social activism, etc.).

4. Invite some local ministry leaders from other backgrounds to an open forum on Christian unity and ecumenism and the ways our church communities work toward those goals.

5. Invite someone from a different Christian denomination or religious group to coffee or lunch.

6. Investigate ways your church community or ministry authentically reflects its surrounding context and its people. Make this a communal initiative and follow it up

with reflection on further action steps beyond observing and learning.

7. Host an ecumenical or interreligious shared meal together, perhaps in honor of a civic or religious holiday all groups can appreciate. Consider making a Scripture conversation about one of the passages named in the "Scripture Study" portion a part of this event.

Scripture Study

- Paul's letters of 1 Corinthians and/or Romans. Read each in view of this chapter's background information, paying special attention to Paul's words regarding unity (e.g., 1 Cor 1:10–17) and how this might have played out—or did not—in each of these contexts.

- John 17 (Jesus's prayer for his followers). Notice especially how Jesus prays not simply for followers in his own day but for those yet to come.

- Ephesians 2:11–20 and 4:1–16, some of the most emphatic words regarding unity in the New Testament.

For Worship

- John Foley, "One Bread, One Body" (*ELW* #496).
- John Oxenham, "In Christ There Is No East or West" (*ELW* #650).

Questions for Reflection

1. What do you think it would have been like to be part of the church communities at Corinth or at Rome? How similar or different do you imagine they would be from your experience today?

2. Imagine living in a society more stratified than your own: where slavery is assumed, society is explicitly patriarchal, social honor and status hinge upon economic resources, and opportunities for improvement are scarce and rare. In such a world as this, how does the message of unity in Christ sound?

3. Reflect on your own church experiences. Have they largely been experiences of unity across divisions, or division across societal lines?

4. Where do we ourselves contribute to ongoing division in our churches and in society—as individuals and as church communities?

5. Where do you experience signs of hope for the church as a place for unity in Christ?

6. Where do you see signs of hope for church communities building constructive bridges with peoples of other faiths?

7. What are your hopes for the church and its message going into the future?

Online Resources for Further Exploration

Lynn H. Cohick, "Women's Work in the Greco-Roman World," https://tinyurl.com/y6sprecp.

Danila Loginov, "Ancient Corinth," https://tinyurl.com/yy5vmelb. A virtual tour of Corinth as it might have been in the second century. An excellent resource for provoking imagination and reflection.

Danila Loginov, "Ancient Rome 320 AD," https://tinyurl.com/y2dlp2uc. A virtual tour of Rome as it might have been in the fourth century.

Katy E. Valentine, "Slavery in the New Testament," https://tinyurl.com/y2x8mx27.

Resources for Further Reading

Bakke, O. M. *When Children Became People: The Birth of Childhood in Early Christianity.* Trans. Brian McNeil. Minneapolis: Fortress, 2005. A focused exploration of evidence for how early Christians and Christianity were instrumental in drawing attention to the value and significance of children.

Cohick, Lynn H. *Women in the World of the Earliest Christians: Illuminating Ancient Ways of Life.* Grand Rapids: Baker, 2009. An excellent entry into the real-life experiences of women in the ancient world, from daughterhood to motherhood, from wives to prostitutes, and from women's work to benefaction and patronage.

Glancy, Jennifer A. *Slavery as Moral Problem: In the Early Church and Today.* Minneapolis: Fortress, 2011. A readable yet informed tackling of the complex issues surrounding slavery among Christians both in antiquity and in the modern world.

Green, Joel B., and Lee Martin McDonald, eds. *The World of the New Testament: Cultural, Social, and Historical Contexts.* Grand Rapids: Baker, 2013. A collection of forty-four brief essays on various topics, including slaves and slavery, women and children, and civic and voluntary associations in the Greco-Roman world.

Hilton, Allen. *A House United: How the Church Can Save the World.* Minneapolis: Fortress, 2018. A reflection on modern realities of division in American society and Jesus's call to unity, with a charge to the church to work toward being a catalyst for constructive change.

3

Being a Body in a
Stratified Society

Paul was calling those in Christian communities to make
the necessary and deep-seated adjustments from their
cultural background. The nature of the church required
a pattern of organization which could not immediately
be transferred from the culture of the day.

—Andrew Clarke

A friend of mine had an interesting experience starting out
as a pastor. She began her ministry at a small congregation, excited to do some new things. Most of all, she had ideas
for changing up worship. She sought out the person identified
by the congregation's leadership board as a "worship" point
person, consulted with her, and together they brainstormed.
Soon afterward, she implemented some things in ways that

Opening Questions:

1. What social dynamics govern your church community? If an outsider were to enter your community, what would she or he experience?
2. Who are the people of influence in your church community? Are they paid staff, professional clergy, longtime members, or other people?
3. What language best depicts what your church community is like? (a club, a melting pot, structured, chaotic, hierarchical, a gathering of equals, serious, playful, traditional, non-traditional, welcoming, restrictive, reserved, expressive, joyful, sullen, etc.)

strove to surprise everyone. The most significant change was a total reorganization of the worship space and its seating. Late one week, she and the worship representative took out several pews, reconfigured the worship orientation, and altered the physical space quite dramatically. They hoped for a real surprise Sunday morning.

The pastor certainly got a surprise—but it was hers to experience. When she arrived Sunday morning, the worship space was back in its original arrangement! And she had no idea who did it. She was a bit distracted leading worship that morning.

Whether or not this response by unknown congregational members was appropriate, the new pastor realized something important that day: this community believed major decisions about worship called for wide input—not "surprises" at the discretion of just two people. It seems the pastor had not consulted some of the *real* decision-makers and leaders in the community. And they made it known.

Social Dynamics and Church Communities

Social dynamics and decision-making patterns are difficult realities to pin down. Typically, there is more to them than meets the eye. The designated leaders of a community may or may not be its true decision-makers. Written policies may or may not accurately describe what actually happens. And one member's experience of a group may differ significantly from another's. Basic questions like "What's this community like?" and "Who's in charge?" can be very complicated to answer.

Before I started teaching at Wartburg Seminary, a friend of mine counseled me, "Make sure you pay close attention, not just to the faculty handbook, but to the 'unofficial' handbook of how things *really* work among the faculty." As the chair of a university department, he knew well the influence that social dynamics, strong personalities, and political alliances can have. And he did not want me to be naïve about them in my new position. His advice applies not only to academic institutions. It applies to any community with leadership roles and social dynamics that are unwritten and unspoken. It applies to most of the groups we affiliate with and participate in whether we realize it or not.

Sometimes churches fare no better than other communities in transparency and honesty about their social dynamics.

Not long ago, a graduate from my seminary left her first church position after just eighteen months due to power struggles she experienced and did not anticipate beforehand. Among church leaders who take leave from ministry positions (temporarily or permanently), "church politics" is an oft-named reason.

These dynamics often compel people to leave or distance themselves from specific church communities as well. The religiously unaffiliated have two prevailing criticisms of church communities: they are more concerned with money and power than people, and they are more focused on rules and politics than spirituality.[1] Well-founded or not, these criticisms arise from some authentic experiences. One of my university students once explained it this way to me: "I like Jesus. I'm just not sure I like church people."

That said, sometimes church communities rise above prevailing social patterns. Many of my seminary students speak emotionally about their home congregations as places where they first experienced acceptance and grace. In many societies, church communities have played instrumental roles in confronting systemic social ills and advocating for justice for the underserved. A pastor friend of mine who spent years working in corporate businesses has characterized the relationships he now experiences in church communities as a "breath of fresh air." Yet another friend speaks of a

> Church communities are capable of both profound virtue and vice when it comes to social dynamics.

church community as the first place she, her partner, and their children truly experienced acceptance as a family.

Clearly, church communities are capable of both profound virtue and vice when it comes to social dynamics. What factors determine which of these rises more clearly to the surface? Why is one community dour, persnickety, and depressed, while another is harmonious, affectionate, and hopeful?

Among the many factors, heritage and history are significant. How a community arose and its historical identity play a major role in who that community is today. Studies of communities in crisis point out that situations of crisis often bring out traits and tendencies that have always been there. In short, a prevailing consistency characterizes the dynamics of many social groups, realized or not.

For this reason, church communities that are asking questions of identity today find it vital to ask, "Who have we *been* from the very beginning?" That is, where have we come from, and how has that shaped who we are? Our questions about what we are like and how our leadership operates can be informed significantly by the experiences of the earliest believers. How they discerned and navigated their own sense of community may richly inform our own ongoing discernment in today's world.

Early Church Communities and the World in Which They Lived

The earliest church communities were no less complicated than the many communities we know today. What is different are the cultural norms believers inherited from surrounding society and the kinds of leadership roles with which they were familiar.

A few examples convey this point well. First, many of us today enter church communities assuming that we will find a community of equals. Many of the earliest believers, in contrast, entered home church-gatherings with assumptions of a community that would be hierarchical, just like other households they knew. Further, many of us today assume that participants in church communities will each have equal say and influence, regardless of financial means and benevolence. Many of the earliest believers probably assumed the opposite: generous individuals of means deserved public gestures of gratitude and honor. In fact, many of us today approach church community with assumptions (or at least ideals) of a virtually classless society. Right or wrong, many of the earliest believers probably approached church gatherings differently, expecting clear marks of social distinction between the enslaved and free, the elite and peasants, men and women, and the old and the young.

Those who gathered in the earliest church communities were deeply influenced by the cultural norms of their world. These realities made up the very air these believers breathed long before they entered a community oriented around Messiah Jesus. And as they entered this community, their cultural assumptions were not checked entirely at the door. In fact, three specific social dynamics weighed heavily upon church communities in first-century Mediterranean society.

Dynamic 1: Public Honor and Shame

In the ancient Mediterranean world, public honor was critical to one's worth. The very Greek word for honor (*timē*) means "worth" or "value," showing how important it was. Aristotle called public honor "the greatest of all external goods" (*Nicomachean Ethics* 4.3). Dio Chrysostom asked, "What is more sacred than honor or gratitude?" (*To the People of Rhodes* 31.37). Bruce Malina likens public honor in ancient Mediterranean culture to the credit rating of individuals in modern developed nations: it directly affected purchasing power, social mobility, and related opportunities.[2] Different from many industrialized cultures today that are essentially individualistic, ancient Mediterranean culture was communally oriented: the opinions and evaluations of others fundamentally determined an individual's worth and sense of self.

To a large extent, public honor was influenced by factors outside one's control: age, nationality, gender, economic class, health, and appearance. At the same time, certain activities could enhance public honor: acts of courage, piety, and benevolence. Likewise, certain acts incurred public shame: infidelity, indecency, and disloyalty. Since opportunities for social mobility were rare and few, activities that risked damage to social honor were carefully avoided.

In a culture oriented around public honor, the Jesus movement faced real obstacles. It was young, misunderstood, and foreign. Many associated it with superstition, women, the uneducated, and the lower classes (Tacitus, *Annals* 15.44; Origen.

Against Celsus 3.44, 55). It boasted no significant opportunities for social honor or public advancement. Even more, its message focused on a crucified Messiah. Since crucifixion was a widespread mark of shame, the cross invited public mockery (see figures 3.1 and 3.2). This may be why we have no evidence for believers from the uppermost elite of Roman society. To swear allegiance to a crucified Galilean peasant as "Lord" (a title conventionally reserved for the Emperor) welcomed real social shame.

Dynamic 2: Economic Distinctions

In the words of Mark Allan Powell, life in the Roman Empire was marked by "grotesque economic inequality."[3] Society was aristocratic, ruled by 2–3 percent of the population (the elite). Meanwhile, nearly 90 percent virtually had no voice, influence, or major opportunities for betterment (peasants). Although a small portion of society lived somewhere in between (specialized artisans, servants of nobility, etc.), Roman society by and large had no concept of a middle class.

Many peasants (the 90 percent) were tradespeople, artisans, farmers, day laborers, and slaves. Nearly a third lived below the subsistence level: primarily widows, orphans, prisoners, and beggars. Virtually all peasants had scarce opportunities for social betterment, formalized education, or change. Instead, peasants were subject to natural calamities like famine, food shortage, and disease—for which there was no social safety net. They also lived

Figure 3.1. Alexamenos Graffito (ca. 200 CE). Public domain, via Wikimedia Commons.

with malnutrition, impure water sources, inadequate waste disposal, and ineffective medical care. On average, peasants lived no longer than forty years.[4] Among those who lived longer, the cumulative toll of infections, diseases, physical labor, and crippling injuries were often visible.

Due to taxes and religious offerings, peasants gave most of their income to rulers, landlords, lenders, and religious sacrifices. David Fiensy estimates that the average peasant farmer in

Figure 3.2. Alexamenos Graffito tracing. Graffiti found near the Palatine Hill in Rome, evidently mocking Christians. The image shows a young man worshiping a crucified, donkey-headed man and reads "Alexamenos worships [his] god." Public domain, via Wikimedia Commons.

first-century Palestine paid about 12 percent or more of their income to a governor or local ruler (such as Herod Antipas), 25 to 50 percent to landlords, additional payments on loans to lenders, and tithes, wave offerings, and temple taxes to the temple in Jerusalem.[5] For most first-century Mediterranean people, the primary goals of life were maintaining family ties and obtaining daily bread.

Dynamic 3: Patrons, Clients, and Loyalty

Amid such economic disparity, virtually everyone in the Roman Empire engaged in transactional relationships with people above and below their status. In these relationships, the wealthy served as benefactors or "patrons," while others served as recipients or "clients."

Patrons assisted others through forms of service: protection, money, legal assistance, employment, or social influence. In fact, this was expected of wealthy individuals. Plutarch noted that people were generally hostile toward wealthy individuals who were reluctant to share (*Precepts of Statecraft* 30.1). And Seneca described the ideal, generous man as helping "one with money, another with credit, another with influence, another with advice, another with sound precepts" (*On Benefits* 1.2.4). Even apart from social pressures, many elite people embraced occasions for charity as opportunities for accumulating social honor.

Although not technically a legal relationship, clients were expected to return patrons' favors with regular—even daily— signs of gratitude and loyalty: morning greetings, public praise, support in court, or various acts of service. In some cases, these tokens of gratitude were small prices to pay. In other cases, they constituted a virtual slavery.[6] Among early Christians, language associated with patron-client relationships offered fitting metaphors to describe God's gracious activity (*charis*) and the human response of faith and faithfulness (*pistis*). Whether they embraced or despised the cultural norms of patronage, early Christians were undoubtedly familiar with them from firsthand experience.

For Reflection: Church-Gatherings as Egalitarian Communities?

Many today have the idea that early church communities were essentially egalitarian: leadership roles were basically shared, and clear organizational structures did not exist. The idea is especially associated with house church gatherings, since these settings imply the metaphor of a family.

Figure 3.3. Roman denarius featuring Marcus Aurelius (second century CE). Photo by Rasiel Suarez. Public domain, via Wikimedia Commons.

But this idea is misleading. Early church communities had designated leaders, even if the roles were neither as universal nor as complicated as those today. More to the point, household settings did not necessarily foster egalitarianism in the modern sense. Ancient Roman households were profoundly patriarchal, with clear roles and lines of authority. Although households fostered ties of love and affection, they were not necessarily at the expense of the distinctions that prevailed in larger society.[7]

Those who hosted church gatherings in their homes would likely have been viewed as functional patrons. This was the case for those who hosted other groups in Roman society (synagogues, voluntary associations), making it likely that similar dynamics played out for home church gatherings. Very few in Roman society had the means to own a home sizeable enough to host large gatherings regularly. Those who could were among society's elite. Such Roman homes were often designed to impress guests, enhancing the perceived honor and generosity of the host. At some level, merely to enter the home of an elite Roman was to become that person's client by virtue of her or his hospitality. In church communities, despite their ideals of equality, hosts may well have been honored by leadership roles, officially or unofficially. In short, ancient homes were not spaces that necessarily nurtured classlessness.[8]

However, not all dynamics associated with homes were negative by our standards. These settings likely gave unique opportunities for leadership to women, since it was space conventionally under their oversight.[9] All four NT references to home church-gatherings, for example, name women among the hosts (1 Cor 16:19; Rom 16:5; Phlm 2; Col 4:15). Domestic spaces also may have allowed more readily for interactions across status, gender, and age. These were real assets to a community that promoted unity in Christ across social distinctions.

Let's stop for a moment to imagine an early church gathering. Envision a gathering of peasants, aristocrats, specialized artisans, and the impoverished. One man has lived his entire life at subsistence level, while another has never experienced physical labor. One woman has seen half her children die, while another has never carried such burdens. One owns spacious living quarters, while another is slave to a cruel master. Patrons and clients are both present, obliging social honors to be displayed. Yet all these people gather as "one in Christ." How should they interact with one another? To what extent should they maintain—or forgo—conventional hierarchies? With such social diversity, how will sharing, leadership, and community take shape?

> Approaching equality takes place not by ignoring the distinctions but by naming them.

These are real questions the earliest believers faced. Even more, these questions are not that different from those we ask—and *should* ask—today. Most of us today approach Christian community as a gathering of equals, whether inspired by our theology or more humanitarian ideals. Even so, we live in a world rife with classism that distinguishes and ranks people based on their income, education level, race, gender, age, occupation, citizenship, place of residency, family, religious affiliation, available assets, and net worth. Even if ours is theoretically a "classless" society, real social distinctions remain. And for most of us, the distinctions that govern our world are remarkably difficult to check at the door—even if we *want* to. Approaching equality takes place not by ignoring the distinctions but by naming them. Despite our ideals, church communities—in antiquity and today—are not classless societies, so we should not pretend as if they are. Just as confession of sin can yield new life, equality in Jesus's name is facilitated by naming our shortcomings—as individuals, people, and as church communities. By naming where we have failed, we open ourselves up to healing. Church communities that in recent years have facilitated deliberate discussion about racism, sexism, and other forms of discrimination find this to be true. By admitting our failures as Christ's people, we welcome an interpersonal healing that moves us forward in sacred ways.

In fact, perhaps counterintuitively, it is encouraging that the earliest church communities did not achieve perfect classlessness. They too struggled to live fully into a vision of equality in Christ. They too struggled to leave behind societal norms for the sake of unity in Christ. Like believers today, early Christians experienced a grace that broke down conventional dividing walls, but the extent to which it empowered them to live out a genuinely countercultural community is unclear.

Leadership and Service in Church Communities

Virtually all social groups have leaders, whether official or unofficial. Church communities are no different. And whether we have positive or negative associations with church leadership roles and structures, they are neither inherently evil nor inherently good. At their best, they guide communities toward shared commitments. At their worst, they become self-serving, manipulative, and destructive.

The same is true for leadership in the earliest church communities. Past generations of interpreters had the vague idea that earliest Christianity was "charismatic" in leadership (Spirit-led, fluid, democratic) and only later reverted to secular models more hierarchical and institutionalizing. But recent studies challenge that idea, showing that social distinctions and hierarchies, however subtle, were present from the very beginning.

In the earliest NT writing, for example, Paul asks believers at Thessalonica "to acknowledge those who labor among you and have charge of you in the Lord and admonish you; regard them very highly in love because of their work" (1 Thess 5:12–13a). Other early NT writings have similar depictions of forms of leadership and service: "Now you are the body of Christ and individually members of it. And God has appointed in the church first apostles, second prophets, third teachers; then deeds of power, then gifts of healing, forms of assistance, forms of administration, various kinds of tongues" (1 Cor 12:28). Enough commonalities exist across NT passages to suggest there were some formalized roles, at the very least in Paul's mind. These roles were neither mutually exclusive nor precisely distinctive. They are more approximations than precise job descriptions. But they do name key forms of service that give us a sketch of leadership as it took shape among some of the earliest church communities.

Founding Leaders: Apostles and Coworkers

In 1 Corinthians 12:28, the first role named is apostle. In the Greco-Roman world, the word "apostle" (*apostolos*) often meant a political ambassador or envoy.[10] For Paul, it was neither a political role nor an established office but a call from Jesus to a particular purpose: to build up church communities

Figure 3.4. The apostle Paul preaching. From the story of the Bible from Genesis to Revelation (1873). Courtesy of Wikimedia Commons.

throughout the gentile world (Gal 1:1; 1 Cor 1:1; Rom 11:13; 2 Cor 10:8; 13:10).

Paul was not the only early church apostle. There were many others, from the twelve disciples to Paul's coworkers and associates, to others who illegitimately bore the name.[11] The role of apostle was more localized than universal, leading Paul to tell believers in Corinth, "Even if I am not an apostle to others, I am to you" (1 Cor 9:2). Still, apostles like Paul were instrumental to the founding, spread, and networking of church communities (Eph 2:20). The preservation and imitation of so many of his writings show how influential an apostle could be. In real ways, an apostle like Paul became a "father" and "mother" to the communities he served (1 Cor 4:14–21; 1 Thess 2:7–8, 11–12; Gal 4:19).

But apostles were not lone rangers. In his letters alone, Paul lists nearly twenty coworkers who served alongside him in critical roles, including many women.[12] Individuals like Timothy, Euodia, Titus, Syntyche, Apollos, Priscilla, Aquila, Urbanus, and Epaphroditus were significant people for many church communities. They served as coauthors of Paul's letters, messengers among believers, founders of church communities, and even as apostles themselves (Phil 2:25; 1 Cor 8:23). Some were itinerant like Paul, while others were local leaders. Some worked closely with Paul, like Timothy, while others apparently worked more independently, like Apollos. Virtually all of them risked their lives and livelihoods for the sake of the gospel. These examples make something crystal clear: from the very start, Paul's ministry was a collaborative undertaking, with something comparable to a ministry staff. And the collaborative nature of his work was a major reason for its lasting impact.

Local Leaders: Prophets, Teachers, and Deacons

Influential as they were, most founding leaders were not consistently part of a church community's daily life. Apostles like Paul founded church communities to thrive in their absence. As highly as we may value the role apostles played, local leaders played larger roles for church communities over the long haul.

Among local leaders in early church communities, prophets and teachers rank first. The roles of prophets and teachers and their respective activities appear regularly, widely, and prominently in NT writings (1 Cor 12:28; Rom 12:4–8; Eph 4:11–12; Acts 13:1). Some prophets traveled between church communities (Matt 10:41; Did. 13:1), but many did not. Christian prophecy was neither decidedly focused on the future nor irrational in nature. It claimed merely to relay "the word of the Lord" in relevant ways to specific communities. Something between ecstatic speech and a prepared sermon, prophecy's goal was the "upbuilding and encouragement and consolation" of faith among church communities (1 Cor 14:3).[13]

Teachers also focused on encouraging, exhorting, and upbuilding communities of faith—making rigid distinctions between teachers and prophets unhelpful.[14] Teachers dealt with conveying, explaining, and interpreting sacred traditions, but their role was not purely intellectual. A bit like Jewish rabbis, teachers used a variety of resources to nurture understandings of the faith in ways that were formative, practical, and faithful—as modeled by the earliest apostles and Jesus himself.[15] From the earliest NT writings on, Christian teachers are associated with nearly every church community named.[16] Paul believed the role worthy of compensation (Gal 6:6; 1 Cor 9:1–12a), and James stressed its significant responsibility (Jas 3:1). Judging from Priscilla and Aquila in Acts, the role was not limited to men (Acts 18:24–28). In time, as sacred Christian traditions continued to crystallize, the role of teaching became more important and increasingly associated with the roles of pastor and overseer (Eph 4:11–12; 1 Tim 4:6, 11, 16; 6:2b; 2 Tim 1:13–14; Titus 2:1, 15).

A third role of leadership/service is that of deacon (*diakonos*). Though the role appears early and widely in NT sources, its specifics are hard to pin down. The related word *diakonia* (ministry, service) can refer to anything from civil service to waiting on tables, from stewarding a collection of money to ministry in service of the gospel.[17] Paul uses *diakonia* language for his apostolic work, as well as for the ministries of Stephanas and his household.[18] Both Paul and Jesus speak of Christ as a servant (*diakonos*) of others, and Paul depicts himself and Apollos the same way.[19] The narrative of Acts describes the organization of a group in Jerusalem for *diakonia* (service) to overlooked widows (6:1–6), but the story neither calls them deacons nor verifies that these men continued in these roles long (cf. 6:8–8:1; 8:4–8, 26–40; 21:8–9). In some cases, the word deacon probably referred to more specific roles such as hosts and overseers of church gatherings, as in the cases of Phoebe and deacons at Philippi (Rom 16:1; Phil 1:1). Later, deacons appeared under the jurisdiction of overseers, with clear ethical expectations (1 Tim 3:8–13).

Leaders in Later Times: Overseers, Elders, and Pastors

Later NT writings—especially the Pastoral Epistles (1–2 Timothy, Titus)—draw attention to three different church leadership roles: overseers, elders, and pastors. Their virtual absence in Paul's undisputed writings suggests they are later historical developments (late first century and afterward). Their respective responsibilities overlap significantly.

Overseers (*episkopoi*) managed and administered care for specific church communities. Outside of Christian contexts, an overseer was typically a local official or officer with administrative responsibilities, which suggests church overseers had similar responsibilities.[20] Many English translations render the Greek word *episkopos* "bishop," but unlike modern synodical and diocesan bishops, these individuals served specific communities, not larger districts. Early on, church communities may have been served by multiple overseers in less hierarchical paradigms (Phil 1:1; Acts 20:28). But from at least the mid-second century on, church communities often each had a single overseer, a bit like a lead pastor in sizeable congregations today.[21] At least in some cases, individuals aspired to this role and came from a church community's council of elders (1 Tim 3:1; 4:14; Titus 1:5–9).

Elders (*presbyteroi*) were local church leaders, often appointed by apostles or other leaders (Acts 14:23; 20:17; Titus

1:5).[22] Church communities typically had many elders, together forming an authoritative group or "council" (1 Tim 4:14; cf. Acts 20:17; Jas 5:14). Within the scope of the New Testament, "elder" sometimes refers to a specific role of oversight (1 Pet 5:1b–4; 1 Tim 5:17–22), and other times suggests an unspecified level of influence (1 Pet 5:1a; 2 John 1; 3 John 1). In the Pastoral Epistles, the roles of elder and overseer overlap almost interchangeably.[23]

The word "pastor" (*poimēn*) simply means "shepherd." But in the context of church communities, shepherding was a core metaphor that defined what it meant to be a pastor: to care for a church community as a shepherd cares for sheep. Jesus used the same language for his ministry (John 10:11–18). Only Ephesians uses the noun to refer to church leaders, but several NT writings use the metaphor for overseeing Christian communities (Eph 4:11; Acts 20:28–29; 1 Pet 5:2–3; John 21:15–17). Many of the same passages associate alternative leadership roles and language closely with pastoring:

- "The gifts God gave were that some would be . . . pastors and teachers" (Eph 4:11).
- "Now as an elder myself . . . I exhort the elders among you: shepherd the flock of God in your midst, exercising oversight (*episkopountes*)" (1 Pet 5:1–2).
- To church elders in Ephesus: "Keep watch over yourselves and the entire flock, of which the Holy Spirit has appointed you overseers (*episkopoi*), to shepherd the church of God" (Acts 20:28).

These examples show that, at least within the period of later NT writings, the role of pastor was not a watertight category. It overlapped a great deal with other roles (teachers, elders, overseers), and in some cases may have been synonymous with them.

For Reflection: Recapturing a Biblical Model of Leadership

Many Christians today believe the best model for church leadership is what the earliest church communities had. The roles and offices named in Scripture are "biblical" ones, and so are worth striving for today.

Certainly, we have things to learn from the earliest models of church leadership, but to embrace them wholesale is not so simple. First off, as this survey shows, the very idea begs the question, *Which* biblical model? Variation, change, and evolution are in place from even the earliest stages, raising questions about which model is the earliest or most authentic.

Second, speaking frankly, what worked well for early believers and their communities may not achieve the same things today. There are enough cultural and contextual differences—around literacy, the role and use of Scripture, interpretive traditions, organizational infrastructure and accountability, and the total numbers of believers—to suggest they may not. The roles of prophecy and teaching changed early on as sacred

> What does it mean to recapture a biblical model of church leadership today?

traditions were canonized and opportunities for studying the faith became more available. Likewise, we regard forms of apostolic ministry today differently in light of the effects of colonialism. In fact, in many parts of our world today, we expect church leaders claiming to offer "a word of the Lord" to have ministry preparation, formalized education, recognized credentials, and organizational accountability. In short, our ministries face different obstacles, pressures, expectations, and realities than first-century believers did.

And so, what does it mean to recapture a biblical model of church leadership today? I do not think it means to adopt the categories of apostles, prophets, teachers, and deacons wholesale—and to rid ourselves of alternative models we now use. But there are some things we may learn from their models and experiences.

First, they fostered connection to the whole church. Apostles and their coworkers founded and nurtured church communities not as independent outposts but as extensions of a larger whole. Apostles like Paul sought to build a network of Christ-following communities that were connected not only to a sending community (like Antioch) but also to other communities throughout the world (see 1 Cor 1:2). This is no small feat, in view of the human tendency to focus primarily on what affects "me and my community."

Second, they prioritized and empowered local leadership. Despite the influence of apostles, the real work of daily ministry in communities was primarily carried on by local prophets, teachers, and deacons. Most of these leaders came from within local communities, though not always. Some denominational structures today excel more than others at this virtue when it comes to raising up church leaders. While credentialed outsiders have much to offer, local community members have distinctive inroads. Many church organizations with leadership shortages today are rightly investing in training and empowering local leaders.

Third, they strove for balance between preserving sacred tradition and relevance to local contexts. Paul's letters reflect this balance well. In 1 Corinthians alone, for example, he refers to Scripture (5:6–8; 10:1–13), traditions (11:23; 15:3), and the practices of other church communities (11:16; 14:33), but at the same time he addresses contextual questions about marriage (chap. 7), food sacrificed to idols (8:1–11:1), and various practices of worship (11:2–14:40). In this way, Paul discerns between sacred heritage and contextual realities to offer what he sees to be word from the Lord for a fledgling community (see 7:10; 14:37). For most church communities, this balance is challenging to navigate, but it protects against an imbalance that yields either stagnancy or rootlessness.

Fourth, they were more fluid and contextual than rigid. If the preceding discussion suggests leadership roles were widely established and clearly defined, it is misleading, since that was hardly the case. For one, they were not the only named roles, even early on. The NT also names patrons (or leaders), laborers, administrators, assistants, and exhorters.[24] Some of these roles overlapped with others, while still others evolved over time. For another, some communities made use of certain leadership roles more than others. Paul names prophets and teachers at Corinth (1 Cor

12:28–29) but overseers at Philippi (Phil 1:1). He also spotlights some distinctive spiritual gifts in 1 Corinthians that he never does elsewhere: deeds of power, gifts of healing, different tongues, the interpretation of tongues, and discernment among spirits (12:9–10, 28). All this implies that different forms of leadership had various levels of significance for different communities. Even more, it suggests that leadership roles among early church communities were less like a static list of offices than a process of emergence and adaptation. Interpreters probing the New Testament for *the* biblical model of church leadership find the picture that emerges to be more fluid and contextual than universal.

Biblical models of church leadership deal less with specific roles and titles than with achieving worthwhile goals, less with universal credentials than with cultivating local resources, and less with canonized forms than with enabling ministry to take root effectively in local contexts. A biblical model of church leadership is not a blueprint handed down from on high—it is a model of adaptability that nurtures deep roots in various contexts.

Evolutions in Leadership: Women as Leaders

Just a century ago, most church organizations across the globe did not authorize the ordination or significant leadership of women. Even half a century ago, women in roles of ordained leadership were profoundly rare. Since then, church denominations and communities are increasingly embracing women as church leaders. However, change is still very slow to come. Today's world offers significantly more opportunities for women to serve as clergy, and yet Christian congregations that have women serving as ordained leaders are in the minority—around 12 percent in the United States.[25]

Modern social, religious, and psychological studies continue to show resoundingly positive results from women serving in church leadership roles.[26] Parodies like Sojourners' video "Seven Reasons Why Men Should Not Be Pastors" can even poke fun at traditional ideas that have fed restrictions on women leaders, and become wildly popular in the process.[27] What restrains church communities and organizations from embracing women in leadership is not new research or modern experiences but historic viewpoints: claims based on Scripture, tradition, and historic church practices. Even so, we discover conflicting and competing voices on this topic among the early church communities. In addition, leadership was not limited to a single role or title. There were many forms of leadership among church communities, changing the question from "Was leadership available to women?" to "What *forms of leadership* were available to women?"

These questions are not merely historical: they directly inform practices today. Both those who advocate for and those who advocate against female church leadership claim that early church practices stand in their support. And so, whether women had leadership opportunities at the outset really matters today.

Did women serve as leaders in early church communities? The short answer is yes. For nearly every leadership and service role named in the New Testament, there is evidence that women occupied it—at least in some contexts.

Among apostles, there is Junia. Paul credits her with being "outstanding among the apostles," giving her a status virtually equal to Paul's among the churches (Rom 16:7). This is no small thing. As proof, male biblical interpreters once fought hard to turn Junia into a man by arguing her name was "Junias"—a male name nowhere attested in any Greek or Latin inscriptions. Today these efforts have been widely discredited.[28]

Among Paul's coworkers, there is Prisca (Priscilla), Euodia, and Syntyche—not to mention the hard-working women Mary, Persis, Tryphaena, and Tryphosa (Rom 16:3–5, 12; Phil 4:2–3).

Among prophets, Paul gives no names, either female or male. But in 1 Corinthians he suggests women can and do prophesy (11:5). Luke's narratives share this assumption, featuring female prophetic figures (Mary, Anna, Philip's daughters) and spotlighting Joel's prophecy at Pentecost: "Your sons and your daughters shall prophesy" (Acts 2:17).[29]

> "I commend to you our sister Phoebe, a deacon of the church at Cenchreae, so that you may welcome her in the Lord in a way fitting for the saints, and help her in whatever practical way she may need from you. For she has been a benefactor of many and of myself as well" (Rom 16:1–2).

Among teachers, there is Prisca (Priscilla), who assumes a teaching role alongside her husband in Acts (18:24–28). More extensive evidence for female teachers in early churches is unavailable, a reality further complicated by later NT voices that bar women from the role (1 Tim 2:12).[30] However, the very same texts, with their forceful prohibitions, strongly suggest that women *were* teachers in some first-century communities. Further, as we have seen, the role of teacher was not so cleanly distinguished from other early church roles (like that of prophets), inviting the possibility that women served in teaching roles for some communities.[31]

Among deacons, Phoebe is the only one named (male or female) by Paul. And his praise for her is loud: "I commend to you our sister Phoebe, a deacon of the church at Cenchreae. . . . For she has been a benefactor of many and of myself as well" (Rom 16:1–2). She probably hosted the church at Cenchreae (outside Corinth), as well as Paul on occasion. Contrary to the Living Bible translation, "deacon" meant far more than merely "dear Christian woman." And contrary to the New Living Translation, the word "benefactor" (*prostatis*) meant more than simply "she has been helpful." The word typically marked someone prominent who served as a patron, whether by monetary funds or social influence. Phoebe was clearly a church leader whose ministry may have entailed hospitality, financial support, human resources, and civic influence. As the first person identified as "deacon" in the New Testament, Phoebe sets a high standard. In later NT writings, women continued to serve as deacons (1 Tim 3:11).[32]

Among overseers, elders, and pastors, the NT writings name no women explicitly. But the church at Philippi may well have had women among its "deacons and overseers" (Phil 1:1), since most of the individuals Paul names in the community were women

(4:2–3). Further, several women in the New Testament hosted church-gatherings in their homes: Prisca, Nympha, Lydia, and perhaps Phoebe. Their service and leadership went beyond providing space: it may more accurately be compared with the work of overseers. When church gatherings took place in domestic spaces, they entered a world normally run by women, suggesting they retained strong roles of influence over gathered communities in these settings. Although later NT writings associate the role of overseer exclusively with men (1 Tim 3:2), many scholars believe that some church communities, especially in their early stages, featured women in genuine roles of pastoral oversight.[33]

At the close of their book *A Woman's Place: House Churches in Earliest Christianity*, Carolyn Osiek and Margaret MacDonald emphasize that women's experiences and contributions to early Christianity were complex:

> We have by no means discovered either utopian communal relations or even distinct roles for women in comparison to the broader society. Nevertheless, we come to the end of this study with greater conviction concerning the influence of women in the creation of early Christian infrastructure, their roles as hosts, teachers, and leaders, and their significant contribution to the expansion of early Christianity in the empire.[34]

Did women serve as leaders among the early NT church communities? Certainly. Were they subjected to sexist and societal biases that limited—and in some cases barred—their involvement and leadership? Absolutely. Were they influential to the formation and growth of early Christian communities? Undoubtedly. And is there far more we do not know about their experiences and opportunities with earliest Christianity? Unquestionably.

For Reflection: Recapturing Not Just Biblical Models, but *Just* Models

Characterizing fairly the experiences of women in early churches is complicated. Conflicting voices stand in tension throughout Scripture, making generalizing unhelpful. So then, we must ask not what a biblical model is for women in church leadership, but *which* biblical models are those most appropriate for emulation and implementation today? Amid the diverse voices within the New Testament, we must distinguish those that most authentically reflect the core of the gospel from those that do not.

This may sound like "picking and choosing" within Scripture. At some level, it is. And it is neither new nor necessarily unfaithful. Consciously or unconsciously, Christians throughout history have always prioritized some portions of Scripture over others, placing some books at their theological center (such as the Gospels and Paul's letters) and others (such as Leviticus and the conquest narrative) on the periphery—at least in practice, if not by conscious choice. Martin Luther did so explicitly, describing some NT writings as "true and certain chief books" and others (such as James and Revelation) as of "a different reputation" ("Prefaces to the New Testament," *Luther's Works* 35:394).

All this relates to our sense of Scripture's authority. As a witness to God's historic work among God's people, Scripture

Figure 3.5. Mosaic in San Zeno chapel of Santa Prassede (ninth century), featuring Theodora (named "episkopa"), Praxedes, Mary the mother of Jesus, and Pudentiana. Although constructed centuries after New Testament times, the mosaic is one of many scattered pieces of evidence from antiquity that women played more significant roles of leadership and service than many mainstream sources imply. Public domain, via Wikimedia Commons.

attests to both redemptive victories and sickening failures among human beings in faith, faithfulness, and living into the reign of God. The same is true with women and church leadership. On the one hand, the NT writings state profound ideals of gender equality and unity in the abstract (e.g., Gal 3:28; 1 Cor 11:11–12). On the other hand, translating these ideals into lived reality is an entirely different thing. We like to believe that Paul, Jesus, and many other church leaders tried and, in many ways, succeeded. But they also encountered limitations from conventional and cultural mores that were not easily changed—much less overturned.

What is more, this taps into matters related to justice. Instead of simply embracing any and all biblical patterns, as Christian interpreters we are called to discern and to embrace more *just* biblical models. We cannot expect that the earliest church communities lived perfectly into ideal, enduring standards of leadership; they were no less fallible and culturally constricted than we are. But we can focus on the ways they tried and embodied their ideals effectively. Where women were welcomed into leadership roles, in the spirit of "there is no longer male and female" (Gal 3:28), we find better, more just models than those that restricted along conventional, patriarchal lines (1 Tim 2:11–15). Amid the plurality of voices in Scripture, we as church people today are called to discern trajectories that best reflected justice, unity, and shalom in Christ-centered ways for the sake of our own living out more faithful models today.

Not long after the first century, Christian churches set a course that identified male leadership as the norm. Various factors influenced this. First, church communities transitioned from domestic spaces (generally under female oversight) to public ones (generally under male oversight), diminishing the opportunities for influence that came to women who hosted home gatherings.[35] Second, society at large was relentlessly patriarchal, deeming women inferior, objects (vs. subjects), and virtual second-class citizens in status and rights. Pressing as our questions are today regarding women in leadership, they were quite jarring to the cultural climate of the Roman Empire.[36] Third, conventional gender roles—which esteemed loyalty, modesty, passivity, and fertility in women—were heavily tied to public honor. Add to this the fact that from the second century on, in view of imperial hostility and misunderstanding, Christians invested in portraying themselves as moral citizens (vs. rabble-rousers) who upheld social decorum and decency. In this environment, advocacy for boundary-breaking female leadership risked inviting significant public shame. Fourth, most of the voices and decision-makers on these matters were male. Even if their aims were well-intended, their insights and experiences were one-sided.

> We are called to name prophetically the signs of patriarchy, sexism, and injustice toward human beings where we see them.

But the trajectory that won out historically is not what is most faithful and just. Although various leadership models exist in Scripture, we as church people are called to go deeper to discern each model's enduring, respective value. And we are called to name prophetically the signs of patriarchy, sexism, and injustice toward human beings where we see them—and not just with regard to women. Like all practices of spiritual discernment, these tasks are neither easy nor clear-cut. Most of the time, they are messy, divisive, and difficult. But they enable us to live more genuinely into the truer and more just visions of Christ-centered community that we find still sounding forth from Scripture, where "all of you are one in Christ Jesus" (Gal 3:28).

Church Communities and Surrounding Culture

From earliest times to today, church communities have lived in tension with surrounding cultural norms. And whether the former have perceived the latter positively or negatively, Christians across the board feel called to reflect divine mercy in who they are and how they live in the world.

Given this, what do the social dynamics of our church communities today say about God? What do they say about the good news of Jesus Christ? Luke Timothy Johnson observes, "If the church's own power arrangements simply mimic those of the world, it offers no challenge to the world, no good news."[37] What social dynamics and power structures do we embrace, reject, assume, endorse, or challenge in our practices of church community?

The earliest Jesus followers also encountered these questions. Their world was marked by stark socioeconomic divisions, rules associated with social honor, and gender biases. However, we find in the NT writings a constructive, alternative vision for leadership and the practice of community as Jesus people.

An Alternative Model of Leadership: Servants

No early NT writing suggests church leadership was to be associated with honor and high status. This contrasts with synagogues and associations elsewhere in the Roman Empire, which entertained more noticeable interests in titles and positions. Mediterranean synagogues, for instance, had offices typically marked by "leader" (*arch-*) language: leader (*archōn*), synagogue leader (*archisynagōgos*), and leader of a council of elders (*gerousiarch*).[38] Voluntary associations had similar titles and roles of honor (*archontes, epistatai, hēgemones*), but with greater variety.[39] Language associated with honor and status was used prevalently for leadership across Greco-Roman society.

But on this point, the earliest churches differed. Although individuals like Jesus and Paul used such language to refer to political and societal leaders, they rejected it for themselves and church community leaders.[40] Vincent Branick states, "It was all work and no play for the Christian administrators, who may have wondered why their non-Christian peers could enjoy extravagant positions of respect"—in contrast to themselves.[41] The most influential voices of the New Testament shared a vision for church leadership that differed from the patterns of their surrounding world. The message of Jesus, it seemed, called for an alternative model.

"Let everyone regard us this way: as servants of Christ and stewards of the mysteries of God. In addition, it is required of stewards that they be found faithful." (1 Cor 4:1–2)

Paul describes this model when he clarifies how believers at Corinth ought to regard him and his ministry associates: "Let everyone regard us this way: as servants of Christ and stewards of the mysteries of God. In addition, it is required of stewards that they be found faithful" (1 Cor 4:1–2). Nowhere else is Paul so carefully reflective about apostolic leadership. The words "servant" (*hypēretēs*) and "steward" (*oikonomos*) are neither honorific nor commanding. In fact, they are downright unimpressive. But for hearers used to bestowing honors on leaders, these titles were instructive clarifications (see also 1 Cor 1:10–17). For Paul, leaders of the Jesus community are called to faithfulness, not status or social honor.

The Gospels emphasize "servant" leadership even more strongly. In instructions preserved by Mark, Matthew, and Luke, Jesus corrects his followers' aspirations for greatness with a countercultural vision:

> And calling [his disciples], he said to them: "You know that those who are supposed to rule the Gentiles lord it over them, and their great ones deliberately exercise authority over them. But it must not be so among you. Instead, whoever desires to be great among you must be your servant, and whoever desires to be first among you must be slave of all. For the Son of Man did not come to be served but to serve, and to give his life as a ransom for many." (Mark 10:42–45; so also Matt 20:25b–28; Luke 22:24–27)

A starker contrast between conventional leadership models and the way of Jesus is hardly possible. John's Gospel includes the same emphasis on servant leadership, rooted in Jesus's humble activity of washing feet:

> You call me Teacher and Lord—and rightly, for that is what I am. So if I, your Lord and Teacher, have washed

your feet, you also ought to wash one another's feet. For
I have set you an example, so that you also should do as I
have done for you. Truly I tell you, servants [or "slaves"]
are not greater than their masters, nor are messengers
greater than those who sent them. If you know these
things, blessed are you if you do them. (John 13:13–17)

In contrast to mainstream patterns of leadership, which aspired
for social honor and status, Jesus challenged his followers to be
"servants" and "slaves."[42] For Jesus, true greatness entailed a
form of leadership fundamentally characterized by servanthood.

Both Jesus and Paul cast related visions of servant leadership
that went against the grain of first-century norms.[43] The call to lead
is characterized by servanthood and stewardship, not lordship and
royalty. At its core, this model takes its cues from the pattern of
ministry set by a crucified Messiah (Phil 2:5–11; Mark 10:42–45).

An Alternative Model of Community: The Body of Christ

The message of Christ crucified calls not only for an alternative model of leadership but for an alternative way of being in
community. Paul fleshed this out through a specific metaphor
for community: the body of Christ. Although later NT writings
employed social distinctions more readily,[44] Paul's early, undisputed letters spotlighted the body of Christ as the foremost guid-
ing metaphor for what it means to practice community together.

Paul lay the groundwork for this metaphor by first undermining conventional patterns of patronage. We see it in his dealings

with believers at Corinth: he refused their financial support (1 Cor 9:1–27; 2 Cor 11:7–11), chastised them for honoring distinctions at the Lord's Supper (1 Cor 11:17–34), and argued for equal honor among community members (12:12–31). He also shamed those who engaged in sexual immorality and those who hauled fellow believers to court (5:1–6:20). And he corrected those who ate food sacrificed to idols with no regard for believers whose consciences were offended (8:1–11:1). All these issues are related. In addressing them all, Paul challenged conventional privileges associated with wealth and status. Only the wealthy and privileged received special honors at banquets, had influence in court, and had regular opportunities to partake in sexual immorality and temple banquets with food sacrificed to idols. Here Paul makes it clear: their privileges do not apply within the community of Christ followers. In stating these things, Paul sought to level the playing field by undermining some very significant cultural norms.[45]

Paul's alternative vision for community is the body of Christ (1 Cor 12:12–31; also 10:17; Rom 12:4–5). The metaphor of community as a "body" was common among ancient writers.[46] But Paul gave it his own distinctive nuances. First, he emphasized the value of "inferior," "less honorable," and "less respectable" members—those typically overlooked and undervalued:

> But rather, the members of the body that appear to be inferior are indispensable, and those that appear to be less honorable we value with greater honor, and our less respectable members receive greater respect—whereas our more respectable members have no need of this. But

God has so arranged the body, giving greater honor to
the inferior member. (1 Cor 12:22–24)

For Paul, the unconventional approach of especially honoring
inferior members is not his idea but God's. It's simply how God
has "arranged" the body, the community of faith. Very likely, the
"more respectable" (socially) community members at Corinth
found Paul's words surprising, as well as displeasing. But for a
community whose core identity was in Christ, Paul deemed a
rebalancing of social statuses and honors to be critical. Those
who knew neither honor nor respect in society deserved special
value within the community of Christ.

> "But God has so arranged the body, giving greater
> honor to the inferior member, in order that there may
> be no dissension in the body, but so that the members
> may have the same concern for one another. And if one
> member suffers, all the members suffer along with it. If
> one member is honored, all the members rejoice together
> with it. Now you are the body of Christ and individually
> members of it." (1 Cor 12:24b–27)

Second, Paul emphasized mutual care for one another.
Other ancient authors using the "body" metaphor emphasized
the interdependence of community members (often as an unfavorable reality). But Paul took it a step further: members not
only depend on one another, they invest in one another by care
and concern. This arrangement is not just to curb dissension but
so that members may "have the same concern" for one another,

sharing in both suffering and rejoicing together (1 Cor 12:25).[47] Such mutual sharing was a character trait of the community united in Christ, which ultimately reflected the "more excellent" way of love (13:1–13).

Third, Paul emphasized unity. At the start of his extended metaphor about the body, he points out, "For just as the body is one but has many members, and all members, though many, are one body, so also is it with Christ: for by one Spirit we all were baptized into one body—whether Jews or Greeks, slaves or free—and we all were given to drink of one Spirit" (1 Cor 12:12–13). For Paul, God's Spirit has united believers in baptism. No matter their social statuses, ethnicities, or backgrounds, they are knit together in Christ. This unity implies equality among members—anchored not in uniformity but in a shared connection to Christ. In the context of this relationship, Paul states elsewhere, "there is no longer Jew no Greek, there is no longer slave or free, there is no longer male and female; for all . . . are one in Christ Jesus" (Gal 3:28).

Conclusion: Church and Culture at the Crossroads

The question named earlier bears repeating: What do the social dynamics of our church communities today say about God? Many church communities today have long histories of honoring specific members—often those who give large sums of money. Affirming generosity is a good thing. But doing so runs the risk of nurturing economic distinctions—a fundamental mark of class divisions. And as Paul's complicated relationship with believers at Corinth shows us, socioeconomic distinctions can easily get in the way of authentic community.

Social divisions are not limited to economics. They may equally stem from years of membership, regularity of attendance, levels of leadership, circles of friends, forms of service, religious education, musical skills, dress or appearance, ethnic pedigrees, cultural heritages, social influence, or civic involvement—not to mention the perennial distinctions of gender, age, and race. In general, human beings gravitate toward social distinctions as ways to self-identify, especially when they boost our own sense of worth.

Paul's vision of the body of Christ undercuts the power of such distinctions among believers. In Christ, the distinctions have no lasting significance. And it is the community's charge to live into this reality authentically. However oppressive the forces of division, injustice, discrimination, and favoritism are for many in daily life, the community of Christ is called to walk to the beat of a different drummer. Followers of Jesus live an alternative reality "in Christ," where distinctions do not have the last word. And even though a countercultural community may not easily influence the customs that rule society at large, its practices still bear witness to a reign of God characterized more by unity than inequality.

In our church communities today, what do people experience? Warmth? Coldness? Grace? Judgment? Equality? Inequality? Welcome? Love? Concern? Humility? Vulnerability? Thoughtfulness? How do these things compare with experiences elsewhere?

Perhaps most importantly, where do people experience God—and marks of divine goodness—in our communities of faith? For many people, divine grace is experienced less often in the abstract or as a church slogan than through the personal warmth of other human beings.

It Starts with Leaders

A countercultural community often thrives with leaders who embody such virtues themselves. For church leaders, that is no small thing. Those with power are those most reluctant to relinquish it. And church leaders of all kinds—no matter their titles, statuses, or training—have power and influence in their church communities. As proof of this, many titles associated with church leaders today subtly suggest honor and superiority: reverend, father, mother, elder, president, doctor, patriarch, and so on. Even though Jesus and Paul did not embrace honorific language for church leaders, in time Christians used it anyway (e.g., archbishop, patriarch, archdeacon). And in today's world, we need not look far to see examples of power abuse by church leaders. As a result, one of the most prevailing criticisms of the US Christian church and its leaders is that they focus too much on money and power.[48]

Both Jesus and Paul instructed believers to blaze different trails with leadership patterns that centered on humility, service, and stewardship. But this is entirely countercultural. Across history, most models of leadership have had strong associations with status, honor, authority, and power. Church communities have not always differed, often struggling more than succeeding at modeling biblical ideals of leadership. But the call remains, for leaders and believers in general, to "have this mind among you that also was in Christ Jesus" (Phil 2:5), who relinquished status and honor to the ultimate end.

One concrete and constructive step toward countercultural leadership is to welcome the excluded (societally) into leadership. An example of this from earliest Christianity is the inclusion of women in leadership. In many early church communities, women occupied roles of leadership. Today's world continues that trajectory, with increasing opportunities for women to serve in leadership as clergy.

But there are many other people excluded and undervalued by larger society: ethnic minorities, immigrants, those without formal higher education, those whose mother tongue differs from the majority, those who identify as LGBTQ+, those with physical disabilities, those with cognitive disabilities, and the young and old, just to name a few. Efforts to bring such individuals into leadership (and not just ordination) are a positive sign that in Christ's community, not only are the undervalued included, they are worth respecting as leaders. A model of inclusive leadership is not a matter of mere political persuasion. It takes

> One concrete and constructive step toward countercultural leadership is to welcome the excluded (societally) into leadership.

seriously the countercultural leadership of Christ, the counter-intuitive message of the cross, and the profound unity shared by people in Christ. It is a way of being that embraces the radical commitments to which Jesus called his followers.

The Contextual Nature of Leadership

As this chapter has shown, the earliest church communities approached leadership more as contextualized realities than a universal pattern, with an approach more adaptive than a "one-size-fits-all" formula. This does not mean NT leadership roles were willy-nilly, lacking discernment and training. It simply means they were especially geared toward the specific needs of specific communities in their respective stages of development. As standardized as church leadership roles are in some contexts today, it has not always been the case.

In most parts of the world in the twenty-first century, church communities are larger and more numerous than those in the first century. This reality calls for more structured patterns of leadership. But it does not mean structured patterns are necessarily better. In fact, the sheer diversity today among church communities regarding leadership patterns suggests how short-sighted it is to think one model is wholly superior. Not only in the first century, but throughout history, church communities have often been at their best when they have adapted to address contextual realities more effectively. This includes patterns of leadership.

The landscapes of church, culture, and society are changing rapidly today in places like the United States and elsewhere. An increasing number of people do not affiliate with religious communities, are critical of institutionalized religion, and are unfamiliar with many religious practices. Many people today regard the tangible difference Christian faith makes in people's lives as far more critical than religious credentials and confessional statements. Meanwhile, the largest increases of church affiliation are taking place virtually everywhere *except* among Euro-American groups, with Latino and Asian American populations leading the charge. Many of these communities are served well by leaders who have been raised up from within their own ranks and who need different kinds of training than the conventional models of years ago. Further, over the next few decades, an increasing number of church communities are expected no longer to be able to pay clergy full-time salaries the way they once did, forcing creative thinking around church partnerships and alternative leadership models.

All these realities call church communities to embrace adaptive thinking and more contextualized forms of leadership training for the church of the future. In many ways, the models we embrace going forward may look more like those used at the church's earliest stages. Potential changes like these will not be easy. Nor will they take place overnight. Nor *should* they. But the good news is that Christ's church has seen such days before, and they have hardly meant the demise of the gospel. Adaptation to new forms of discipleship and leadership for an uncertain world requires imagination, creativity, working together, and a lot of hard work. But where communities of Christ gather to face such challenges, the Holy Spirit is prone to activate the distinctive gifts most needed for building up the church of tomorrow, starting today.

Bringing It Home: Ideas and Conversation for Implementation

1. Invite someone new to worship or an event in your church community. Ask him or her afterward what he or she experienced and saw.
2. Speak with your pastor(s) or other church leader(s) about what biblical models they deem especially informative to their work.
3. Lead a group in conversation or Bible study on 1 Corinthians 12:12–31 and the metaphor "the body of Christ."
4. Invite a group of Christians to a conversation—in person or online—about what characteristics they most value in church leaders and why.
5. Ask a church leader with ministry training (seminary or otherwise) what some of the most formative experiences they had in that training were. What do they think is most important for church leadership training?

Scripture Study

- Teachings of Jesus on leadership in the Gospels: Mark 10:42–45 (parallels: Matt 20:25b–28; Luke 22:24–27) and John 13:1–17. See also Mark 9:35; Matthew 23:11; Luke 9:48; John 6:15; 15:13.

- The Acts of the Apostles, especially portions that relate to leadership in various communities: 6:1–7; 13:1–3; 14:23; 18:24–28; 20:17–38.
- 1 Corinthians 12:1–14:40, especially Paul's words regarding the "body of Christ" in 12:12–31 (see also Rom 12:3–8).

For Worship

- John Fawcett, "Blest Be the Tie That Binds" (*ELW* #656).
- Latin Antiphon, "Ubi Caritas et Amor (Where True Charity and Love Abide)" (*ELW* #642 and #653).
- Rusty Edwards, "We All Are One in Mission" (*ELW* #576).

Questions for Reflection

1. Think about some of the social dynamics that governed the lives of early believers (early part of this chapter). What do you find most interesting? Which of these do you think posed some of the greatest challenges for practicing community as Christians?
2. This chapter generally emphasized that leadership in the earliest church communities developed in more contextualized ways than universal paradigms. Is this similar to— or different from—leadership forms in churches today?

3. Evidence shows that women participated in leadership in many early church communities, with various levels of acceptance and opposition. How do these experiences compare with those of women in leadership today, in church communities and in larger society?

4. The last portions of the chapter deal with ways some NT voices challenged cultural norms of the surrounding society (regarding leadership and social distinctions). Where do church communities challenge cultural norms in today's world? Where should they do so more?

5. Imagine a church community that genuinely lived out Jesus's call to live and lead as servants. What would that look like?

6. Where do you see signs of hope that church communities can (or do) embody the message of Jesus by how they live and treat one another?

7. For you, what does a community centered on Christ look like?

Online Resources for Further Exploration

"Women Clergy: A Growing and Diverse Community," *Religion Link*, May 15, 2015, https://tinyurl.com/y2tz36kr.

David Masci, "The Divide over Ordaining Women," *Fact Tank*, September 9, 2014, https://tinyurl.com/y5nz3l3x.

Resources for Further Reading

Clarke, Andrew D. *Serve the Community of the Church: Christians as Leaders and Ministers*. Grand Rapids: Eerdmans, 2000. Discusses leadership and organization practices among various groups in Roman society—the city, voluntary associations, synagogues, the household—and the extent to which they influenced early church communities. Clarke highlights several ways that Paul differed from conventional patterns of leadership in his day.

Malina, Bruce J. *Windows on the World of Jesus: Time Travel to Ancient Judea*. Louisville: John Knox, 1993. A readable and enjoyable exploration of the customs and cultural world in which Jesus lived. The book includes sixty vignettes, each featuring a twentieth-century North American who encounters foreign cultural realities in ancient Judea.

Madigan, Kevin, and Carolyn Osiek, eds and trans. *Ordained Women in the Early Church: A Documentary History*. Baltimore: Johns Hopkins University Press, 2005. A collection of all primary sources from the Latin and Greek-speaking world for women deacons and presbyters in the early church, from its beginning to around 600 CE.

Osiek, Carolyn, and Margaret Y. MacDonald. *A Woman's Place: House Churches in Earliest Christianity*. Minneapolis: Fortress, 2006. A careful and well-researched look at the context of ancient households and the challenges and opportunities for women within the emergence of earliest Christianity. An excellent and readable resource from authors who have contributed extensively to this field of study.

4

Practicing the Things That Matter

[Gathered] assemblies were not a new or specifically Christian invention. In gathering as associations or clubs, in regarding each other as a kind of family, in meeting in households, in sharing meals, Christians were making use of a widespread pattern in Greco-Roman society.

—Gordon Lathrop

What practices really matter for Christian worship? There are many answers to this question. The Lutheran *Augsburg Confession* identifies worship as essentially preaching the gospel and administering the sacraments (articles 5 and 7). John Calvin, based on Acts 2:42, characterized it as attending to the word, prayers, Eucharist, and sharing (*Institutes of the Christian Religion* 4.17.44). Roman Catholic and Eastern

Opening Questions:

1. What practices are core to Christian worship?
2. What practices are central for nurturing church community?
3. When you think of a first-century church gathering, what do you imagine took place?

Orthodox traditions emphasize the Eucharist as the center of worship. For Quakers, "expectant waiting" is the essence of worship. A popular song (by Matt Redman) from the late 1990s characterized the "heart of worship" as simply "all about you, Jesus." Clearly, there are many answers to the question of what practices really matter for Christian worship.

In fact, the question is very much alive today. Just ask a random sampling of Christians what they think is most essential to worship. In my experience, a lot of input I hear today revolves around the notion of "relevance." For this reason, many church communities go to great lengths to capture a spirit of relevance, whether by way of a style of music, multimedia, alternative spaces (e.g., taprooms, coffeehouses), packaging of its message, or availability of services. The challenge, of course, is that what is relevant to one person may not be relevant to the next, and what is relevant now will not be in a few years.

On the flip side, in recent years many millennials and others have expressed a desire to return to sacred tradition and the spirituality they embody. The desire is for spiritual practices that run deeper than current trends, offering a sense of connection to the saints of the past—and the future. For these worshipers, "relevance" looks less like a modern worship band and more like simple forms of plainclothes authenticity. All these considerations only beg the question, What practices really matter for Christian worship?

To answer this, we must start with where we came from. However we define relevance and its significance today, a sense of the earliest practices of church communities are essential to setting a course for how we define and approach worship practices today.

As a young person growing up in a church community, I assumed all our worship practices basically came from Jesus. In fact, when I first started to read the Bible, I expected to learn how these practices came to be. Only later on, when I experienced the variety of worship practices across different Christian traditions, did I realize how widely church communities differ.

My assumptions as a young person are not isolated ones. At some level, most of us believe the worship traditions familiar to us not only make sense but also reflect the principles and best practices of early church communities. In other words, we tend to think our own practices are "biblical"—however we define that—or at least historically grounded. Liturgically oriented communities, for instance, often characterize their traditions not only as historic but also as having roots that reach back to the earliest churches. Nonliturgical communities often pride themselves on being less bound by tradition but at the same time strive to reflect biblical ideals more directly. Ultimately, virtually every church community under the sun sees itself as somehow grounded in the practices of NT church communities.

But how comparable are our worship experiences today to those of the earliest church communities? There are some significant differences between then and now. Even communities that spring out of the modern house church movement cannot replicate early church practices pristinely, hard as they may try, simply because of the vast differences of time and context.

What practices were at the heart of early Christian worship? Addressing this question will help us think about the practices of worship that most matter for our own day and age.

Gathering and Worship: First-Century Style

Imagine you are a resident of Corinth, a freed person, living in the first century of the common era. Your friend has invited you to attend a gathering of people at the home of man named Gaius. You are told it will entail a meal, and afterward time for discourse. Your friend tells you the group is devoted to a deity named "Christos."

Your friend has told you a few things about this religious association: it has significant ties to the religion of Jews, though most participants are not ethnically Jewish; they gather regularly, especially when specific prophets or teachers are in town; they share resources among themselves and with outsiders, as they are able; they practice rituals that involve water baths, eating together, prophesying, and teaching. Finally, the association is not limited to men, adults, or people of certain social standings. In fact, the community's unity across social distinctions is emphasized. Since your friend has invited you, personal honor—as well as your own curiosity—leads you to accept the invitation.

When you arrive, you see Gaius's home is spacious: about 2,500 square feet in area, clearly owned by an elite member of society. Being welcomed into such a home is not an everyday occasion for a freed person as yourself. This hospitality, you anticipate, comes with an expectation that you will honor Gaius favorably in public (where possible) as a generous man. But you regard this to be a fair price to pay for the occasion.

At the door that opens to the street, a slave receives you, asks whose invitation brings you, and welcomes you into the atrium (see figure 4.1 for an example). Several other people have also entered and are now being greeted by the host, Gaius. After speaking with them, he greets you warmly and welcomes you into his home. He emphasizes the honor it is to have you present, points out the votive altar honoring his ancestors and family, and directs you to the courtyard where other guests are mingling and enjoying hors d'oeuvres.

As is obvious from the diversity of clothing, hairstyles, and social mannerisms, the people gathered reflect a wide range of social statures. In some ways, this mixture of social statuses is refreshing. In other ways, it feels awkward, since you are naturally concerned with appropriately honoring anyone there who may socially be your superior.

After some time mingling, Gaius and his wife enter the courtyard to extend a public welcome to all guests, introducing some by name—especially an "apostle" named Paul. Gaius invites Paul to lead the community in prayer before dining. Paul

Figure 4.1. View of atrium of the House of Menander (Pompeii, before 79 CE), with a peristyle courtyard visible in the distance. The photo replicates what a visitor would have seen upon entering the home. Photo by Carole Raddato.

does so, offering a prayer that sounds in some ways Jewish, and in other ways like prayers you have heard at other sacred meals. He often names a certain "Jesus" in this prayer—someone unfamiliar to you—calling him "Messiah" and "Lord." After Paul's prayer, Gaius welcomes a selection of guests to recline in the triclinium for the meal. The rest remain in the courtyard, to eat reclining on available ground area as they are comfortable.

At a certain point during the meal, Paul invites everyone's attention toward a sacred act he performs. He holds up bread from the meal and states the following words: "The Lord Jesus on the night when he was betrayed took a loaf of bread, and when he had given thanks, he broke it and said, 'This is my body that is for you. Do this in remembrance of me.'" Then Paul and Gaius offer bread portions to each group of guests, who take and share it among each other, partaking in it like food that has been offered in sacrifice to a god.

Paul then asks again for everyone's attention, while holding up a cup of wine. He says, "In the same way our Lord Jesus took the cup also, after supper, saying, 'This cup is the new covenant in my blood. Do this, as often as you drink it, in remembrance of me.' For as often as we eat this bread and drink the cup, we proclaim the Lord's death until he comes." Then, as with the bread, Paul and Gaius offer the cup to each group of people, who take and pass it one to another, allowing everyone the opportunity to drink. All this takes place in ways that remind you of other religious banquets you have attended. After that, the meal resumes.

Not long afterward, Gaius invites a reconfiguring of seating in the courtyard—the only space in the house able to accommodate the thirty-some people present. Once convened, Paul begins to speak, teaching those assembled about Jesus the Messiah. Paul says things like the following:

"Though he was in the form of God, he did not regard equality with God as something to be exploited, but emptied himself, taking the form of a slave, being born in human likeness. And being found in human form, he humbled himself and became obedient to the point of death—even death on a cross. Therefore, God also highly exalted him, and gave him the name that is above every name, so that at the name of Jesus every knee should bend, in heaven and on earth and under the earth, and every tongue should confess that Jesus Christ is Lord, to the glory of God the Father."

After Paul teaches for some time, those gathered join in singing a hymn—one unfamiliar to you. Then some individuals begin to pray, some quietly and others more audibly. After a few minutes of this, a woman stands before the assembly to say something: "This is the word of the Lord: we are called to be one body, united in purpose and in love, and not to honor divisions among us. We are united in Christ, and are called to be united in Spirit with him." Other individuals stand before the assembly to say similar words about love, unity, humility, perseverance, and practices of holy living. Some words address the entire community, while others concern specific individuals, and still others address the context and society in which they live. The gathered community responds to these words with affirmations ranging from loud and pronounced to quiet and inaudible. Throughout this time, you hear foreign words like "Amen," "*Maranatha,*" and "Hallelujah." This goes on for nearly an hour.

After these events conclude, the community joins in a prayer led by Gaius's wife. Afterward, some people depart by greeting one another with a kiss of peace, just as many did when they first entered the assembly at the start of the evening. All seem distinctively gracious and warm toward one another. Gaius himself ushers you and some others outside, reiterating his welcome for you to return next week when they gather again.

Christian Worship in First-Century Context

The preceding story gives a glimpse of what a mid-first-century church gathering in Corinth might have looked like. In past generations, NT interpreters portrayed earliest Christianity as unstructured when it came to rituals and practices. It was, if compared with cults elsewhere in the Roman Empire, which boasted sacred structures, physical monuments, traditional sacrifices, and public festivals.[1] But that comparison is unfair, since church communities in the first century not only lacked dedicated buildings, they also lacked consistent tolerance by governing authorities (imperial and regional) to carry out religious activities publicly.

Regardless, early Christians certainly had core rituals that they practiced regularly. Rituals, after all, are forms of communication: they convey a community's central values and beliefs to themselves and observers. Rituals communicate who we are and what we believe.

As Gordon Lathrop points out, it may be misleading to use the word *worship* to refer to the wide variety of practices among early church gatherings.[2] Certainly the earliest believers gathered, and certainly they worshiped. But they also engaged in a broad spectrum of activities at different kinds of gatherings: they ate together, talked with one another, listened to readings of letters, addressed matters of conflict, made decisions together, shared their resources, prayed, sang hymns, laid hands on the

> Early Christians certainly had core rituals that they practiced regularly.

sick, engaged in prophetic discourse, and many other activities as well. These are only the activities suggested by the New Testament, and not all of them fit a narrow definition of "worship." For this reason, it is more accurate to see early church assemblies as *gatherings* that incorporated worship as well as other activities.

Over a half-dozen times in 1 Corinthians, Paul refers to occasions when the church community at Corinth "gathers" or "assembles" together (5:4; 11:17–18, 20, 33–34; 14:23, 26). At least some of these occasions involved the entire church gathering "in one place" (11:20; 14:23). Paul's language implies these were regular occasions. Several NT references suggest weekly gatherings on Sundays were a norm (1 Cor 16:2; Acts 20:7; also Rev 1:9–10). That Jewish synagogues gathered weekly (on the Sabbath) may have encouraged a similar practice among Christians. By the second century, many sources describe Christians as gathering on "the Lord's Day" (Sunday).[3]

Like synagogue communities and other groups in the Roman Empire, participants in early church communities gathered at different times and places and for different reasons. Even so, virtually all these gatherings had religious goals at heart.[4] And one of the most attested took shape around a meal.

Shared Meals and the Lord's Supper

Shared meals were fundamental to early Christian assembly and life together. There are two reasons for this: the influence of Jesus traditions and the prevalence of shared meals in the first-century Mediterranean world.

First, Jesus started a tradition of eating together in his remembrance. As described in several NT writings, at what is referred to as the Last Supper, Jesus gave a new spin to the Passover meal, consecrating bread and wine as his body and blood (1 Cor 11:23–25; Mark 14:22–25; Matt 26:26–30; Luke 22:14–23). Certainly, this influenced ensuing Eucharist practices. But it is not the only influence from the traditions of Jesus. Many early stories of his ministry feature meals and lavish distribution of food as signs of God's reign. In a context where most hearers were peasants, these acts of provision were no small thing. In fact, some scholars suggest these acts of food sharing across economic distinctions were so central to Jesus's ministry that they—no less than the Last Supper—were primary influences on later eucharistic practices.[5]

Second, shared meals were a basic social and cultural norm for people across the Mediterranean. Eating together fostered community, shared values, and connection with the divine. Meals and banquets in the Greek and Roman world were influenced by traditions of the symposium, an extended banquet that featured drinking alongside entertainment or discourse. These traditions are at least as old as Plato and Xenophon (fourth century BCE). They include a meal of several courses, with guests reclining together according to positions of status and sacred acts accompanying most courses. Afterward was the symposium proper: drinking wine while engaging in either entertainment or high-minded discussion (symposium = Greek *sympinein,* "to drink together"). Entertainment may have involved music (often by a flute girl), party games, dramatic presentations, or bawdier activities.[6] In the Greek philosophical tradition, the symposium hosted discussion about enlightened themes—a form readily adapted for church usage.

If there is one thing true about early Christian meal gatherings, it's that their practices varied. Some meal gatherings featured either the bread or the cup, but not both. Some eucharistic rituals blessed the cup first, while others the bread.[9] Others featured a full meal with the Eucharist ritual. In short, uniform Eucharist practices are a product of later centuries, when centralization and uniformity became virtues. Gordon Lathrop points out, "Meals are always local events, with local food, local meeting places, local participants, local customs. Of course, they are diverse, especially so in a time when Christian communities had no particular instruments of extensive uniformity."[10]

> Early church communities clearly saw the Eucharist as an act of social formation.

The earliest Eucharist reference appears in 1 Corinthians. Paul calls the meal "the Lord's Supper," implying a genuine meal—not just a ritual act (11:20). Elsewhere the word *supper* (*deipnon*) commonly refers to the main meal of the day, sometimes even a formal banquet or a cultic meal. Unlike later depictions of the Eucharist, Paul speaks of "eating" (vs. "partaking") the meal. He mentions no official or presider (cf. Justin, *1 Apology* 67.5; Didache 10.7). This particular meal gathering probably entailed all believers in Corinth gathered together at once (1 Cor 11:20; also 10:16–17; 14:23).

Figure 2. Fresco of female figure holding chalice in the Agape Feast. Catacomb of Saints Pietro e Marcellino (Saints Marcellinus and Peter), Via Labicana, Rome, Italy. Courtesy of Wikimedia Commons.

Like or unlike some modern associations, the Eucharist was primarily an identity marker for early church communities: it served to draw distinctions between them and their surrounding world. Association groups in the Roman Empire held festival meals for similar purposes, making early Christian practice nothing extraordinary. Paul, for example, depicted the Eucharist as incompatible with joining in pagan meals (1 Cor 10:21). Soon after Paul's time, several Christian writings explicitly restrict the Eucharist to the baptized (Did. 9.5; Justin, *1 Apol.* 66). Though it is not clear, Paul's churches may have done the same (see 1 Cor 5:11; 14:23–25). In short, early church communities clearly saw

> "Now in the following instructions I do not commend you,
> because when you come together it is not for the better
> but for the worse. . . . When you come together, it is not
> really to eat the Lord's supper. For when the time comes
> to eat, each of you goes ahead with your own supper,
> and one goes hungry and another becomes drunk. What!
> Do you not have homes to eat and drink in? Or do you
> show contempt for the church of God and humiliate those
> who have nothing? What should I say to you? Should I
> commend you? In this matter I do not commend you!"
> (1 Cor 11:17–22).

the Eucharist as an act of social formation: aimed at uniting a community in a shared identity in relation to Jesus as Lord.

Some early sources speak of a "love feast" (*agapē*), a kind of shared meal similar to the Eucharist (Jude 12). But while some sources differentiate it from the Eucharist, others virtually equate the two.[11] Around 200 CE, Tertullian characterized the love feast as a shared evening meal accompanied by prayers, hymns, and teaching:

> We do not recline at the table before prayer to God is
> first made. Then we eat as much as satisfies the hungry,
> and drink as much as is beneficial to the modest. We sat-
> isfy ourselves as those who remember that even during
> the night we are to worship God; we converse as those
> who know that the Lord is listening. After the washing
> of hands and lighting of lamps, each one who is able is
> called into the center to chant praise to God either from

Figure 4.3. "Miracle of the Loaves and Fishes," Basilica di Sant' Apollinare Nuovo (Ravenna), sixth century. Public domain.

the holy scriptures or from one's own talents; that itself tests how much each has drunk. And in like manner, prayer concludes the meal. (*Apol.* 39.16–18)

Tertullian's emphasis on modesty aims to distinguish Christian dining practices from slander that insinuated they were gatherings for immorality. In time, the Eucharist ritual became clearly distinguished from shared meals, a distinction likely spurred on more by the restrictions of physical spaces than by theological ideas.

Many other questions remain about early Christian Eucharists. Did men and women recline together? Were social distinctions honored more than we realize? Did women preside over the Eucharist, especially when they hosted gatherings? The truth is, the answer to each of these questions likely is, *It varied*, from community to community, from region to region. The same is true for the Eucharist ritual itself, which sometimes was part of a larger meal and other times stood alone.[12] Clearly, eucharistic practices were more diverse than standardized.

In the second century, Justin described eucharistic practice as it took place in Rome:

> When we have finished praying, bread and wine and water are brought up, and the president likewise sends up prayers and thanksgivings to the best of his ability, and the people assent, saying the Amen; and the [elements over which] thanks have been given are distributed, and everyone partakes; and they are sent through the deacons to those who are not present. (*1 Apology* 67)[13]

Although nearly a century after Paul's day, Justin's description is closer in time and practice to the traditions of NT church communities than our own, making his words more helpful than not for our imagining church practices as they first took shape.

Baptism

From the earliest stages, church communities practiced Christian baptism. Paul mentions individuals whom he personally baptized (1 Cor 1:13–17). Even more, he regularly depicts baptism as a fundamental point of unity for all believers (Gal

3:17–18; 1 Cor 6:11; 12:13; Rom 6:1–11). Other NT writings only confirm that baptism was practiced widely and across different contexts, typically as a ritual of initiation into the believing community.[14]

Rites of water immersion were common throughout the ancient world. But Christian baptism's deepest roots are Jewish rituals associated with purification and repentance.[15] The word baptism (Gk *baptisma*) means "immersion" or "dipping," making clear it was fundamentally an act of water immersion. Paul's comparison of baptism to "burial with Christ" (Rom 6:4; also Col 2:12) also implies full immersion was typical, though by the end of the first century sprinkling is an attested alternative (Did. 7.3). By that same time, if not earlier, communities baptized "in the name of the Father and of the Son and of the Holy Spirit" (Matt 28:19; Did. 7.1; Justin, *1 Apol.* 61).

Early NT writings do not state where baptisms took place, but late first-century references suggest rivers were common venues.[16] In fact, the Didache (late first or early second century) declares rivers preferable, likely for hygienic reasons (7.1–2). That Jesus was baptized in a river may also be an influence. Though some buildings had resources for water immersion (public baths, synagogues), they were not necessarily available for Christian rituals. And most homes boasted water receptacles no more than a few feet deep, at best (the impluvium). This suggests baptisms happened not at shared meal gatherings, but on separate occasions in alternative spaces—a reality in play at least in the second century (Justin, *1 Apol.* 65).

Paul's baptism references suggest two things about its practice in his churches. First, the baptized participant probably undressed before and reclothed after immersion. Paul associated baptism with "clothing" the self "with Christ," with "put[ting] on the Lord Jesus Christ" a prevalent symbol for the new life (Gal 3:27; Rom 13:14; also Rom 13:12; Col 3:10, 12; Eph 4:24). Though metaphors, these words suggest the shedding and donning of new clothes was a baptism practice that was in place in Paul's day.[17] Second, Paul's letters and Acts attest to baptizing women, servants, and whole households. This suggests the ritual was not restricted to adults of a certain age, status, or gender.[18]

"Now concerning baptism, baptize this way: after addressing all these things, baptize in the name of the Father and of the Son and of the Holy Spirit in running water. But if you do not have running water, then baptize in other water; and if you are not able in cold water, then do so in warm water. But if you have neither, then pour water on the head three times in the name of the Father and of the Son and of the Holy Spirit. And before the baptism, let the one baptizing and the one being baptized fast, as well as any others who are able. You will also instruct the one being baptized to fast one or two days beforehand." (Didache 7.1–4)

Beyond these details, we may only speculate. We wonder how early baptism was associated with anointing (see 2 Cor 1:21; 1 John 2:20, 27). We also wonder when credal professions became a regular part of baptisms. And we wonder where and

Figure 4.4. The Baptism of Jesus, domed ceiling mosaic in Baptistry at Ravenna. Photo by José Luiz Bernardes Ribeiro. Wikimedia Commons.

when patterns of formation took place in preparation for baptism. Although later sources depict extensive preparation as a pattern (*Apostolic Tradition* 17), the NT writings give no indications of comparable practices early on. Even fasting in preparation for baptism is not well-attested until the second century (Did. 7.4; Justin, *1 Apol.* 61). We also wonder how uniform the practices of baptism were across regions and communities. Regardless of these variations, Christian baptism clearly was the fundamental ritual of initiation and inclusion into the community of faith.

Forms of Spiritual Discourse (Hymns, Prayers, Teaching, Prophecy, Tongues)

In 1 Corinthians, Paul describes the activity of the assembled this way: "When you gather together, each one has a hymn, another has a teaching, another has a revelation, another has a tongue, and another has an interpretation. Let all things take place toward the purpose of building up" (14:26). Clearly these early church gatherings were participatory, with many participants joining in offering instruction and forms of spiritual discourse. In fact, Paul's words suggest the flow of this gathered time was more disorderly and chaotic than consistent and structured (14:26–33). C. K. Barrett aptly writes, "Church meetings in Corinth can scarcely have suffered from dullness."[19] Still, Paul's words identify some common patterns of spiritual discourse for their assemblies.

Hymns, Psalms, and Singing

Hymns, psalms, and singing likely were regular features of early Christian gatherings. Singing to deities was a common practice for gatherings of Jewish and Greek religious groups.[20] And several NT writings depict "psalms, hymns, and spiritual songs" as activities familiar to believers (Col 3:16; Eph 5:19; Mark 14:26). Pliny attested in the early second century that early Christians sang songs "in honor of Christ as if to a god" (*Ep.* 10.96.7). Some early Christian hymns may even be reflected by lyrical phrases and portions we find in our NT writings (e.g., Phil 2:6–11; Col 1:15–20; 1 Tim 3:16).

"[The Christians I interrogated] asserted, however, that the sum and substance of their fault or error had been that they were accustomed to meet on a fixed day before dawn and sing responsively a hymn to Christ as to a god, and to bind themselves by oath, not to some crime, but not to commit fraud, theft, or adultery, not falsify their trust, nor to refuse to return a trust when called upon to do so. When this was over, it was their custom to depart and to assemble again to partake of food—but ordinary and innocent food." (Pliny the Younger to Emperor Trajan, *Epistles* 10.96)

By modern-day music standards, the hymns and songs of early Christians would likely seem metrically imprecise—more like chanting than what we today call "songs." But for early believers, hymns and songs served teaching purposes far more than most songs do today. This is why many NT references to singing associate it with teaching and instruction. In Colossians, for example, psalms, hymns, and spiritual songs are associated with teaching and admonishing one another in wisdom (3:16; see also 1 Cor 14:26). Specific songs and hymns may have been shared and used across individual church communities, generating shared practices of hymnody.

Prayer

Certainly, early church gatherings included forms of prayer. Paul speaks often of praying for his churches.[21] He composes various prayers in his letters, offering thanksgivings, blessings, and requests for harmony, peace, and encouragement.[22]

Jewish prayer practices likely influenced early Christian prayer. Jewish tradition largely assumes prayer as a daily practice for the faithful, especially at morning and evening (Ps 92:2).[23] Surviving prayers from Jews in antiquity often reflect a fairly consistent structure: an address to God ("Blessed be God . . ."), words of praise, specific petitions for particular needs, and concluding thanksgivings. Paul uses words, phrases, and patterns in his prayers that resonate with these precedents, suggesting their influence on his practices and those of his church communities.[24] For example, the Hebrew word *Amen* saw prevalent use early on, as did the phrase "in the name of Jesus" (Col 3:17; Eph 5:20). We know little more regarding early Christian forms and patterns of prayer. We simply know that early believers prayed often, for others and themselves, at gathered assemblies, and at various occasions and circumstances.[25]

Teaching

Some people today assume early church gatherings centered on reading and interpreting Scripture—what Christians now call the Old Testament. The assumption comes from practices associated with first-century synagogues, if not modern church practices. But hard evidence for this among first-century churches is more elusive than real. Paul nowhere states explicitly that early gatherings centered on Scripture. Instead, he and most NT authors refer generally to "instruction," "teaching," and "admonition"—activities that may or may not have used Scripture as a starting point.[26] Paul certainly alludes to scriptural traditions in his letters, however, implying they were a significant influence on his teaching. By the second century, public reading of Scripture was central for many gatherings (2 Tim 4:13; Justin, *1 Apol.* 67).

> "When you gather together, each one has a hymn, another has a teaching, another has a revelation, another has a tongue, and another has an interpretation. Let all things take place toward the purpose of building up."
> (1 Cor 14:26)

Paul's letters offer a glimpse of what early Christian teaching looked like. While some are quite situational (e.g., Galatians, Philemon), all his letters sought to teach early communities of believers. And some specific portions—especially those that encourage holy living (e.g., Rom 12:1–15:13; Phil 2:1–18; Col 3:1–4:18)—reflect the kind of teaching leaders probably issued at church gatherings. In fact, these gatherings provided the most likely contexts where Paul's letters were first publicly read (see 1 Thess 5:26–27; Col 4:16). In due time, the role of teaching grew in importance for church gatherings, while other forms of spiritual discourse (like prophecy) diminished.

Prophecy

For many Christians today, prophecy is a foreign concept. But for early Christian assemblies, it was a regular and common experience.[27] First-century believers were likely more familiar with the concept of prophecy, due to the legacy of Israel's prophets and prophetic oracles of Greek and Roman traditions (e.g., the oracle of Delphi). More importantly, early Christians lived in a predominately oral culture. *Hearing* the word of God from an individual was an experience far more normal than reading it privately.

Contrary to some modern assumptions, early Christian prophecy focused very little on the future; it was primarily focused on discerning God's word for the present. For Paul, prophecy exposed the inner realities of human hearts, encouraged believers, built up the community, and promoted order (1 Cor 14:3, 24–33a). Prophetic messages were subject to both the prophet's discretion and the community's discernment (1 Cor 14:29, 32; 1 Thess 5:21). Paul encouraged all believers to pursue prophecy as a spiritual gift (1 Cor 11:5; 14:1, 5, 39; cf. 12:29).

On the one hand, prophecy was not the same as preaching, since it was not sustained exposition of sacred texts. It was also not exactly teaching, although prophecy served some instructional purposes. In contrast to both Jewish patterns of Scripture interpretation and Greek and Roman prophetic oracles, early Christian prophecy tended to be less formulaic, more unsolicited and extemporaneous, and less prompted by specific questions.[28] The value Paul placed on community discernment also shows that prophecy was a communal practice.

On the other hand, prophecy was also not necessarily ecstatic and irrational. In contrast to speaking in tongues, Paul associated prophecy with intelligible speech and rational thinking (1 Cor

14:13–19). He may even have seen his letters as falling within the general realm of prophetic speech, at least in places where he claims to bear the word of the Lord: "Anyone who claims to be a prophet or to have spiritual powers, must acknowledge that what I am writing to you is a command of the Lord" (1 Cor 14:37). For these reasons, Christian prophecy is best described as applied exposition (or application) of the Christian message to the hearers' situations.[29]

We do not know more specifics about what early Christian prophecy looked like: whether it was more spontaneous or premeditated, more extemporaneous or reflective, or more passionate or cognitive. What characterized it most of all was not its feel or form, but its claim to be a word from God.[30] In centuries soon after Paul's day, prophecy became less central for Christian assemblies—a shift partially influenced by the rise of unorthodox movements like Montanism, which placed great emphasis on the role of prophecy. In time, Christian preaching and teaching took over the role prophecy once had in articulating norms of the faith.[31]

Speaking in Tongues

Speaking in tongues (*glossolalia*) involved unintelligible words inspired by God's Spirit. Whether they corresponded with known languages is debated.[32] Paul's discussion in 1 Corinthians presumes these words were unintelligible to both hearers and speakers, requiring interpretation (or translation) for others to understand (1 Cor 14:1–25).

> "If anyone is speaking in a tongue, let there be two or at
> most three, and each in turn; and let someone interpret.
> But if there is no interpreter, let them be silent in the
> assembly and speak only to themselves and to God. Let
> two or three prophets speak and let others discern what is
> spoken. If something is revealed to another person sitting,
> let the first be silent. For you are all able to prophesy in
> turn, so that all may learn and be encouraged. And the
> spirits of prophets are subject to prophets, for God is not
> a God of disorder, but of peace." (1 Cor 14:27–33)

Paul himself spoke in tongues (1 Cor 14:18). He characterized it as a kind of irrational prayer, and "a sign not for believers but for unbelievers" (v. 22).[33] This contrasts with the more
cognitive activity of prophecy, which Paul believed did more
to build up church communities: "I thank God that I speak in
tongues more than all of you; still, in the church I would rather
speak five words with my mind, so as also to instruct others, than
ten thousand words in a tongue" (vv. 18–19; also 22–25). However, Paul did not devalue tongues entirely. He simply desired
it be practiced in ways that built up church communities. He
assumed those speaking in tongues could regulate their activity
and should use it for the community's good (vv. 27–32).

Speaking in tongues was not unique to Christians in antiquity.[34] Within Christianity, the practice continued well beyond the
New Testament period.[35] Today speaking in tongues continues
to be a prevalent practice among certain segments of Christianity
(typically labeled "charismatic"). For most Christians, personal

experiences with speaking in tongues—or lack thereof—heavily overshadow their understanding and appreciation of the practice for early church communities. Regardless, it played a vital role among the practices of many early communities.[36]

Sharing and Service

According to many NT writings, early church communities shared resources with those in need. They did so not only in response to specific needs but as a general habit. They shared not only with those within the community but also in some cases with those outside. These practices of sharing were not entirely unique to Christians in the ancient world. Synagogues and associations in the Roman Empire shared resources in similar ways to assist community members, often with clearer protocols and guidelines.[37] For early church communities, sharing resources was fundamentally part of what it meant for them to practice community in Jesus's name.

The earliest references to resource sharing appear in Paul's letters, associated with a collection of funds he gathered among his churches for Jerusalem.[38] This collection may have stemmed from a relief initiative focused on Jerusalem, possibly catalyzed by a famine or shortage (Gal 2:10; Rom 15:26; cf. Acts 11:27–30). In time the project took on larger significance: as a sign of unity with Judean churches, a response of gratitude from largely gentile churches, and an act of worship all its own.[39] Church communities from several regions joined in Paul's collection (2 Cor 8:1–6; Rom 15:26). More important is how he instructed believers in Corinth (and Galatia) to set aside on Sunday "whatever profit you earn" (1 Cor 16:2). These words suggest that, if Sundays were indeed a day of regular gathering, then sharing resources was a regular practice of their assemblies.

Later Christian writings, in and outside the NT, portray church communities sharing regularly—even exorbitantly—so that no one among them be in need. Acts offers the classic example, highlighting the generosity of the earliest church in Jerusalem just after Pentecost:

> All those who believed were united, and they held all things in common. They would sell possessions and goods and distribute the proceeds to all, just as each had need. (2:44–45)

> Now the entire community of those who believed were one in heart and soul, and no one claimed private possession of their resources, but everything was held in common. . . . For there was not a needy person among them, since whoever owned lands or houses sold them and offered the proceeds from what was sold. They laid it at the feet of the apostles, and they distributed to each just as anyone had need. (4:32–35)

At some level, these portrayals are overstated—or at least one-sided—since soon afterward in Acts there are examples of deception and economic discrepancies (5:1–11; 6:1–7). Still, the radical sharing of the earliest community reflects virtues emphasized by a long list of early Christian writings.[40] What is more, the emphasis on radical generosity hardly diminishes in the ensuing

early centuries of Christianity. And several witnesses from surrounding society—that also esteemed communal sharing very
highly—suggest that, among the ancients, the depiction of Acts
was heard with more admiration than shock or surprise.[41]

For many early Christian authors, sharing was a natural and
faithful use of wealth—like offering the "first fruits" of their pro-
duce (2 Cor 8:13–14; 1 Cor 16:2; Did. 13:1–7). These gifts were
not shared simply with teachers and leaders. They were shared
especially with those in need: widows, orphans, traveling guests,
and those in prison. In fact, early Christian writings depict caring for the needy as a regular practice for church communities—
one with ancient roots in Judaism.[42] Justin described the kinds
of people whom Roman Christians in the second century served
by sharing their resources: "And the wealthy who so desire give
what they wish, as each chooses; and what is collected is depos-
ited with the president. He helps orphans and widows, and those
who through sickness or any other cause are in need, and those
in prison, and strangers sojourning among us; in a word, he takes
care of all those who are in need" (1 Apol. 67, trans. Jasper and
Cuming). More a habit than a response to specific needs, sharing resources appears to have been a widespread practice among
early church communities across the Mediterranean.

Other Gatherings and Activities

There are other activities and special gatherings in which early
church communities participated. Paul's letters and Matthew's
Gospel both refer to gatherings for confronting and disciplining

community members (1 Cor 5:3–5; Matt 18:15–20; also 2 Cor 2:5–11). These passages lack conventional gathering language, implying they were not regular assemblies but special meetings instigated by leaders. Other groups in antiquity handled matters of discipline similarly.[43] Paul encouraged this approach for settling community disputes as opposed to using public courts (1 Cor 6:1–11).

Early church communities likely practiced funerary rites, though we know no specifics about them. Many synagogues and associations in the Roman Empire tended to the disposition and burial of members, treating them like extended family. Church communities probably did the same. Memorial meals in honor of the deceased were also common in Roman society, and in time—if not early on—they were so among Christians as well.[44] In many Mediterranean societies, families of means erected inscriptions to honor their dead. Unfortunately, early surviving inscriptions either did not belong to Christians or did not honor them in markedly Christian ways. Paul refers in passing and enigmatically to a baptism "for the dead" (1 Cor 15:29), but it is highly debated whether this was a practice he endorsed—and whether believers actually did it. Early church communities almost certainly honored their dead, but we do not know what specific and distinctive practices they used.

Finally, early Jesus followers gathered to pray—apart from regular meal gatherings of larger assemblies. The letter of James encourages calling church elders together to anoint and pray over the sick (5:14). The narrative of Acts portrays believers gathered for prayer on several occasions.[45] And the sheer number of Paul's references to prayer suggests not only that it was central to the gatherings of believers but also that they gathered on occasion *primarily* to pray.[46] Where, when, and how often these gatherings took place is uncertain.

For Reflection: Unity and Diversity among Church Practices, Then and Now

Many today explore the practices of early church communities in hopes of bringing modern practices more closely in line with them. This is a worthwhile cause. Ancient forms such as the eucharistic prayer from the Didache, the Lord's Prayer from Matthew's Gospel, and sacramental language from various NT writings—just to name a few examples—may enrich our practices today with substance, heritage, and a sense of ecclesial grounding.

The challenge, however, is that early church practices were more diverse than streamlined. For example, whether early communities gathered weekly on Sunday is likely but not certain. Although meal sharing was a core practice, specifics evolved and varied widely for centuries. Although baptism was a mark of unity for believers early on, there was no clear consensus on the ritual's location, form, preparation, and circumstances. And as for forms of spiritual discourse (hymns, prayers, teaching, prophecy, tongues), clearly some communities valued some practices more highly than others (e.g., tongues at Corinth). And so, in wrestling with the question, "What did the earliest church do?" we find our question changed: "What marks of unity *and diversity* characterized early church practices?"

In the first and early second centuries, standardizing forms and practices was not a high priority, for reasons that were organizational, circumstantial, and theological. First, structures of leadership, lines of communication, and paths to unified governance were not readily available. Second, the spread of earliest Christianity—especially among non-Jewish peoples, scattered across geographical areas—compelled church communities to adapt, embracing contextual forms and customs. Third, for early church communities, diversity of practice was not simply an unintended consequence: it stemmed from the way believers' unity lay elsewhere. That believers were baptized into Christ mattered, not necessarily *how* they were. Likewise, it mattered that their shared meals reflected unity in Christ, not necessarily *how* they did. In general, diversity pervaded early church practices in ways that counterintuitively accentuated the core sources of unity that were most highly valued.

In today's world, unity among churches can feel profoundly elusive. Stark differences in theology, practice, political leanings, ministries, and governance lead some Christians to look at others and ask, "Are we really part of the same religion?" Some of these differences have split church bodies into separate denominations. Some large denominations, although unified in theory, have such diversity among members that questions of authentic unity are no less real. Not long ago (2017), Christian bodies observed the five hundredth anniversary of the Reformation led by Martin Luther, which led to one of the most significant splits in church history. As a Lutheran seminary professor, I have had many recent opportunities to consider this question with colleagues of other traditions: "What does church unity look like for all of us, going forward?" Questions about church unity, it seems, loom larger today than in days past.

Questions about unity were no less important for early church communities. And the divisions they faced fell along relatively similar lines (ethnic, cultural, geographical, theological, etc.). If Paul's experience is representative, unity across these lines was hardly assumed. Whether the Jerusalem church leaders, for instance, recognized his ministry among largely gentile churches was an open question throughout his lifetime (see Rom 15:30–32). Fostering a sense of unity across such distinctions requires openness to dialogue from both sides—and often persistent advocacy, persuasive arguments, and thick skin.

> Questions about church unity, it seems, loom larger today than in days past.

Paul saw a fundamental unity, however, not in particular practices but in a shared connection to Christ. No matter their demographics, geographical locations, economic standings, cultural norms, or distinctive pieties, all believers were finally united "in Christ."[47] For this reason, Paul could name and claim a unity among church communities he had never even met. Although other commonalities were undoubtedly present, for Paul being "in Christ" was the unifying bedrock for churches far and wide.

We can learn something from Paul here. Anchoring church unity in so simple a thing relieves pressure to streamline other practices that differ. For example, if the earliest church communities differed in their Eucharist practices, perhaps differences today need not be so threatening. If similar differences existed regarding baptism preparation, purity practices, and forms of spiritual discourse, perhaps similar discrepancies today may not just be tolerated but celebrated. Church communities throughout history have rightly sought to preserve and continue sacred traditions. But at the same time, they have rightly adapted, as needed, to circumstances and contexts that call for new forms.

As Richard Ascough points out, the goal of NT study is not to portray early church practices as *the* model we "must replicate in order to be truly Christian." Instead, exploring these early practices shows us how "they reflected the environment within which they were first formed, and the fact that they also adapted to the various situations which Christians faced in the early period."[48] Like church communities today, the earliest communities preserved practices and adapted them, revered sacred traditions and changed them, and fostered a sense of heritage and improvised within it. The earliest practices were not holy in and of themselves so much as were the *ways* early Christians *used* them to foster authentic encounters with the risen Christ.

Still, the historic practices and sacred traditions of early Christianity matter—and they should. They invite believers of later times to share in a larger community, reminding us the church is more expansive than our personal experience of one small corner of the world. And they ground us in practices that have built up the community of Christ for centuries.

Further, the earliest churches *did* entertain some consistency in practices and patterns, which fostered a clear sense of shared identity. A fine example of some appears in Luke's depiction of the church at its inception in Jerusalem: "Now they devoted themselves to the apostles' teaching and to the community, to the breaking of bread and to the prayers" (Acts 2:42). Several key things are emphasized: teaching, community (and sharing), meal sharing, and forms of prayer. To these we may add baptism, a practice named just a few verses before (vv. 37–39). This short list of practices corresponds to many of the activities discussed earlier in this chapter. They offer a representative snapshot of practices widely shared by early believers across diverse contexts and communities.

> Rituals and practices . . . serve to shape reality and identity.

For newly formed communities, practices such as these were remarkably formative to a new way of life oriented around Jesus as Lord. Rituals and practices, after all, are not just things we do: they serve to shape reality and identity. As such, these practices molded new believers into a newfound identity "in Christ," giving birth to a lasting transformation (see Rom 12:1–2).

How do church communities today continue practices as these—ones that foster authentic encounters with Christ, shared identity with one another, and lasting transformation? How do church communities today preserve sacred connections to the universal church and at the same time adapt faithfully to today's contexts? These important questions today are the same kinds of questions first faced by the earliest church communities in their own times and places.

Guiding Metaphor: The Church as Gathering

There is a core activity, however, that holds all others together: *gathering*. In fact, the NT word for church (*ekklēsia*) suggests it is.

Contrary to modern associations, NT references to "church" refer neither to buildings nor to membership rosters but to *gatherings* of people. Stemming from a verb that means "call out" (*ekkaleō*), outside Christian literature the word *ekklēsia* refers to casual gatherings, legislative assemblies, and sometimes communities with shared beliefs and practices. In classical Greek literature, the word often refers to official assemblies of a city's voting citizens; in Jewish literature, it typically refers to public assemblies of all Israel.[49] While both of these nuances appear in the New Testament (Acts 7:38; 19:39; Heb 2:12), virtually all NT occurrences of *ekklēsia* refer to communities of Christ followers.

Based on its use elsewhere, to ancient hearers the word *church* (*ekklēsia*) likely implied a particular *gathering* of people more than a specific group. In other words, the word suggested an *activity* (of gathering) more than a static list (of members). Though a noun, the word for "church" implied activity more than a static object.[50] For example, in addressing matters around the Lord's Supper, Paul often used the language of "coming together" (*synerchomenōn*), "as church" (*en ekklēsia*), and "in one place" (*epi to auto*) (1 Cor 11:18, 20). The emphasis on "gathering" is significant. It stands in contrast to activity that might take place "at home" (11:22; also 14:35)—even though most church gatherings in Corinth took place in homes! For Paul, it seems space distinctions did not differentiate "church" from "home"—the purpose of *gathering together* did.

The purpose of gathering was to "build up" (*oikodomeō*) the church.[51] For Paul, "building up" referred less to individuals than to the well-being of communities. Early believers like him had virtually no concept of living out their faith in isolation from the regular gatherings of community. For them, the modern idea "I can be a Christian without being part of a church" would have seemed foreign, if not impossible. Early believers gathered to learn together, to address needs together, to eat together, to pray together, to discern together, and to be together—all of which "built up" the whole. Early Jesus followers gathered together regularly because that's essentially what it meant to be "church" (*ekklēsia*).

This emphasis shows how significant community was to spiritual formation. The faith of early believers was nurtured more by communal formation than by individualistic instruction. A Pharisee by background, Paul was familiar with more individualistic models of instruction such as those between rabbis and pupils. Yet, he saw his calling as geared primarily toward "building up" the faith of communities. He devoted years of ministry to being with and supporting specific communities, sharing this ministry with coworkers and local leaders. And he wrote most of his letters not to individuals but to communities, encouraging and informing their faith. In short, Paul's vision for nurturing faith was more communal than individualistic.[52]

How does this emphasis apply to communities in the Western world, where individualism and autonomy are virtues? We who live in these contexts tend to approach spirituality individualistically, to regard our faith as a personal matter, and to engage church communities with more interest in what we may gain than what we may contribute. More to the point, in recent decades in the US, worship attendance has declined at a steady pace. The statement "I attend worship regularly" once meant at least weekly; it now means at least monthly. Even as church communities work hard to offer worship experiences that are more concise, more engaging, more conveniently scheduled, and more accessible, the decline continues. Few people outrightly *dislike* gathering to worship. They just apparently deem it less important today.

On this point, early church communities acted differently. Whatever believers *did* together, they *got* together. In gathering together as community, they became God's temple, the body of Christ, and the sacred space where God's Spirit dwelled (1 Cor 3:16–17; 6:19; 12:27). Together they were what they were not on their own.

What does it mean for Christians today, especially in the Western world, to reclaim this legacy of gathering? It starts with a vision of community as the primary place for spiritual formation. It starts with viewing community as a spiritual practice, necessary to the individual soul. It starts with the conviction that in community individuals become more Christlike than they can be on their own. These ideas, which are visible in the New Testament and in the practices of early church communities, may be transformative to our way of thinking and being in radically positive ways.

Conclusion: Practicing the Things That Matter Today

What are the practices we prioritize as church communities? What spiritual practices characterize our shared life together?

What we do shapes us. Our activities and habits form us. Even if we try to differentiate our identities from the things that take up most of our time, those things inevitably become formative to who we are.

The same is true with church communities: what we do shapes us. Whether or not we identify as "liturgical," we have habits and practices (aka liturgies) that shape who we are. In fact, some of these practices are so ingrained that we cannot do otherwise, making the words "It's just what we do" a natural explanation for why we do them.

As church communities, what are the spiritual practices that we prioritize and foster?

In the US context, church communities often focus on programs. Many congregations—especially larger ones—identify themselves heavily with the activities and programs they oversee (e.g., a food program, an after-school program, a visitation ministry, a youth ministry program). These programs are great things. But they can also mask key questions about whether a community engages deliberately in basic practices of spirituality.

As human beings, we like what is tangible and concrete. This is especially true when it comes to ministry. We like programs, results, and tangible evidence that we can point to, measure, and be proud of. But faith and spirituality, by nature, are intangible realities. Though they bear fruit and make their presence known, they are neither quantifiable nor measurable. For this reason, many of us find it easier to focus on ministry programs and activities than on the practices that form us into spiritual people. We find it easier to focus on building projects, attendance numbers, fundraising goals, and innovative programs than the basic practices of prayer and worship.

A congregation I know recently issued a request for donations for a new ministry to college students. Within a couple hours, the request was filled. The same congregation issued another request for people willing to be faith mentors for their youth. Over several years, it has received nothing but silence. The comparison is striking. For many people, giving money to a cause is far easier than investing in the intangible practice of faith formation.

The needs that surround church communities are endless— as are the ways we address them. But the church exists not merely to address worthwhile needs. If that's all the church is for, then it's one humanitarian agency among countless others. It offers nothing remarkably distinctive to the world. First and foremost, church communities are called to tend to the things that nurture genuine faith and transformative spirituality. This is the heart of spiritual formation. Many people in professional ministry inadvertently miss this basic point. They revolve their ministries around addressing needs around them. And after a few years, they often burn out and leave the ministry. It's not hard to identify pressing needs that we, as people of faith, should address. But church communities and Christians are called not only to address the needs around us but also to attend to the deep spiritual needs within us.

We are called first and foremost to practice the things that matter, the kinds of things church communities have practiced since the start: receiving God's gifts, hearing God's word, sharing together, eating together, praying together, and worshiping together. Though these practices are hardly new, they help us know who we truly are—or better, *whose* we are. Basic grounding in this identity is the core of Christian spirituality from which healthy and effective service springs.

What we do shapes us. But the activities most formative to us are rarely tangible achievements. Instead, they involve simply making space to breathe, reflect, and be. These core practices of spirituality help us focus more on receiving and giving up than on accomplishing and doing. By modern Western standards, acts like praying, listening, meditating, singing, and eating are not very productive. They don't accomplish tasks or achieve results, making them worthless by many results-based standards. But they are the very things that center us in our core identity as children beloved by God.

In reflecting on these questions, Scripture and early church practices make it clear to me that the things that most matter spring from activities associated with worship. While some practices of early church communities have shifted in significance (e.g., prophecy), most have not dramatically. Then and now, worship is *the* core activity of Jesus followers. Christians engaged in worship reflect who the church truly is.

When all is said and done, Christians identify themselves as people who worship the God made known in Jesus Christ. And the things we do in worship are not meaningless rituals; they are training for life. They teach us to stop doing and talking. They teach us to listen to God and to one another. They teach us to receive graciously and to give thanks in response. They show us who we are in relationship to God and help us live into that identity. Amid all the activities that fill our days, these practices are what most matter to who we are as church communities.

Bringing It Home: Ideas for Conversation and Implementation

1. Invite a Christian—or a few—from different denominational traditions to coffee or lunch, and ask, "Where do you see signs of church unity today? Where would you *like* to see more?"

2. Join in worship with believers of a different Christian tradition. Consider what practices stand out in their worship. Ask someone among them what practices most matter for their worship.

3. Ask a pastor or ministry leader about worship attendance trends in recent years in their experience and how they make sense of these things.

4. Consider your church's core values in relationship to the activities that most often occupy the community's calendar. Do these things correspond well?

Scripture Study

- Read 1 Corinthians 11–14 in one sitting. These chapters are all associated with activities of worship at Corinth. What themes stand out to you as most important to Paul? What concerns and problems are present? What topics are left unaddressed that you would like to know more about?

- Read Acts 2:37–47, Luke's account of the start of the church in Jerusalem. Notice the practices emphasized. What can church communities today learn from this account? What questions remain for you about these early communities?

For Worship

- Huub Oosterhuis, "What Is This Place" (*ELW* #524).
- Fred Pratt Green, "God Is Here!" (*ELW* #526)

Questions for Reflection

1. Revisit the chapter's opening narrative of an experience of early church gathering in ancient Corinth. What surprises or interests you about it? What questions remain?

2. Do you think churches today are more in line with—or different from—the church community you encountered in the first few pages of this chapter? Why?

3. Consider the discussion of ancient church practices in this chapter. What do you think are the most central practices—the nonnegotiables—for church communities today?

4. What church practices are most important to your faith? What practices do you think are most important to your community? Why?

5. This chapter suggests the practices of the earliest church communities were not nearly as uniform and streamlined as we might assume. Does that bother or encourage you?

6. What practices today are most important for church communities to foster authentic encounters with Christ, shared identity with one another, and lasting transformation?

7. How do church communities today preserve sacred connections to the larger church yet adapt faithfully to today's contexts?

Online Resources for Further Explanation

The Didache 7–16 (late first century) and Justin's *1 Apology* 61–68 (esp. 61 and 65–67) (mid-second century), both available at New Advent: https://tinyurl.com/2ldshx and https://tinyurl.com/yycnesed. These post-NT writings give detailed depictions of early church practices in later times in two specific church contexts.

Resources for Further Reading

Heath, Elaine A. *Five Means of Grace: Experience God's Love the Wesleyan Way.* Nashville: Abingdon, 2017. Using five spiritual practices highlighted by John Wesley—prayer, searching Scripture, receiving the Eucharist, fasting, and community—this book explores the extraordinary grace experienced by simply engaging these ordinary practices.

Hippolytus, *Apostolic Tradition* (third to fifth century). Considerable debate surrounds the traditions reflected in this writing: their date, their origins, how descriptive of reality (vs. prescriptive of ideals) they are, and how representative they are of the larger church. Regardless, it has certainly been influential to liturgical reflection in recent times.

Lathrop, Gordon W. *The Four Gospels on a Sunday: The New Testament and the Reform of Christian Worship.* Minneapolis: Fortress, 2012. A cross-disciplinary study by a foremost scholar of worship and liturgy. The book explores how the NT Gospels may have interacted with and shaped early church assembly practices.

Smith, Dennis E. *From Symposium to Eucharist: The Banquet in the Early Christian World.* Minneapolis: Fortress, 2003. Whereas many Christians today assume early Eucharist practices started with traditions of Jesus and the Last Supper,

Dennis Smith argues that the prevalence of meal-sharing practices across the ancient world played a much bigger role in giving Eucharist practices traction. The book places these practices helpfully into the context of communal meals throughout ancient Mediterranean societies.

Witherington, Ben, III. *A Week in the Life of Corinth.* Downers Grove, IL: InterVarsity, 2012. A work of historical fiction that offers an informed narrative reconstruction of what things might have been like in the first-century church community at Corinth. Informative sidebars and images illumine the ancient world in ways descriptive text alone simply cannot rival. The last regular chapter ("The End of the Day") depicts a meal gathering of the church community at Gaius's home.

5

Bearing Distinctive Witness

In short, even if we allow for similarities with other groups of the day . . . early Christianity was distinctive.

—Larry Hurtado

How distinctive are Christians today within broader society? How distinctive should they be?

Some Christians believe their faith calls them to a demonstrably different way of life, an alternative lifestyle that sets them apart from a society marred by corruption. Other Christians believe their faith calls them to robust engagement with their surrounding world, with wholehearted investment into influencing societal norms for the good. Both sides of this spectrum address the question of distinctiveness with integrity. Both sides

Opening Questions:

1. Do you find church communities today more similar to—or distinctive from—other groups in society?
2. What words would you use to describe the relationship church communities have with surrounding society? Is the relationship hospitable, hostile, supportive, antagonistic, respectful, indifferent, engaged with, appreciative, or other?
3. Do you think church communities should act demonstrably differently from the rest of society? If so, how? If not, why not?

have passionate devotees. Both approaches are also met with positive and negative responses from those who do not share these views.

Evidence of how ancient peoples experienced the earliest Christians is mixed. We see an emphasis on distinctive living that set Christians apart from their contexts, and we see deep engagement with their surrounding world. In some ways, the earliest church communities looked like other groups in the Mediterranean world. In other ways, they blazed new trails of living in relationship to nonbelievers and society at large.

The anonymous Epistle to Diognetus (second century) briefly describes some of the profound dichotomies in how early Jesus followers lived in relationship to surrounding society:

> But while they reside in both Greek and Barbarian cities
> . . . and they follow the local customs in dress and diet

and the rest of life, still they demonstrate the remarkable and admittedly paradoxical character of their own citizenship. They live in their own countries, but as non-residents; they partake in everything as citizens, but endure everything as foreigners; every foreign place is their country, and for them every country is foreign. (Diogn. 5.4–5)

As these words show, early Christians often saw themselves as both citizens and yet foreigners, participants in society and yet ostracized from it, at home with local customs and yet decidedly removed from them. The letter's word "paradoxical" (Gk *paradoxon*) is a fitting descriptor indeed.

How did outsiders view and experience this paradoxical people? From what we know, reactions varied—from acceptance to indifference to antagonism. For historical perspective, we will consider some comparable groups that existed at the time this new Jesus movement began.

Early Church Communities and Other Social Groups in the Roman Empire

To outside observers, early church communities may not initially have looked like anything new. Their participants and activities probably resembled those of a Jewish synagogue, a voluntary association, or a philosophical school. These groups were the closest models of comparison for outsiders to make sense of communities devoted to Jesus the Messiah.

Synagogues

Though the origins of Jewish synagogues are unknown, by the first century CE they were scattered all over the Mediterranean world, serving as vibrant hubs for Jewish community, education, and religious activities.[1] Synagogues existed in large cities and rural villages, from Jerusalem to places thousands of miles away. They served entirely different purposes from the Jerusalem temple. A first-century CE Greek inscription from Jerusalem describes some of these: "Theodotus, son of Vettenos, the priest and synagogue leader... who built the synagogue for purposes of reciting the Law and studying the commandments, and as a hotel with chambers and water installations to provide for the needs of itinerants from abroad."[2] First and foremost, synagogues were dedicated to the study of Scripture. Still, other functions were also important, prompting most synagogue buildings to be multipurpose in nature. Men and women of all ages participated in synagogue life, although leadership offices were often reserved for benefactors and those with higher social status.

Many synagogues adapted to their contextual settings, offering various ways for participants to honor their cultural and religious identities. Though interpreters once characterized synagogues as isolated from their surrounding contexts, recent studies have disproven that. Forms of cross-cultural assimilation were common, especially in the Diaspora: Jewish residents attended theater performances, participated in gymnasiums, assisted their cities financially, joined trade associations, observed the Roman calendar and local customs, and fostered connections with civic leaders.[3] While Jewish residents retained their distinctive traditions, they also participated in Roman civic life.

Early church communities certainly shared certain commonalities with synagogues. Both used domestic gathering spaces in their early stages. Both used "coming together" language for gathering (*synagōgeō, synerchomai*). Both retained a sense of belonging to a local community and a larger movement. Most importantly, both drew from shared sources of religious tradition (Scripture, prayer, almsgiving). Further, several NT narratives portray critical events of Jesus's and Paul's ministries taking place in synagogues, portraying them as starting points for their ministries. For these reasons, many have traditionally viewed church communities as direct descendants of synagogues, fundamentally based on the blueprints of local Jewish gatherings.[4]

But early church communities also differed from synagogues—in leadership roles, participation, initiation rites, use of Scripture, gathering activities, gathering spaces, and more. The NT portrayal (in Acts) that Paul's mission work started with synagogues may be more a theological claim than objective history, since he never mentions it in his letters. There is also no evidence an early church gathering ever took place in synagogue spaces—a natural thing, if church communities patterned themselves after synagogues. Despite their shared traditions and history, the extent to which early church

> Early church communities certainly shared certain commonalities with synagogues.

gatherings looked and acted like synagogues entails more questions than answers. Recent studies, in fact, have shown commonalities between synagogues and voluntary associations—a group to which we now turn.[5]

Voluntary Associations

Voluntary associations (henceforth "associations") were social groups that united people around shared interests such as occupations, religious devotions, and social ties.[6] Eating and drinking together was a staple activity for most gatherings. Many associations were small (fifteen to twenty members). Some were larger (up to a few hundred), but they were the exception more than the rule.[7] Membership size was often constrained by a group's gathering space, typically the home of a wealthy member. A small number of associations possessed dedicated buildings, often bestowed by a generous patron. While some groups were religious (e.g., the Dionysus and Mithras cults) and others occupational (e.g., a society of ship merchants), virtually every association integrated religious devotion into its ethos. For example, most associations arranged for member burials, many hosted sacrifices, and virtually all held offerings and acts of devotion to deities. In the Roman world, religion was not an isolated component of life; religion infiltrated all of life.

Associations flourished throughout the Roman Empire, largely because they gave opportunities for social ties and local leadership. They often appeared in urban centers (vs. rural communities), where large civic communities did not foster intimate social ties. Some associations encouraged equality among participants, but many reinforced social distinctions from society at large (e.g., slave and free). Some associations featured members from diverse socioeconomic statuses, while others were quite homogeneous (esp. occupational associations). Many associations were exclusively male or female. Some mixed associations gave women significant positions (esp. benefactors), while others restricted women's roles to spouse and mother.[8]

It's not hard to see the commonalities between early church communities and associations: both tended to be small in size; both typically met in homes; both were theoretically open to various participants; both engaged in religious activities; and both gathered often around eating and drinking. Further, Dennis Smith points out that many associations had basic social expectations for banquet meetings, many of which Paul shared for the church community at Corinth: there was to be no quarreling or fighting, no taking someone else's assigned place, no speaking out of turn or without permission, no fomenting factions, and no accusing members in public court (1 Cor 1:10–17; 6:1–8; 11:17–34; 14:26–40). Further, associations often had instructions for settling internal disputes and hosting worship activities.[9] These commonalities suggest the social dynamics of associations and early church communities were comparable.

In fact, by the second century, outsiders were comparing church communities to associations: Pliny the Elder characterized a Christian group as a religious association (*hetaeria*), Celsus compared Christianity to a religious club or similar association (*thiasos*), and Lucian of Samosata called Christianity a "new initiation rite" with gatherings comparable to religious associations.[10] In time, many outsiders made sense of early church communities by comparing them to religious associations.

Philosophical Schools

Philosophical schools (*philosophiai*) were groups of people committed to a distinctive way of thinking and living. They were widely known to the Greco-Roman world, even though they were not as common as associations and synagogues. The earliest known examples of philosophical schools took shape in Athens in the fourth century BCE: Plato's Academy, Aristotle's Lyceum, Zeno's Poikile (Stoicism), and Epicurus's Garden. In the first century CE, two philosophical groups were certainly active: the Neopythagoreans (based in Croton, Italy) and Epicureans (based in Athens). But less formal schools existed wherever an individual practiced a philosophy and gathered others of like mind.

These "schools" were tied far less to physical structures than to individual founders who taught by means of lectures, letters, meditations, and public speaking. Philosophical schools often engaged in distinctive forms of communal living and patterns of dress, diet, and lifestyle. They typically focused more on practical instructions for virtuous living and the pursuit of happiness (*eudaimonia*) than on abstract theory alone, which made them more akin to modern religious communities than philosophy groups.[11]

To ancient observers, Paul's apostolic ministry and church communities looked more like philosophical schools than many

Figure 5.1. School of Athens by Rafael (1511). Public domain.

twenty-first-century people realize. Both fostered loyalty to particular teachers and their moral convictions (see Gal 4:12–20; 1 Cor 1:10–17).[12] Both Paul and many philosopher-teachers traveled, using different forms of instruction (gatherings, letters, colleagues) to nurture local communities (or "schools"). Related, Paul used language familiar to the exhortations of philosophers in his day: "sibling love" (*philadelphia,* 1 Thess 4:9; Rom 12:10), "taught by God" (1 Thess 4:9), "mind your own affairs" and "work with your hands" (4:11), and so on.[13]

Authors from diverse backgrounds in antiquity even explicitly compared Judaism and Christianity to philosophical schools.

In the first century CE, Jewish authors like Josephus character-ized Judaism as a philosophy superior to other alternatives.[14] In the second century, Christian writers did the same with their movement. Justin Martyr, for example, characterized Christian-ity as the truest philosophy: "I found this philosophy alone to be safe and profitable. Thus, and for this reason, I am a phi-losopher" (*Dialogue with Trypho* 8).[15] Even more interesting is the perspective of an outsider: Galen, a second-century Roman physician. He ridiculed physicians and philosophers of his day by comparing them to the philosophical schools of Moses (Juda-ism) and of Christ (Christianity), which used "undemonstrated laws" and asked pupils to "accept everything on faith" (*On the Pulse, On the Prime Mover*). Yet elsewhere Galen praises Chris-tians' ability to live virtuously:

> Just as now we see the people called Christians . . . some-times acting in the same way as those who practice phi-losophy. For their contempt of death is patent to us every day, and likewise their restraint in cohabitation. For they include not only men but also women who refrain from cohabiting all through their lives; and they also num-ber individuals who, in self-discipline and self-control in matters of food and drink, and in their keen pursuit of justice, have attained a pitch not inferior to that of genuine philosophers. (*Summary of Platonic Dialogues*)[16]

For Galen and others in the early centuries, church communities were most comparable to philosophical schools in their ethical living and commitments to a distinctive lifestyle.

For Reflection: When Churches Look like Everybody Else

To many today, church communities may not look much different from other social or humanitarian groups: they get together, do things together, and assist with beneficial causes together. To outsiders especially, these traits are not terribly distinctive. Is that a bad thing?

As a rule, human beings make sense of *new* things through the lens of *known* things. So, it's not only understandable that outsiders identify (and label) church communities today in comparison to other groups—it's inevitable. Outsiders did the same with church communities in the early centuries, and for good reason. Church communities had a lot in common with synagogues, associations, and philosophical schools. The similarities do not mean early church communities *tried* to emulate other groups. In antiquity and today, many factors play into why one community may look like another, from the intentional to the unintentional and the deliberate to the accidental.

> To many today, church communities may not look much different from other social or humanitarian groups.

At the end of the day, the basic human need for community influences most social groups to do similar things to address this need. The same is true today. Church communities are not unique in striving to nurture positive social connections. And cultural realities in larger society influence church communities, just as they influence other social groups. For this reason, in fact, evolutions in things like church leadership structures, musical resources, worship styles, and social decorum often have more to do with cultural shifts than theological convictions alone.

More to the point, the fact that a church community may look like other groups is not inherently bad. It does not automatically mean the community is less spiritual or more "worldly." It may in fact mean it's engaged and spiritually vital. For example, if a church community invests heavily in advertising, does that mean that community is lacking faith or is committed to evangelism? Is a church engaged in interreligious dialogue unclear on its convictions or proactively hospitable? Is a church's choice to build a multipurpose building—without a steeple, cross, and Christian symbols—wishy-washy or in tune with its community's needs? Is a church radically committed to humanitarian causes lacking in focus or living out Christ's calling? Depending on who you ask, answers will vary, proving the basic point: "It's complicated."

It's not simply the distinctive traits of churches that reflect divine grace. Foreignness and strangeness are not inherent signs of faithfulness. Commonalities between churches and surrounding groups make churches *approachable* and *understandable*— they make sense, are accessible, and at some level are welcoming to outsiders. Some assume that the more foreign and peculiar a church is, the more authentic it is, but the reality is more complicated.

For Reflection: When Churches *Don't* Look like Everybody Else

Sometimes differences between church communities and other groups are more pronounced than their similarities. The same was true for early church communities. For them, five differences were especially noticeable.

First, early church communities believed they were an interconnected, global movement—not a random smattering of local groups. The NT letters testify to their interconnectedness, often identifying recipients in relationship to a wider web of communities: "To the church of God that is in Corinth. . . together with all those who in every place call on the name of our Lord Jesus Christ, both their Lord and ours" (1 Cor 1:2).[17]

Second, church communities shared a distinctive commitment, even a divine calling, to engage all peoples. Though other groups generally welcomed new participants, they did not prioritize incorporating all nations and peoples so explicitly. In a survey of groups in antiquity, Richard Ascough points out that "the strong, universal missionizing tendency seems to have been unique to Christianity."[18]

Third, early church communities generally displayed a wider mix of people than other groups did—in gender, class, ethnicity, age, economic status, and age. Though many groups had similar kinds of social variety (esp. synagogues), church communities often exceled more at reflecting cross-sections of surrounding society.[19]

Fourth, as described in chapter 3, early church communities did not readily embrace titles and honorary offices the way other groups tended to—especially synagogues and associations. For early church communities, leadership roles were not revered as positions of high social honor the way contemporary groups esteemed them.

Fifth, as mentioned in chapter 2, early church communities reflected a high level of social intimacy not characteristic of many other groups. They characterized their ties as "family bonds," visible in the way the NT writings use sibling language (sisters, brothers) for church participants. Early NT voices also assume and encourage acts of solidarity and intimacy, including greeting one another with a holy kiss, exhorting one another to sisterly and brotherly love, assisting one another's needs, expressing mutual concern for each other's well-being, and emphasizing the virtue of loving one another.[20] While contemporary groups engaged in similar activities, early Jesus followers practiced them more widely and consistently.

These traits raise a natural question: To what extent are our church communities today *unlike* other groups around us? The distinctions associated with early churches named above are, by most standards, virtues. Though these traits existed in other groups, among Jesus-following communities they were more pronounced. May we say similar things about church communities today?

> To what extent are our church communities today *unlike* other groups around us?

In *theory*, many churches might be distinctive along these lines. But in *practice*, often these distinctive virtues are not terribly pronounced.

For instance, virtually all church communities value diversity, global focus, and connectedness, but putting them into tangible practice is quite another matter. While our core values sometimes directly influence our practices, at other times our practices bear little resemblance to our core values.

Perhaps the question is better asked: In what ways do our church communities *differ* from surrounding groups? How are they distinct? We will return to these questions later in the chapter.

In the Eyes of Outsiders: How Do Others View the Church?

This past year, the faculty of my seminary spent time engaging people—students, alums, friends, and unaffiliated people—in conversation about the question, "What is the church?" Of course, answers have varied. The vast discrepancy between favorable and unfavorable responses has been the most interesting. For example, one person said the church is a "place of hope," while another said it's a "coercive environment." Another said the church is a "place to be who I am and be accepted," while yet another said it's a "dangerous, unchecked minefield of takers and manipulators." Clearly, whatever the church is, people's impressions and experiences of it are not only varied but also fraught with personal significance and baggage.

Things were not radically different in the first century. Despite vast contextual differences between then and now, like today people in the first century rarely reacted to early Jesus followers with apathy.

In the Eyes of Outsiders, Part 1: Negative Responses

For many today, perhaps the first thing that comes to mind regarding reactions to early Christ followers is persecution. Certainly, early church communities encountered hostility. Perhaps the most famous—and vivid—depiction of this hostility comes from the second-century historian Tacitus, who describes persecution under the reign of Emperor Nero (54–68 CE):

> Nero blamed [the fire of Rome on] the Christians, who are hated for their abominations, and punished them with refined cruelty. Christ, from whom they take their name, was executed by Pontius Pilate during the reign of Tiberius. Stopped for a moment, this evil superstition reappeared, not only in Judea, where was the root of the evil, but also in Rome, where all things sordid and abominable from every corner of the world come together. Thus, first those who confessed [that they were Christians] were arrested, and on the basis of their testimony a great number were condemned, although not so much for the fire itself as for their hatred of humankind. Before killing the Christians, Nero used them to amuse the people. Some were dressed in furs, to be killed by dogs. Others were crucified. Still others were set on fire early in the night, so that they might illumine it. Nero opened his own gardens for these shows, and in the circus he himself became a spectacle, for he mingled with the people dressed as a charioteer, or he rode around in

his chariot. All of this aroused the mercy of the people, even against these culprits who deserved an exemplary punishment, for it was clear that they were not being destroyed for the common good, but rather to satisfy the cruelty of one person. (Tacitus, *Annals* 15.44)[21]

Clearly, the message and movement of early Jesus followers were not received warmly by all.

But some caveats are needed. Many today have the idea that persecution against early Christianity was persistent, widespread, and systematic. That perspective is exaggerated. First, persecution was more sporadic and periodic than consistent and more localized than universal. In his account, Tacitus even suggests most found Nero's persecution extreme, implying it was neither desired by all Romans nor the norm after Nero's time. Sources indicate that explicit and sanctioned persecution took place primarily during the reigns of four emperors: Nero (54–68), Domitian (81–96), Decius (249–51), and Diocletian (284–305).[22] Some of these persecutions were fairly regional. Nero's persecution, for instance, is not attested outside Rome. Domitian's, likewise, is not outside Asia Minor. In the late second century, Origen even suggested the number of martyrs was not terribly high: "For a few, whose number could be easily enumerated, have died occasionally for the sake of the Christian religion" (*Against Celsus* 3.8). These factors lead many modern historians to think the number of Christian martyrs in the first century was lower than popular martyrdom accounts from antiquity suggest.[23]

Why were early Jesus followers persecuted at all? Many readers in the Western world find this difficult to understand.

To start with, two cultural differences play a major role. First, ancient Mediterranean societies were communal, not individualistic. In such a world, I am inherently connected to my neighbors, my community, my nation, and my people. If my neighbor is an unethical, impious jerk, then I may fear my neighborhood will be struck by the gods with disease, invading armies, or death—and justly so. The same holds true for my community, my nation, and my people. In such a world, my neighbor's activity—and religious devotion—matters. Second, religious devotion intermingled with political loyalty. To be Roman was to revere Roman gods, and to be Jewish was to worship Israel's God faithfully. To do otherwise was to dishonor a people's patron divinity. In Western societies today, we often deem religious commitments to be personal and unrelated to civic realities. Things were entirely different for first-century church communities. Their situation was more precarious, more directly influenced by how their neighbors perceived them.

Very early on, Jesus followers received an unfavorable reception from some Jewish people and their leaders. Paul was once an example. Throughout his letters, he confesses that he once "violently" tried to "destroy" the church (Gal 1:13; 1 Cor 15:9; Phil 3:6). As a pious Jew, he probably saw his attacks against Jesus followers as a legitimate disciplining of heretical beliefs. Many Jews, after all, believed their subjection to Rome was due to Jewish unfaithfulness. A new wave of teaching by a group identified as an unorthodox sect of Judaism, therefore, would only further their people's demise and impede their fidelity.[24] Many NT writings attest to Jewish hostility against followers of

Jesus.[25] Though some passages are more rhetorical than descriptive, their volume and wide attestation show there were clearly fierce conflicts—to the extent that Emperor Claudius felt compelled to expel all Jews from Rome in the mid-first century (Suetonius 25.4). In time, Jesus followers became distinguished as "Christians" (see Acts 11:26; 26:28; 1 Pet 4:16), a distinction that did not enhance their safety, since the empire recognized Judaism as an established religious tradition (Tacitus, *Hist.* 5.5; Origen, *Against Celsus* 5.25, 41).

The more significant proponent of hostility against Jesus followers was the Roman Empire and its people. There are several reasons—all visible in Tacitus's account of Nero's persecution (above). First, some emperors deemed the Jesus movement a "superstition" (*superstitio*), a slanderous mark that justified its persecution. Rome was not a religious free-for-all: "No Roman propounded the view that Rome should respect the religious liberty of other peoples."[26] What distinguished "superstition" from respectable "religion" (*religio*) was subjectively decided by Rome, with few limits on how "superstition" may be oppressed. Thus, from Nero on, simply being "Christian" in the Roman Empire was basically a crime—something second-century Christian writers protested.[27]

Second, many Romans associated Jesus followers with a "hatred of humankind." Why? Many unfounded accusations circulated against them (e.g., cannibalism), prompting Christian writers in the ensuing centuries to complain: "By the Jews [Christians] are assaulted as foreigners, and by the Greeks they are persecuted, yet those who hate them are unable to give a reason for their hostility" (Diognetus 5.16). Tertullian lamented in the early third century: "If the Tiber river reaches the walls, if the Nile river does not rise to water the fields, if the sky yields no rain, if the earth quakes, if there is famine, or if there is plague, the cry at once arises: 'The Christians to the lions!'" (*Apology* 40.2).

But not all Roman animosity toward Jesus followers was unfounded. For traditional Romans, respect (*pietas*) and reverence (*eusebeia*) for one's family, fellow citizens, country, and divinities (including the emperor) were crucial to preserving the social order. To disrespect these in any way was not just unpatriotic—it was abominable and degenerate, even evil.[28] Virtually from the start, Jesus followers were associated with "atheism" (or "godlessness")—the charge named for the execution of Flavius Clemens and Flavia Domitilla in the late first century (Cassius Dio, *Rom. Hist.* 67.14). Romans accused Jesus followers of many things: cannibalism, incest, human sacrifice, obstinacy, and preying on the uneducated. But "atheism" was the most persistent accusation.[29]

And the accusation was not unfounded. The NT writings attest that Jesus followers maintained an exclusivist devotion that refused to honor any alternative divinity—turning "to God from idols, to serve a living and true God" (1 Thess 1:9).[30] In the early second century, Pliny gave accused Christians opportunity to invoke the gods, make an offering to the emperor's image, and curse Christ—"none of which, I understand, those who are genuine Christians can be induced to do" (*Epistles* 10.96.5–6; also 10.97). Pliny's tactic narrows in on the Romans' core problem with followers of Jesus: their refusal to participate in basic national, religious piety. For Romans, this was ungodly, un-Roman, and basically treasonous. It cut against the very fabric of what it meant to be Roman.

In practice, followers of Jesus were most often prosecuted in response to local reports from credible witnesses. In the early second century, for instance, Emperor Trajan felt compelled to punish confirmed Christians since their faith was illegal, but still he advised the Bithynian governor Pliny not to hunt them out— and to reject anonymous accusations (Pliny, *Epistles* 10.97). Pliny's unfamiliarity with Roman procedures for Christians suggests prosecuting them was not terribly common. Trajan himself suggests there was no universal protocol, "for it is impossible to lay down a general rule to a fixed formula." Clearly, the plight of early Jesus followers depended heavily on local circumstances, local authorities, and the good will of neighbors. Not until the early fourth century would the Jesus movement have official sanction by the Roman state.[31]

Whether or not many Jesus followers died for their faith, many lived in fear that they may. They lived as identified outlaws and illegals. Though most were never formally accused, the identity entailed its own traumas. Forms of harassment may have taken place, furthering the fear that interpersonal tensions may escalate into tangible acts. And the baselessness of many accusations against Christians gave little confidence their beliefs would be judged fairly. Whether or not imperial persecution was widespread, church communities knew the experience of being identified as a persecuted people.

For Reflection: Comfortable Christianity

Especially in Western countries like the United States, some describe effective church ministry as making the faith accessible, comfortable, undemanding, and convenient. Fair reasons stand behind this idea. Since people are busy, some reason, churches should work around their schedules. Since people face many pressures in daily life, churches should not ask more of them. Since many young people have school demands, they should not be asked to study more at church. Since life itself is already hard, church should not add to people's burdens by making it harder. What people most need, after all, is a message of grace and unconditional love. Church ministries convey this best by asking as little as possible of their people.

But the problem with this approach is that this vision bears very little resemblance to the ministry of Jesus and the experiences of early church communities. Both took shape in ways that were remarkably demanding: people were asked to put their lives, livelihoods, and reputations at stake. To be a follower of Jesus entailed giving up old patterns of living, sharing generously from one's resources, and forsaking devotion to rival divinities. In the NT writings, hardship and persecution were regular experiences of church communities, their people, and their leaders. Jesus warned his followers to expect all manner of imprisonments, trials, and persecutions.[32] Most other NT writings envisioned similar hostilities as regular experiences for believers.[33] The author of 1 Peter summarizes the idea this way: "Beloved, do not be surprised at the fiery ordeal that is taking place among you to test you, as though something strange were happening to you" (4:12).

What is more, by virtually any standard of historical comparison, life was much harder for people in the first-century Mediterranean than today. In this context, early church communities and their practices did not aim to make following Jesus comfortable. And yet counterintuitively, church communities grew and thrived.

Comfortable Christianity is not the answer to the woes of the twenty-first-century church. Though accessibility and relevance are virtues in ministry, convenience and comfort at the expense of discipleship are not. Throughout history, seasons of spiritual renewal in Christian communities have most often happened in the face of challenge and difficulty—not leisure and convenience. The latter qualities are not inherently bad; they just neither inspire nor challenge people to be transformed. Grace without spiritual transformation rarely yields lasting change. Comfortable Christianity runs more against the grain of following Jesus than with it. The experiences of early church communities demonstrate that the Christian faith did not take root among armchair theologians of leisure, but rather by people risking their lives to follow Jesus.

> To be a follower of Jesus entailed giving up old patterns of living, sharing generously from one's resources, and forsaking devotion to rival divinities.

Our twenty-first-century contexts are different. And it does no good to seek out hardships that are artificial to our cultural worlds. What we can learn, however, is that the faith of Christ has faced remarkable challenges in history—and thrived. In view of this, challenges that face church communities today are not insurmountable: they may even be what church communities actually need.

How Do Followers of Jesus Respond to Hostility?

In today's world, when hostility takes place against the faith of Christians, they respond in different ways. Some call such hostility persecution, thereby identifying with the experience of a victim. Some find the hostility to be evidence their faith is authentic. Some try to engage the hostility, seeing it as an opportunity for dialogue, bearing witness, or correcting misinformation. Some try to learn from the hostility, believing negative responses must stem from things worth addressing. Some strive to ignore it, looking instead for other opportunities for constructive public witness. None of these responses is inherently bad or good. The value of each depends on the situation and form of hostility.

The New Testament shows a similar diversity among early followers of Jesus. Their characterizations of the Roman Empire— the most persistent source of hostility—are a prime example. On the one hand, the book of Revelation portrays the empire as fundamentally aligned with evil, with no future except destruction by the hand of God (see esp. 12:18–13:18; 17:1–19:21). On the other hand, several NT writers portray the empire and its ruler as entities put in place by God. In writing Roman believers, for instance, Paul characterizes all ruling authorities as God's servants: "Let everyone submit to the ruling authorities, for no authority exists except by God's doing, and those now in authority are appointed by God. So those who oppose them oppose the authority God has appointed, and those who do so will incur judgment. For rulers are not sources of fear to doers of good but to doers of evil . . . for they are servants of God for your good" (Rom 13:1–4a; see also 1 Pet 2:13–14). Ironically, later Christian tradition credits Paul's death—as well as Peter's—to the very emperor who ruled at this time, Nero (Eusebius, *Eccl. Hist.* 2.25.5).

This variety of responses may be natural for a powerless people caught between two realities: imperial hostility on the one hand, and the ethical call to love others (including enemies), respect authorities, and respond with nonviolence on the other. In time, the trajectory of love, respect, and nonviolence is the one that prevailed. Later NT writings like the Acts of the Apostles characterize the empire more neutral than decidedly evil, with Roman authorities depicted as trying to ensure fair trials of Jesus followers. Similar traits appear in the Pastoral Epistles (1–2 Timothy and Titus), which envision a peaceful existence for believers in the empire: "I urge requests, prayers, intercessions, and thanksgivings to be made for all people, for emperors and all those in authority, in order that we may lead a peaceable and quiet life in all godliness and dignity. This is right and acceptable in the sight of God our Savior" (1 Tim 2:1–3).

This line of thinking encouraged followers of Jesus to lead lives that were socially respectable, free of offense and scandal, and esteemed by outsiders.[34]

In the second and third centuries, Christian writers increasingly engaged external hostilities by clarifying misinformation, addressing criticisms, and showing the upstanding nature of the faith. These writers (commonly called "apologists") did not vilify imperial society but rather pled for fairer consideration of their beliefs. To that end, they argued their presence in larger society contributed to its good. The second-century Epistle to Diognetus is a classic example:

> [Christians] marry like everyone else, and have children, but they do not expose their offspring. They share their food but not their wives. They are in the flesh, but they do not live according to the flesh. They live on earth, but their citizenship is in heaven. They obey the established laws; indeed in their private lives they transcend the laws. They love everyone, and by everyone they are persecuted. They are unknown, yet they are condemned; they are put to death, yet they are brought to life. They are poor, yet they make many rich; they are in need of everything, yet they abound in everything. They are dishonored, yet they are glorified in their dishonor; they are slandered, yet they are vindicated. They are cursed, yet they bless; they are insulted, yet they offer respect. When they do good, they are punished as evildoers; when they are punished, they rejoice as though brought to life. By the Jews they are assaulted as foreigners, and by the Greeks they are persecuted, yet those who hate them are unable to give a reason for their hostility. In a

word, what the soul is to the body, Christians are to the world. (Diogn. 5.6–6.1)

Of course, these pleas for respect and fair treatment of Christians were not persuasive to all.

We learn both positive and negative lessons from these responses by early Jesus followers. Negatively, some of them answered hostility with hostility, as seen in the book of Revelation and in many NT characterizations of Jewish opposition. Though these responses aimed to encourage believers in the face of resistance, they fostered no inroads outside church communities. (Worse still, in centuries to come their words fueled acts of anti-Semitism at the hands of Christians.)

Positively, in time followers of Jesus increasingly strove to engage their surrounding world in ethical ways: with respect, affirmation, prayer, and attempts to address prevalent concerns. These efforts were neither always successful nor received well. In some cases, they were arguably naïve. But they tried. And in doing so, they took seriously the call to bear a constructive, positive witness in the contexts where they lived.

How do church communities respond to hostility today? There is no single, textbook way to do so. The value of our response depends a great deal on the situation, the audience, and contextual realities in play. Both in antiquity and today, many

> Befriending, inviting, and engaging others in dialogue do far more to alter negative ideas of church than watertight arguments alone.

negative impressions of "the church" come from either misinformation or bad personal experiences. Both are worth addressing, not so much by rousing apologetic as by personal relationship. Befriending, inviting, and engaging others in dialogue do far more to alter negative ideas of church than watertight arguments alone. Like Jesus did with his first followers, a basic invitation to "come and see" may be the best starting point of all.

In the Eyes of Outsiders, Part 2: Positive Responses

Of course, positive responses from outsiders are what most church communities today desire and work toward. But strategies for yielding such reactions vary profoundly. Some church communities build rapport through community service, while others use targeted forms of evangelism. Some use media or traditional advertising, while others simply rely on personal relationships. Some forge ties with local businesses, while others form partnerships with religious groups. Some focus on invitation to worship, while others focus on alternative programs and activities for making connections.

Most discussions today about constructive witness, or evangelism, focus a great deal on studies of modern cultural and societal realities. The thinking is: if we can crack the code on what people today want, we can offer a positive witness by addressing their needs most effectively. Be that as it may, we ought first to pause and learn a few things from the witness of early church communities. After all, their ratio of growth—what some evaluations would call "success"—was provocatively high. Over just a few centuries' time, the fledgling Jesus movement exponentially grew in an extraordinary way. The numbers estimated by modern historians speak for themselves.

Year (CE)	Number of Christians	Percent of Empire's Population
40	1,000	0.0017
100	7,400	0.013
150	40,000	0.07
200	210,000	0.35
250	1,100,000	2
300	6,300,000	10.5
350	34,000,000	56.5

Figure 5.2. Christian growth in the first few centuries.

Overall, these numbers depict a growth rate of about 40 percent per decade—about 3.5 percent growth per year.[35] Although this is merely an estimated reconstruction, even the most generous margin of error does not wash over the impressive rate at which the Jesus movement spread and grew.

To the surprise of some, this growth did not happen through highly organized evangelism programs or aggressive missionary campaigns. During the earliest centuries, church communities were scarcely oriented around converting outsiders, at least in measurable ways. Many were more secretive than public, gathering primarily to edify those already devoted. Further, apostles and missionaries were not dominant forces that catalyzed massive conversions. Though they helped the church's spread, very few from early centuries are named, suggesting they played a less significant role in the larger story of growth than we may assume.[36] Finally, the imperial label of "outlaws" was hardly an attractive selling point. In the third century, Origen points out that Christians experienced a "disgrace among the rest of society" (*Against Celsus* 3.9), making the church's growth an unlikely success story, to say the least. "And yet," Alan Kreider notes, "improbably, the movement was growing. In number, size, and geographical spread, churches were expanding without any of the probable prerequisites for church growth."[37]

From what we can tell, the overwhelming majority of those persuaded to join the Jesus movement were introduced to it by neighbors, friends, and acquaintances whose lives bore credible witness to their faith. These introductions did not likely take shape at public events or in sacred spaces, but in shops and marketplaces, in homes and at workplaces, and all within the context of personal relationships. Certainly there were influential leaders: teachers who held public debates (Justin, Origen), and individuals associated with miracles (Gregory Thaumaturgus). But far more of early Christianity's growth came from the work and witness of anonymous people whose names are now lost to history.[38]

The Distinctive Way of Early Jesus Followers

What was so compelling about the witness of early Jesus followers? Countless historians have tried to answer the question definitively. All we can say with certainty is their witness *was* compelling, for reasons we may speculate about with humility and caution.

From the outset, participants in church communities were encouraged to live lives that reflected the character of their faith. Paul, for example, wrote:

- For this is God's desire: your holy living (1 Thess 4:2–3a).
- Do all things without murmuring and arguing, so that you may be blameless and innocent, children of God without blemish in the midst of a crooked and perverse generation, in which you shine like stars in the world (Phil 2:14–15).[39]

This trajectory of holy living persisted well beyond Paul's undisputed letters:

- Conduct yourselves wisely toward outsiders, making the most of the time. Let your speech always be gracious, seasoned with salt, so that you may know how you ought to answer everyone (Col 4:5–6).
- Conduct yourselves honorably among the Gentiles, so that, though they malign you as evildoers, they may see your honorable deeds and glorify God when God comes to judge (1 Pet 2:12).[40]

Many of these writings give special significance to believers' words, crediting them with bearing "the very words of God" (1 Pet 4:11). Especially after Nero's persecution, NT authors encouraged believers to be always ready to articulate their faith

(Col 4:6; 1 Pet 3:15). In word and in deed, integrity of character was a widespread aspiration.

And it was not just an aspiration. In some cases, devotion to Jesus resulted in death. Perhaps hundreds died for this in the first century, and certainly more in the next two. Many readers today find the early believers' willingness to die foreign and off-putting, if not implausible or even masochistic. But most scholars believe their accounts reflect historical perspectives and events.[41] For one, martyrdom paralleled the experience of Jesus. For another, it gave a public stage to the ultimate act of faith profession, which itself solidified enduring social honor. Those who died for their faith—like Ignatius of Antioch, Polycarp, and Perpetua—were thereafter revered, and not just among believers. Justin states that Christians' "fearless" embrace of death impressed him long before he joined their ranks (2 Apology 12), and Galen respectfully admits "their contempt of death is patent to us every day" (Platonic Dialogues). Tertullian gives classic expression to the sentiment among early believers in the late second century:

> But have at it, O fine magistrates! You will be held all the more in honor before the populace if for their sake you sacrifice, torture, condemn, and crush us Christians. Your cruelties are all the more proof of our innocence. . . . But nothing whatever is achieved by your cruelties, each more choice than the last. It is all the more an invitation to our school. We multiply when by you we are cut down. The blood of Christians is a seed. (Apology 50.12–13)

"But among us you will find uneducated persons, and artisans, and old women, who, if they are unable in words to prove the benefit of our doctrine, yet by their deeds exhibit the benefit arising from their persuasion of its truth: they do not rehearse speeches, but exhibit good works; when struck, they do not strike again; when robbed, they do not go to law; they give to those that ask of them, and love their neighbours as themselves." (Athenagoras, *Plea for the Christians* 11, trans. B. P. Pratten)

Despite such words, martyrdom was not the primary path of devotion for early believers. Most lived a distinctive way of life by other means. Many chose the path of generosity, sharing resources to assist those in need. Several NT writings portray sharing as a core activity of early church communities, making it a central piece of their public witness.[42] Their practices evidently made a favorable impression. Henry Chadwick suggests early Christian practices of generosity were "probably the most potent single cause of Christian success" in spreading as they did.[43]

Early Jesus followers also cared for those in need of healing, attended to people in prison, took in widows and orphans, and prioritized hospitality toward guests.[44] They also united with Jews in mounting the only widespread criticism against the practice of discarding unwanted infants.[45] In these ways, Jesus followers earned a reputation for attending to people who were overlooked. In the late second century, Tertullian summarizes:

[Our offerings] are not taken and spent on feasts, and drinking-bouts, and eating-houses, but to support and bury poor people, to supply the wants of boys and girls who lack property and parents, and then for old slaves and mariners who have suffered shipwreck, and those who are in mines, on islands, or in prisons, for nothing but their loyalty to the cause of God's school, becoming the pensioners of their confession. But this work of great love puts a mark on us in the eyes of some: "Look," they say, "how they love one another . . . and how ready they are to die for one another." (*Apology* 39.6–7)

Early Jesus followers also blazed a counter-cultural trail regarding entertainment, indulgence, and sexuality. They encouraged modesty in food and drink. They accused gladiatorial games of violence and idolatry (Tertullian, *The Shows*). They not only condemned adultery (as did the Romans), they also condemned prostitution, the sexual use of slaves, the sexual use of children (pederasty), and any sexual activity outside of marriage. As the second-century Epistle to Diognetus quips, "They share their food but not their wives" (5.7).[46]

This differed markedly from the prevailing culture of the Greco-Roman world, which had no issue with males engaging in sexual activity with prostitutes, slaves, and others under their power—including boys. In fact, many ancient Romans encouraged men who were of age to avail themselves of prostitutes as a hedge against adultery—a transgression against another man's wife. A line from Demosthenes, though centuries earlier than Christianity, reflects some of the attitude prevailing still in later

"For [the Christians'] contempt of death is patent to us every day, and likewise their restraint in cohabitation. For they include not only men but also women who refrain from cohabiting all through their lives; and they also number individuals who, in self-discipline and self-control in matters of food and drink, and in their keen pursuit of justice, have attained a pitch not inferior to that of genuine philosophers." (Galen, *Summary of Platonic Dialogues*)

times: "We [men] have mistresses for pleasure, female slaves for our daily [sexual] needs, and wives to give us legitimate children and to be guardians of our households" (*Against Neaera* 3.122). In contrast to this, the sexual modesty of early Jesus followers was viewed by outsiders only with respect and admiration.[47] At the same time, virtually all Greek and Roman authors encouraged nothing but the strictest marital chastity for women—making for a profoundly inequitable and hypocritical double standard. Early Christian sexual modesty, therefore, was hardly "prudish" in the eyes of women, children, and men of low social stature. It was a direct and forceful challenge only to the selfish social liberties of wealthy men of leisure.

In short, early Jesus followers lived differently—and it showed. From the earliest writings down throughout the early centuries, believers embraced a call to live holy lives that served as "beacons in the world" for their confession (Origen, *Against Celsus* 3.29). This played a major role in the public witness of church communities: they knew who they were, why they existed, and what they were called to stand for. In other words, early believers embodied an integrity that was credible and visible. They not only professed an alternative faith, they embodied its ethos, however imperfectly.

For Reflection: Public Witness and Integrity

Many approaches to effective witness and evangelism today start with studies of our surrounding society and its people. As church, we need no less to reflect on who we are and why we are here. Early believers did not have a well-organized marketing strategy: they simply lived out their faith in Jesus with integrity. A community that lacks purpose and conviction about who it is, no matter its evangelism strategies, is neither inviting nor compelling. At the end of the day, church communities are called by God to proclaim a message of good news that has changed them, their identities, and their sense of purpose in the world. They are called to love and live in ways that reflect their experience of divine grace.

> A community that lacks purpose and conviction about who it is, no matter its evangelism strategies, is neither inviting nor compelling.

A friend of mine ("Ron") is actively involved in his church community. In fact, he thinks of it like family. When Ron had a personal crisis, the church community cared for him. They drove him to appointments, helped with childcare, prayed for him, and assisted in other ways. They didn't help because of any congregational program; they helped because they knew him, appreciated his need, and responded with love. Although a more personal than a public act, this kind of service bears genuine witness—a kind that Ron knows is certainly genuine.

Guiding Metaphors: Saints and Bearers of Light

What does it mean for Christians to live "distinctively" in our world today? Two metaphors appear in the NT and early Christian writings that inform our thinking about this question: saints and bearers of light.

The word *saint* (*hagios*) simply means someone whom God sets apart as holy or sacred. In his letters, Paul regularly calls church participants saints (or holy ones) and encourages them to live in light of it.[48] Aside from sibling language, it is the most common designation Paul gives to believers. Most of his letters, in fact, begin with the introduction: "to the saints in . . ."[49] Paul does this even though some communities were "unsaintly" in behavior (1 Cor 1:2), and others were unknown to him personally (Rom 1:7). Simply by virtue of being believers in Christ, they were not only "sisters and brothers" in the faith, they were "saints"—people set apart by God as holy.

In today's world, the idea of being "set apart" may not seem positive. After all, some church communities today are more clannish and reclusive than actively engaged with their world. And the very idea of being set apart implies a division that seems judgmental. But NT authors, including Paul, describe this being "set apart" not in terms of exclusion but as the bestowal of a divine significance: it aims to distinguish a way of life that reflects the nature of God. First Peter captures this thinking well: "Just as the one who called you is holy, so be holy yourselves in all your manner of living, since it is written: 'you shall be holy, for I am holy'" (1:15–16).

Being "set apart" or "holy" as saints means simply to reflect the character and nature of God. More importantly, the call and power to be saints comes not from within but from God.[50] It is something believers neither earn nor achieve: they embrace and live into it. As Paul declares to the church at Corinth, a community with behavioral issues: "Do you not know that you are God's temple and God's Spirit dwells among you? . . . For God's temple—who you are—is holy" (1 Cor 3:16–17). Though being set apart is grounds for living differently, it is God who makes followers of Jesus holy and enables them to live accordingly, however imperfectly. In the perspective of NT writers, believers in Jesus *are* saints—and so are set apart by God for God's purposes in the world.

The second metaphor deals with bearing light. It uses a variety of language—children of light, children of the day, light of the world, light for the nations—to convey with different nuances the same basic idea: Christians are a people called to bear light in an otherwise dark world. "For you are all children of light and children of the day" (1 Thess 5:5).[51]

Probably the most well-known form of the metaphor occurs early in Matthew's Sermon on the Mount, acting like a lens through which to hear all the sermon's ensuing ethical instructions: "You are the light of the world. A city built on a hill cannot be hid. No one lights a lamp and puts it under the bushel basket, but instead on the lampstand, and it gives light to all in the house. In the same way, let your light shine before others, so that they may see your good deeds and give glory to your Father in heaven" (Matt 5:14–16).

Most forms of the metaphor emphasize that the light borne by Jesus followers comes not from themselves but from the one who called them (2 Cor 4:4–6; Eph 5:8). God is a source of eternal light, enabling followers of Jesus to experience and extend divine light to the world.[52] In a string of metaphors, 1 Peter captures both the call to holiness and the comparison of light and darkness: "You are a chosen race, a royal priesthood, a holy nation, God's own people, in order that you may proclaim the great acts of the one who called you out of darkness into God's marvelous light" (2:9).[53]

These two metaphors, *saints* and *bearers of light*, depict a distinctive calling and contribution Jesus followers have in the world. As a people set apart and enlightened by God, they become tangible signs and reflections of the one who has called them so that others may catch a glimpse of the character of their God. This made early church communities a distinctive movement and people.

Do our church communities today embody this identity—a people set apart to bear light in a dark world? The world needs a constructive witness (or light) that stands in protest against the dark things that flourish at the expense of people's lives— including such things as materialism, sexism, isolationism, religious discrimination, racism, human trafficking, pornography, militarism, misguided nationalism, consumerism and commercialism, substance abuse, systemic oversight of the impoverished, and other forms of dehumanization. Do we, as church, stand in protest in order to shed light on the shortcomings in need of addressing?

Conclusion: A Patient Ferment Today?

What is the role of church communities in local contexts of the world today?

To some extent, church communities are no different than other groups. They gather together at set times. They do things together. They eat and drink together. They know and care for each other. They have leaders of various kinds. They support one another in their joys and sorrows. They help each other when in need. They collect resources to share toward good causes. They gather for specific purposes. In these things, church communities do not look any different from another social club down the street.

But is that all?

In increasing measure in the Western world, young people coming of age have no interest in a Christianity that looks like just another social club. It's not that these young adults have no interest in God or Jesus or spirituality. It's that they are indifferent and skeptical toward a religious group—*any* religious group— that is more institutionalized, stagnant, and conventional than it is authentic, passionate, and relevant. And these people are smart. They can sniff out inauthenticity where it appears. An undergraduate student of mine once worded it this way: "I'm really interested in learning more about Jesus; I just don't know whether the church really helps with that."

Of course, not all church communities are stagnant. Maybe people like my undergraduate student are simply not looking in the right places. Still, surveys in recent years show a fair share of people are religiously unaffiliated due to discontent with existing religious communities and their leaders.[54] How do church communities remember, recover, and retain a vibrant sense of their calling to live distinctively in the world?

> How do church communities remember, recover, and retain a vibrant sense of their calling to live distinctively in the world?

In many Western contexts, the Christian faith and surrounding culture have historically overlapped more than they differed. But in many of those same contexts, things today are changing dramatically. In the United States, for instance, the fastest growing religious group today is the unaffiliated. If the trend continues, very soon church communities will feel far more like a minority movement than a force in society. The need will only increase for the voice and calling of church communities to be more distinctive, identifiable, and clear. Their role as bearers of light, in a society increasingly apathetic to them, will become all the more significant.

Alan Krieder attributes the improbable rise and dramatic spread of Christianity in early centuries to their "patient ferment": a persistent resistance to mainstream culture marked by distinctive character, intentional communities, deliberate formation, and authentic commitment. He describes the attractiveness of this resistance this way:

> The churches grew in many places, taking varied forms. They proliferated because the faith that these fishers and hunters embodied was attractive to people who were dissatisfied with their old cultural and religious habits, who felt pushed to explore new possibilities, and who then encountered Christians who embodied a new manner of life that pulled them toward what the Christians called "rebirth" into a new life. Surprisingly, this happened in a patient manner.[55]

Patient and undramatic as this growth was, within a few centuries the fledgling band of Jesus followers attracted and welcomed most of the empire.

What can church communities today learn from their experience?

Many struggling church communities today turn for help to charismatic leaders and staff, innovative outreach approaches, creative forms of advertising, or capital appeal programs. While some of these things may prove helpful, they are not long-term solutions to the decline they now face. In lieu of quick-fix solutions, what would a patient, persistent stirring by communities of Christian character look like today?

For starters, church communities may join together in tangible forms of radical generosity and compassion, beginning with needs close to home. No matter where a church community is, there are pressing needs close at hand: hunger and malnutrition, cycles of poverty, lack of affordable housing, deficient education opportunities, children in need of care, the incarcerated, the lonely, and the isolated. While some locations have more abundant needs than others, all church communities live in places where people are in real need.

Some of the most vibrant congregations I have known personally have made reputations for themselves along these lines: "That's the church that helps kids," or "Those people are making a difference here," or "That community really cares about homeless people," or "That church is serious about welcoming people new to the community," or something similar. Reputations like these speak louder than billboards, advertisements, and cutting-edge media. It is one thing to care for social needs in theory; it's quite another to get hands dirty doing it. Doing so not only gives purpose to a community, it shines a beacon of grace in dark places.

How might church communities and believers today live distinctively so as to shine a steadfast and constructive witness in ways the world desperately needs? The question is best answered not by our words but by our deeds.

Bringing It Home: Ideas for Conversation and Implementation

1. Take a poll among those near your church community. What impressions have they—positive and negative—of your church?

2. Connect with a small group of young adults in their early twenties. Ask them what difference they think the church makes in the world and in their lives.

3. Interview someone who has experienced being a Christian in a context of the world where Christianity is a minority religion. In that context, how did believers approach public witness and hospitality toward neighbors?

4. Ask your church members: "Who are we (as a church)? Why are we here? What is our purpose here in this place?" Find ways to bridge these questions to dialogue about your community's ministry and mission.

5. Consider: What central thing is your denomination or local church community most known for? If you could change this, what do you *hope* it would be most known for?

Scripture Study

■ Read 1 Thessalonians, noticing especially the focus on holy living in chapters four and five. This letter is our earliest glimpse of how Paul encouraged believers to live. How did he envision their distinctions from the surrounding world?

■ Read Matthew 5:13–16, reflecting on how it serves as a lens for reading all the ethical instructions to follow in the Sermon on the Mount (Matthew 5–7). If these chapters show what it means to be "the light of the world," what does that mean for us today?

- Meditate on 1 Peter 2:9–10, with its rich language for the community of Jesus followers. The recipients saw themselves as "aliens and exiles" (2:11) in a hostile world. What do we learn from their approach in such an environment?

For Worship

- David Haas, "We Are Called" (*ELW* #720).
- Marty Haugen, "Gather Us In" (*ELW* #532).

Questions for Reflection

1. Imagine starting a church community from scratch, in a cultural context where there are no conventional expectations of what "church" should look like. What social models might inform your imagination?
2. In the late first-century Roman Empire, early church communities arose amid prevalent hostility toward them. How might this have influenced them negatively and positively?
3. What if your own context were suddenly to become hostile toward Christianity? How would that influence your faith?
4. This chapter suggests early church communities intentionally lived differently from their surrounding culture. How do church communities today do the same? How do they not?

5. Christianity experienced dramatic growth in the early centuries (see figure 5.2). This was not due to an organized evangelism program but to what Alan Krieder calls a "patient ferment," a persistent, counter-cultural devotion to Christian faith and character. What would a patient ferment today look like?

6. How important is it for Christians to live lives that authentically reflect their faith? Why?

7. What areas of the predominant culture are "dark places," where the light of Christ is needed from Christian believers?

Online Resources for Further Exploration

The Pew Research Center: PewResearch.org. The website offers current research on growth and decline of religious groups and people in society today, with data to help flesh out reasons for the trends.

Resources for Further Reading

Ascough, Richard S. *What Are They Saying about the Formation of Pauline Churches?* Mahwah, NJ: Paulist, 1998. Although now a few decades old, the book is a readable yet informed comparison of early Pauline churches with four social models from Paul's world: synagogues, philosophical schools, the ancient mysteries, and associations.

Hurtado, Larry W. *Destroyer of the Gods: Early Christian Distinctiveness in the Roman World.* Waco, TX: Baylor University Press, 2016. In a discussion that looks carefully at a host of early NT and later Christian sources, Hurtado argues early church communities lived in ways that were distinctive and directly challenging to widespread Roman cultural norms.

Justin's *1 Apology,* the Epistle to Diognetus, Origen's *Against Celsus,* and Tertullian's *Apology.* These writings by four early Christian apologists give glimpses into the criticisms, concerns, and tensions church communities faced in relationship to larger society.

Krieder, Alan. *The Patient Ferment of the Early Church: The Improbable Rise of Christianity in the Roman Empire.* Grand Rapids: Baker, 2016. The book addresses how and why Christianity took root and spread so dramatically in antiquity, arguing believers embodied a patient and persistent approach, counter-cultural to surrounding society, that slowly but surely won over the empire.

CONCLUSION

On Being Both Rooted and Renewing

Study the past, if you would divine the future.

—Confucius

When I served full time as a congregational pastor, I regularly read publications on church ministry practices and trends (periodicals, magazines, newsletters). After a few years of it, I became frustrated. On the positive side, they often covered new programs and creative initiatives that could spark my imagination. On the negative side, it seemed that all they *ever* covered were new programs and creative initiatives—ideally with social media, young adults, tattooed pastors, and anything at all in a bar or taproom. Rarely did something focus on core spiritual activities like worship, prayer, discipleship, or Scripture study— things I yearned for as a pastor struggling to foster deeply grounded discipleship in my community. Apparently, these core activities were not provocative or sexy enough to earn attention. This naturally made me pause and ask: "Are we attending to the things that most matter in our ministries today?"

Many questions haunt us church people and ministry leaders. With declining worship participation, we wonder about the church's future. With decreasing loyalty to established church structures, we wonder whether current practices are sustainable. With increasing numbers of the religiously "unaffiliated," we wonder what will make the church more relevant. And with shifting church demographics, we wonder whether the faith is being passed on to the next generation. These questions keep some of us up at night. And in response, we feel the need to do something—*anything*.

I suggest answers to these questions will not come simply from tattoos and taprooms. They are far more likely to come from returning first to our roots. Yes, as a church we need to think outside the box, try new things, and adapt to changing contexts. But creativity without substance will yield short-lived, superficial results. If we learn anything from church people in the earliest centuries, it is that authentic spirituality matters more, in the end, than creative attempts at favorable public relations. The uncanny rise of Christianity sprang from a distinctive profession and way of life that were somehow compelling to outsiders, however counterintuitive that may be to us.

As church people, we need to remember that a tree without deep roots will not flourish—it will die. As we listen for the Spirit's stirring and prodding among us, we must attend not only to the contexts and circumstances around us but also to how the Spirit has energized and revitalized God's people in times past—and most of all, at the very start. The world of the twenty-first century is a far cry from the first-century world that birthed the church, but the challenges, questions, and obstacles we now face are not entirely new. In many ways, the questions we ask are the same; we simply ask them from new vantage points. As we discern, listen, imagine, and experiment, we do so together most wisely with a keen awareness of where we have come from.

> As church people, we need to remember that a tree without deep roots will not flourish—it will die.

Observations and Questions

Allow me to summarize some observations from the book to help us ponder where we go from here. First, church communities never started out with dedicated buildings; that development happened centuries down the road. Instead, believers gathered in homes and other available spaces. Today, most of our church experiences happen in dedicated buildings. And while buildings offer benefits, they also tie our spiritual practices to sacred spaces, ultimately separating our spirituality from the places where we live. The stability of buildings can create a sense of routine to our practices of faith. Earliest Christianity flourished in a very different environment: one that mandated adaptability.

In that setting, church was tethered less to specific spaces than to people gathered as community. They identified themselves as "the Way" because they were not an established institution but a people on a journey.

In a world where most people think of "church" as institutionalized, structured, and even walled off from the world, we need a vision for being a people "on the Way." We need a renewed sense that we are a people in motion, on a journey, in transit, continually evolving and being changed. It does not mean we have to sell all our church buildings. It simply means we need to regain a vision marked less by stability and routine than by movement, adaptability, and transformation. From the outset, Christ called followers to be people on the move, following someone who had no permanent place to lay his head (Matt 8:20; Luke 9:58). As he called more followers, he charged them with bearing witness to the farthest reaches of the world (Acts 1:8). In short, Jesus called his followers to be a people always going somewhere. His call still stands today. How can we, as church people, recall a vision of being a people identified as "the Way"?

Second, unity has long been a characteristic of church communities and their witness. From the start, participants in church communities identified as "sisters and brothers." In doing so, they professed a unity that cut across social strata, political loyalties, gender distinctions, ethnic divisions, age discrepancies, and economic differences. In comparison to many other groups in society, church communities were a more diverse crowd that practiced a more distinctive equality. At least in theory, church communities were where "there is no longer Jew or Greek, there is no longer slave or free, there is no longer male and female; for all of you are one in Christ Jesus" (Gal 3:28).

Especially in the US, many people long to see signs of unity—and all the more from church communities. Yet interestingly, unity does not often work as a goal in and of itself. Authentic unity is more often a byproduct of an inspiring, shared purpose. Hurricane Harvey, for example, brought countless people together in the name of helping those in need. The events of 9/11, similarly, compelled a nation to unite against fear and hatred. As a church, then, perhaps we need less to sloganize "unity" than to clarify our source of unity (Christ) and to unite around purposes consistent with our unity.

Discussing what unites us is helpful, but what is more influential are shared acts of solidarity. A student of mine, for example, once recalled an antiracism march in which he and his community participated. He described the march as the most profound experience of Christian unity for his community in recent memory. Another congregation I know experienced deep solidarity among its members in the shadow of a sudden accident, as they resolved to stand with the grieving. In a community where I served as pastor, the faith formation of youth during the year after a major flood brought Lutheran churches together in ways never achieved before. As these examples show, putting unity into practice makes it visible and tangible. Here is where church communities may shine. Building on our unity in Christ, we as church are called to embody and work toward fostering a unity the world longs to see and hear. How may we do that more genuinely and more visibly?

Third, the church leadership models we use today did not fall directly from heaven. In the early centuries, forms of church leadership existed, but they varied from community to community and changed over time. Even more, the leadership vision of Jesus and Paul was one of servanthood. Rather than hand us a divine paradigm of leadership offices, they promoted the ideals of servant leadership, which may be lived out in various ways. For many people today, "church leaders" are associated with traditional hierarchies, power dynamics, and exclusive opportunities. True enough, past forms of church leadership have restricted the voices of women, ethnic minorities, LGBTQ people, and young people. In contrast, the message of Jesus compels us to use models that are just, theologically informed, contextually appropriate, and adaptive. Even more, it compels us to foster patterns of servanthood among those who lead.

> The leadership vision of Jesus and Paul was one of servanthood.

A related challenge is to cultivate a blend of both adaptability and high standards. In some rural and immigrant congregations in the US, for example, it is not feasible to expect traditional master's degrees of all leaders. At the same time, these leaders are no less in need of training, theological education, and spiritual resources. In fact, in my experience, most leaders crave these things. Going forward, we will need not fewer but *more* opportunities and possibilities for leadership training—and people to take advantage of them.

These opportunities will not just be for potential clergy but for all—in ways that are accessible, edifying, and empowering. We also need to tap the resources of congregations further, giving them greater ownership in leadership training and ongoing discipleship. These are just a few changes to come. We live in an age of change for the church that is not entirely different from the age of the earliest church communities. The Spirit calls us, as church, to discern, adapt, and strive for ongoing faithfulness as the realities around us continue to shift. Where today do we see signs of hope that we are discerning and adapting faithfully?

Fourth, among all the things church communities do, what matters most are the practices that gather and form us into a people oriented toward God. In these practices, early church communities displayed more diversity than uniformity. What prevailed, however, were the practices that built up communities and deepened their dependence on God: receiving God's gifts, hearing God's word, sharing together, eating together, praying together, and worshiping together. These activities were not terribly complicated. But they helped people to stop, to listen, to be open, and to know more fully whose people they were.

In the Western world today, many Christians approach spirituality as an individualistic endeavor, prioritizing practices that require no interaction with others. John Crist pokes fun at this individualized approach in a video about the "Virtual Reality Church," where people can choose a worship experience customized to their individual interests and inclinations. The virtual church menu allows individuals to choose a theological tradition, music, type of sermon (including the level of interaction expected by the speaker), and more. The video is a farce, but the grain of truth behind it is what makes it funny: many people today might *prefer* this virtual reality church over existing alternatives. But in the end, the Virtual Reality Church is a church without people.[1]

For Jesus, however, church is not an individualistic experience—it's a community. For this reason, *gathering* together as Christ's people is a core spiritual practice. When the Spirit sparked a movement at Pentecost, people were called into community (Acts 2:42–47)—not to be individuals who profess, "I can worship God on my own." Today many church communities face pressures to measure up to performance ideals, influenced by a cultural consumerism that views church through the same lens. Igniter Media Group has a spoof video that takes this mentality to its fullest degree. The video advertises a church called "Me Church," which starts when you show up, invites you to be as disruptive as you like, gives your car an oil change and a tune-up during worship, discloses others' giving (without asking the same of you), and hands out free ponies and Super Bowl tickets. The closing tagline is: "Me Church: Where It's All About You."[2] Although a spoof, the demands this church claims to meet are funny because they mirror some of the similarly unreasonable demands (albeit less exaggerated) placed on many church communities today.

Right or wrong, church communities have rarely excelled at meeting individualistic, consumerist demands. In its early centuries, the church flourished by uniting people into a new identity and enabling them to grow deeper in their awareness of God.

Among the many activities churches do today, what matters most are the practices that lead us into community in Christ, nurture within us openness to God, and inspire us to love authentically. Are we practicing the things that most matter today, or do we find ourselves more often focused on other things?

Finally, the most constructive witness today is less likely to come from catchy outreach strategies than from church people being who Christ called us to be. Important as it is to ask questions about our church's public image, neighborhood, and local needs, no less crucial are the basic questions, "Who are we?," "Why are we here?," and "What is our purpose?" Programs that meet local needs are excellent, but if we as church have no keen awareness of our core identity, then we offer nothing authentic or lasting.

The witness of early church communities shows us that authentic spirituality and tangible acts of love carry more weight than short-lived strategies and words alone. The earliest church grew not because of strategic public relations campaigns but because they lived out their faith genuinely in a hostile environment. This distinctive faith is not rocket science—it's just authentic spirituality. For our public witness today, we would do well to begin with our core message and how we live that out before giving sole attention to things outside ourselves.

Challenges and hardships are not entirely unwelcome. Hardships did not deter the earliest believers from their distinctive way of life but rather encouraged and enhanced it. The more they were oppressed, the more they multiplied (Tertullian, *Apology* 50.12–13). If, as predicted, challenges are only to grow for church communities, it is not simply bad news. With challenges come new opportunities. After all, it is often amid seasons of difficulty that God's Spirit is most at work refining, revitalizing, and renewing our dependence on God.

The Church of the Future and the Church of the Past

Though there are vast differences between the twenty-first century and first century, I propose the church of the future will look increasingly like the church of the past. This church will be less tied to physical buildings. It will be less wedded to denominational infrastructures. It will sense more acutely the significance of its professed unity. It will focus more on spiritual practices that gather, deepen, and forge community ties. It will feel compelled to take public witness seriously among audiences increasingly unfamiliar with Christian basics. It will focus more on what distinguishes church from alternative options. It will attend more deliberately to embodying a faith that matters to the world. Though our contexts today differ markedly from the early centuries, the church today will be called increasingly to return to our historic roots.

The church today will be called increasingly to return to our historic roots.

These changes will come neither easily nor quickly. Some of them may take place only in the wake of a crisis. But as Christendom fades in glory and the church imagines where the Spirit calls us going forward, we can be assured our future is a hope-filled one, regardless of the challenges ahead. After all, amid the skepticism and cynicism we sometimes entertain, we must remind ourselves the church was Jesus's idea, not ours. As Carey Nieuwhof observes, "[The church] will survive our missteps and whatever cultural trends happen around us. We certainly don't always get things right, but Christ has an incredible history of pulling together Christians in every generation to share his love for a broken world. As a result, the reports of the church's death are greatly exaggerated."[3]

In short, there is no reason to fear the church will ultimately roll over and die. Christ's people have seen far worse crises than ours, and they will outlast many more. No matter how bleak things sometimes appear, the Spirit has not abandoned us but is alive and well among us. And as Christ's cross shows us, sometimes precisely when things look their worst, God is up to something most profound.

Questions for Reflection

1. How can we, as church people, recapture a vision of being a people identified as "the Way"? What does that look like to you?

2. How might we, as church people, embody and foster a unity the world longs to see and hear? How does our unity in Christ (Gal 3:28) give us a foundation for this?

3. Are we practicing the spiritual practices that most matter, or do we find ourselves more often focused on other

things? What practices, do you think, will become increasingly important going forward?

4. Which is easier to ask: questions about our neighborhood and its needs, or questions about ourselves—like "Who are we?," "Why are we here?," and "What is our purpose?" Why?

5. Do you agree with the author's suggestion that the church of the future will look more like the earliest church—or not? Why?

NOTES

INTRODUCTION: WHY CHURCH ROOTS MATTER

1. Attributed to George Santayana, *The Life of Reason: The Phases of Human Progress* (1905–1906).

2. Frank Viola, *Finding Organic Church: A Practical Manual for Planting a Church from Scratch* (Colorado Springs: David C. Cook, 2009), 14. A predecessor book of Viola's with a similar focus is *So You Want to Start a House Church?: First-Century Style Church Planting for Today* (Gainesville, FL: Present Testimony Ministry, 2003).

3. Robert W. Gehring, *House Church and Mission: The Importance of Household Structures in Early Christianity* (Peabody, MA: Hendrickson, 2004), 1.

4. Edward Adams, *The Earliest Christian Meeting Places: Almost Exclusively Houses?* (London: T&T Clark, 2013).

5. For example, Elisabeth Schüssler Fiorenza, *In Memory of Her: A Feminist Theological Reconstruction of Christian Origins* (New York: Crossroad, 1983); Robert A. Atkins Jr., *Egalitarian Community: Ethnography and Exegesis* (Tuscaloosa: University of Alabama Press, 1991).

6. John H. Elliott, "The Jesus Movement Was Not Egalitarian but Family-Oriented," *Biblical Interpretation* 11 (2003): 173–210; Andrew D. Clarke, *Serve the Community of the Church: Christians as Leaders and Ministers* (Grand Rapids: Eerdmans, 2000); Jack

Barensten, *Emerging Leadership in the Pauline Mission: A Social Identity Perspective on Local Leadership Development in Corinth and Ephesus* (Eugene, OR: Pickwick, 2011); Richard Last, *The Pauline Church and the Corinthian Ekklēsia: Greco-Roman Associations in Comparative Context* (Cambridge: Cambridge University Press, 2016).

CHAPTER 1: SACRED SPACES FOR A CHURCH ON THE WAY

1. Nadine Ellsworth-Moran, "What Makes Space Sacred?," *The Presbyterian Outlook*, March 1, 2017, https://tinyurl.com/y2al8bun.
2. All New Testament quotations in this book are my own (from the Greek of the Nestle-Aland 28th edition).
3. Murphy-O'Connor, *St. Paul's Corinth: Texts and Archaeology* (Collegeville, MN: Liturgical Press, 2002), 178–80. See also Murphy-O'Connor, *St. Paul's Ephesus: Texts and Archaeology* (Collegeville, MN: Liturgical Press, 2008), 193–95.
4. So traditional estimates (e.g., two hundred people per acre, Vincent Branick, *The House Church in the Writings of Paul* [Eugene, OR: Wipf & Stock, 2012], 42–43). More recent research suggests lower numbers. Glenn R. Storey, "The Population of Ancient Rome," *Antiquity* 71, no. 274 (Dec. 1997): 966–78.
5. David Balch, "Rich Pompeiian Houses, Shops for Rent, and the Huge Apartment Building in Herculaneum as Typical Spaces for Pauline House Churches," *Journal for the Study of the New Testament* 27 (2004): 27–46.
6. The "place" where believers gather in Acts 4:23–31 after Peter and John's release by the authorities may also have been a house, given precedents earlier in the narrative (2:46; 1:12–26). Since Acts 1:15 gives the full number of believers as 120, Adams disputes the "upper room" was part of a house (*The Earliest Christian Meeting Places: Almost Exclusively Houses?* [London: T&T Clark, 2013], 55–57). But whether all 120 gathered at the same time is not entirely clear (cf. 2:1). Regardless, Roger W. Gehring notes the upper room is portrayed as "an example of a house church in the fullest sense" (*House Church and Mission: The Importance*

of Household Structures in Early Christianity [Peabody, MA: Hendrickson, 2004], 66).

7. The language of "encourage" (*parakaleō*) is often used for preaching in Acts (2:40; 11:23). Also in Philippi, after the baptism of the jailer and his household, he invites Paul and Silas to his home for shared dining and rejoicing (16:25–34)

8. So Bradley Blue, "Acts and the House Church," in *The Book of Acts in Its Graeco-Roman Setting*, ed. David W. J. Gill and Conrad Gempf (Grand Rapids: Eerdmans, 1994), 119–222; Roger Gehring, *House Church and Mission*, 62–228. A skeptic of this idea is Edward Adams, *Earliest Christian Meeting Places*, 51–67.

9. Adams, *Earliest Christian Meeting Places*, 51.

10. Luke 10:38–42; 11:37–54; 14:1–24; 19:1–10; 24:28–32, 36–49; John 13:1–17:26; 20:19–23, 26–29.

11. See Hans-Josef Klauck, *Hausgemeinde und Hauskirche im frühen Christentum*, SBS 103 (Stuttgart: Katholisches Bibelwerk, 1981), 56–62; Gehring, *House Church and Mission*, 28–61.

12. Gehring, *House Church and Mission*, 55.

13. Barna Group. "How Many People Really Attend a House Church? Barna Study Finds It Depends on the Definition," August 31, 2009, https://tinyurl.com/y3p57byl.

14. Gehring, *House Church and Mission*, 1.

15. Peter proclaims in the temple (3:1–4:3), while Paul most often preaches and teaches in synagogues (9:20; 13:5, 14–43; 14:1; 17:1–3, 10, 17; 18:4, 19; 19:8). Still, Paul does the same at the city gates of Lystra (14:13–18), at a "place of prayer" at Philippi (16:13), in the marketplace of Athens (17:17), in the Areopagus at Athens (17:22–31), at the lecture hall (*scholē*) of Tyrannus in Ephesus (19:9–10), and very possibly at a harbor at Miletus (20:18–38).

16. Some believe this "place of prayer" (*proseuchē*) refers to a synagogue, but if so, then why does Acts not simply call it that (a *synagōgē*)—as it does every other Jewish gathering space?

17. Adams, *Earliest Christian Meetings Places*, 198.

18. See Donald D. Binder, *Into the Temple Courts: The Place of the Synagogues in the Second Temple Period*, SBLDS 169 (Atlanta: Society of Biblical Literature, 1999); Adams, *Earliest Christian*

Meeting Places, 124–32. On Jewish gatherings at waterside areas, see Philo, *On the Life of Moses* 2.41–42; *Against Flaccus* 122; Josephus, *Jewish Antiquities* 14.257–58; Tertullian, *On Fasting* 16.

19. Didache 7.1; Tertullian, *Baptism* 4.3, *Testamentum Domini* 21.1–2; *Acts of Paul* 3.23–27; *Acts of John* 62–86; Eusebius, *Ecclesiastical History* 7.11.10.

20. See esp. Edward Adams, *Earliest Christian Meeting Places*; David L. Balch, "The Church Sitting in a Garden (1 Cor 14:30; Rom 16:23; Mark 6:39–40; 8:6; John 6:3, 10; Acts 1:15; 2:1–2)," in *Contested Spaces: Houses and Temples in Roman Antiquity and the New Testament*, ed. David L. Balch and A. Weissenrieder (Tübingen: Mohr Siebeck, 2012), 201–35; Richard Last, *The Pauline Church and the Corinthians Ekklēsia: Greco-Roman Associations in Comparative Context*, SNTSMS 164 (Cambridge: Cambridge University Press, 2016), 43–82.

21. Another excavation of interest is the Christian prayer hall at Megiddo, built around 230 CE, attached to what was apparently a residential building associated with the Roman army. See Yotam Tepper and L. Di Segni, *A Christian Prayer Hall of the Third Century CE at Kefar 'Othnay (Legio): Excavations at the Megiddo Prison 2005* (Jerusalem: Israel Antiquities Authority, 2006).

22. L. Michael White, *The Social Origins of Christian Architecture, Volume II: Texts and Monuments for the Christian Domus Ecclesiae in Its Environment*, Harvard Theological Studies 42 (Valley Forge, PA: Trinity, 1997), 135–257.

23. An example is Wolfgang Simon, *The House Church Book: Rediscover the Dynamic, Organic, Relational, Viral Community Jesus Started* (Carol Stream, IL: Barna, 2009).

24. Titus and Jude alone do not use sibling language this way (cf. Jude 1:1), and 1 Peter uses it infrequently (5:12). For more on this, see chapter 2.

25. John 2:16; 4:21, 23[2]; 5:17, 19, 20, 21, 22, 23[2], 26, 36, 37, 43, 45; 6:27, 32, 37, 40, 44, 45, 46[2], 57[2], 58, 65; 8:16, 18, 19[2], 28, 38, 42, 49, 54; 10:15, 17, 18, 25, 29[2], 30, 32, 36, 37, 38[2]; 11:41; 12:26, 27, 28, 49, 50; 14:2, 6, 7, 9[2], 10[3], 11[2], 12, 13, 16, 20, 21, 23, 24, 26, 28[2], 31[2]; 15:1, 8, 9, 10, 15, 16, 23, 24,

26[2]; 16:3, 10, 15, 17, 23, 25, 26, 27, 28[2], 32; 17:1, 5, 11, 21, 24, 25; 18:11; 20:17[3], 21). The narrative and other characters do so as well (1:14, 18; 3:35; 5:18; 8:27, 41; 13:1, 3; 14:8). The letter of Ephesians also uses this designation for God frequently: 1:2, 3, 17; 2:18; 3:14; 4:6; 5:20; 6:23.

26. Eph 5:21–6:9; Col 3:18–4:1; Titus 2:1–10; 1 Pet 2:13–3:7. See also 1 Tim 2:18–15; 5:1–6:2; 1 Clement 1:3; 21:6–9; Polycarp, *To the Philippians* 4:1–6:2.

27. Branick, *House Church,* 137.

CHAPTER 2: BEING TRUE SIBLINGS IN A DIVIDED WORLD

1. "Meet the Press" interview with Martin Luther King Jr. (April 17, 1960), conducted by NBC. Viewable online at https://tinyurl. com/yc37bas8.

2. Jennifer Harvey, *Dear White Christians: For Those Still Longing for Racial Reconciliation* (Grand Rapids: Eerdmans, 2014), 15–16.

3. Michael Lipka, "The Most and Least Racially Diverse U.S. Religious Groups," Pew Research Center, July 27, 2015, https://tinyurl.com/ojcxgyp.

4. Pew Research Center, "The Political Preferences of U.S. Religious Groups," February 23, 2016, https://tinyurl.com/y52jm2l2.

5. Jerome Murphy-O'Connor, "The Corinth That Saint Paul Saw," *Biblical Archaeologist,* September 1984, 147.

6. Engels estimates fifty-six thousand residents, and Taylor seventy to eighty thousand. Donald Engels, *Roman Corinth: An Alternative Model for the Classical City* (Chicago: University of Chicago Press, 1990), 79–84, 179–81; Walter F. Taylor Jr., *Paul: Apostle to the Nations* (Minneapolis: Fortress, 2012), 162.

7. Plato and Aristophanes (both Athenians) wrote around 400 BCE. Strabo was not from Athens and wrote later (about 7 BCE), but his sources may well have been Athenian (see Murphy-O'Connor, "Corinth That St. Paul Saw," 152). Both Strabo and Horace record the proverb, "It is not for every man to venture to Corinth" (Strabo, *Geography* 8.6.20; Horace, *Epistles* 1.17.36).

8. See 1 Cor 5:6–8; 7:18; 9:8–10; 10:1–13; Acts 18:4–8. On Jews in Corinth, see Philo, *On the Embassy to Gaius* 281; Justin, *Dialogue with Trypho* 1.3.

9. Richard Last estimates ten, Jerome Murphy-O'Connor forty to fifty, Craig de Vos one hundred, Richard Hays 150 to two hundred, and Chrys Caragounis several hundred. Last, *Pauline Church,* 77–82; de Vos, *Church and Community Conflicts: The Relationships of the Thessalonian, Corinthian, and Philippian Churches with their Wider Civic Communities* (Atlanta: Scholars Press, 1999), 204; Murphy-O'Connor, *St. Paul's Corinth,* 182; Hays, *First Corinthians* (Louisville: Westminster John Knox, 1997), 7; Chrys Caragounis, "A House Church in Corinth: An Inquiry into the Structure of Early Corinthian Christianity," in *Saint Paul and Corinth: 1950 Years since the Writing of the Epistles to the Corinthians*, ed. C. J. Belezos, 2 vols. (Athens: Psichogios, 2009), 1:365–418.

10. Last, *Pauline Church,* 77–80; Dennis E. Smith, "The House Church as Social Environment," in *Text, Image, and Christians in the Graeco-Roman World: A Festschrift in Honor of David Lee Balch*, ed. Aliou Cissé and Carolyn Osiek (Eugene, OR: Pickwick, 2012), 3–21.

11. Wayne O. McCready, "*Ekklēsia* and Voluntary Associations," in *Voluntary Associations in the Graeco-Roman World*, ed. John S. Kloppenborg and Stephen G. Wilson (London: Routledge, 1996), 59–73; Philip A. Harland, *Dynamics of Identity in the World of the Early Christians: Associations, Judeans, and Cultural Minorities* (New York: T&T Clark, 2009), 32–34; Richard S. Ascough, Philip A. Harland, and John S. Kloppenborg, eds., *Associations in the Greco-Roman World: A Sourcebook* (Waco, TX: Baylor University Press, 2012).

12. Minucius Felix, *Octavius* 36.3–7; see also Justin, *2 Apology* 10.8; Tatian, *Oration to the Greeks* 32.

13. Gerd Theissen, "Social Stratification in the Corinthian Community: A Contribution to the Sociology of Early Hellenic Christianity," in *The Social Setting of Pauline Christianity: Essays on Corinth*, ed. and trans. John H. Schütz (Philadelphia: Fortress, 1982), 102.

14. So Abraham Malherbe, *Social Aspects of Early Christianity* (Baton Rouge: Louisiana State University Press, 1977), 31; Theissen, "Social Stratification," 106; Wayne Meeks, *First Urban Christians: The Social World of the Apostle Paul*, 2nd ed. (New Haven: Yale University Press, 2003), 51–73.
15. Glenn R. Storey, "The Population of Ancient Rome," *Antiquity* 71, no. 274 (Dec. 1997): 966–78.
16. James S. Jeffers, *Conflict at Rome: Social Order and Hierarchy in Early Christianity* (Minneapolis: Fortress, 1991), 10; H. J. Leon, *The Jews of Ancient Rome* (Philadelphia: Jewish Publication Society of America, 1960), 135–36.
17. Not, as some translations (like the NRSV) say, "relatives." Cf. Rom 9:3 (*syngeneis*).
18. 1 Clement; Ignatius, *Romans*; The Shepherd of Hermas; Justin Martyr; Dionysius's letter (Eusebius, *Eccl. Hist.* 4.23.9–12), and Hippolytus of Rome. See also Tacitus, *Annals* 15.44. The NT writings Hebrews and 1 Peter also have associations with Rome (Heb 13:24; 1 Pet 5:13), and the Apostles' Creed is traditionally attributed to the church at Rome (Ambrose of Milan, *Letter* 42.5).
19. Mary, Rufus, Julia, Andronicus, and Tryphaena. Only the first three (Mary, Rufus, Julia) are attested among Jews in the city of Rome. Peter Lampe, *From Paul to Valentinus: Christians at Rome in the First Two Centuries*, trans. Michael Steinhauser, ed. Marshall D. Johnson (Minneapolis: Fortress, 2003), 74–75.
20. Peter Lampe suggests that, already in Paul's day, the Roman church was more ethnically gentile than Jewish, fostered especially by Emperor Claudius's expulsion of Jews from Rome in 49 CE (see Suetonius, *Claudius* 25.4; also Acts 18:2). Lampe, *From Paul to Valentinus*, 69–79.
21. 1 Thess 1:1; 1 Cor 1:2; 2 Cor 1:1; Phil 4:15; see also Col 4:16; Rom 16:1; 2 Thess 1:1. Cf. Gal 1:2 ("churches in Galatia"); 1 Cor 16:1 ("churches of Macedonia"). Paul does use the word *church* (*ekklēsia*) in the phrase "church-gathering at home," but in all these instances the qualifying adjectival phrase *at home* (*kat' oikon*) is added (1 Cor 16:19; Rom 16:5; Phlm 2; also Col 4:15).

22. Murphy-O'Connor, *St. Paul's Corinth,* 182–83.

23. So Vincent Branick, *The House Church in the Writings of Paul* (Eugene, OR: Wipf & Stock, 2012), 70; Lampe, *From Paul to Valentinus,* 359; Meeks, *First Urban Christians,* 76. On the Jewish community at Rome, see Silvia Cappelletti, *The Jewish Community of Rome: From the Second Century B.C. to the Third Century C.E.* (Leiden: Brill, 2006). Cappelletti sees evidence of a "cultural unity" in the synagogues' use of language and rituals (198).

24. 1 Clement prescript; Ignatius, *To the Romans* prescript; *Martyrdom of Justin* 2 ("Justin said, 'I live above one Martinus, at the Timiotinian Bath; and during the whole time—and I am now living in Rome for the second time—I am unaware of any other meeting [in Rome] than his'"). See also Eusebius, *Eccl. Hist.* 4.23.9–12; Justin Martyr, *1 Apology* 67.3.

25. Mark Button and Fika J. Van Rensburg, "The 'House Churches' in Corinth," *Neotestamentica* 37, no. 1 (2003): 10.

26. E.g., 1 John 2:18–19, 26–27; 4:1–6; 2 John 7–11. See also 3 John 9–10; Jude 12–13; Rev 2:14–16, 20–25.

27. For the sake of brevity, the discussion here is admittedly a binary one, but do note there were early church participants who very likely would not have identified entirely and comfortably with one gender or the other (e.g., the Ethiopian in Acts 8:26–40).

28. They worked alongside Paul: Rom 16:3–4, 9, 12; Phil 4:3; Phlm 1 (also Col 4:12–13); they carried letters for him: 1 Cor 16:17–18; Phlm 12 (also Col 4:7–9); they spent time with him in prison: Rom 16:7; Phlm 10, 23; they preceded him in faith: Rom 16:7; they were dearly beloved to him: Rom 16:4, 8–9, 12.

29. Acts names fifty-two male believers versus twelve female, excluding "certain women" in 1:14 and the male leadership groups in 11:1–18, 15:6–21, and 20:17–35.

30. Women: Junia (v. 7), Prisca (vv. 3–5), Mary (v. 6), Tryphaena, Tryphosa, and Persis (v. 12; see also Rufus's mother, v. 13). Men: Andronicus (v. 7), Aquila (vv. 3–5), Urbanus (v. 9; see also Apelles, v. 10, and Rufus, v. 13).

31. See Lee A. Johnson, "Paul's Letters Reheard: Performance-Critical Examination of the Preparation, Transportation, and Delivery

of Paul's Correspondence," *Catholic Biblical Quarterly* 79, no. 1 (2017): 60–76.

32. See Carolyn Osiek and Margaret Y. MacDonald, *A Woman's Place: House Churches in Earliest Christianity* (Minneapolis: Fortress, 2006), 95–117; Jennifer A. Glancy, *Slavery in Early Christianity* (Minneapolis: Fortress, 2006).

33. See Pliny the Younger, *Epistles* 9.21, 24; Justinian, *Digest* 21.1.17.4; 21.1.43.1.

34. Lampe, *From Paul to Valentinus*, 164–83.

35. 1 Cor 1:16; 16:15; Acts 10:24–48; 16:15, 33–34; 18:8.

36. O. M. Bakke, *When Children Became People: The Birth of Childhood in Early Christianity*, trans. Brian McNeil (Minneapolis: Augsburg Fortress, 2005), 259.

37. Exod 22:22; Deut 14:28–29; Jer 7:6; Ps 68:5; 82:3; 146:9; Prov 23:10; Job 29:12; 31:16–18.

38. Within the context of the metaphor of the body of Christ, Paul does use the language of "members" (1 Cor 12:12–31; Rom 12:4–5; also Eph 4:25; 5:30), but simply because the metaphor calls for it. Outside of this metaphor, no NT author calls church participants "members."

39. Rom 1:13; 7:1, 4; 8:12, 29; 10:1; 11:25; 12:1; 14:10, 13, 15, 21; 15:14, 30; 16:14, 17, 23; 1 Cor 1:1, 10–11, 26; 2:1; 3:1; 4:6; 5:11; 6:5–6, 8; 7:12, 14–15, 24, 29; 8:11–13 [4]; 9:5; 10:1; 11:33; 12:1; 14:6, 20, 26, 39; 15:1, 6, 31, 50, 58; 16:11–12, 15, 20; 2 Cor 1:1, 8; 2:13; 8:1, 18, 22–23; 9:3, 5; 11:9; Gal 1:2, 11, 19; 3:15; 4:12, 28, 31; 5:11, 13; 6:1, 18; Phil 1:12, 14; 2:25; 3:1, 13, 17; 4:1, 8, 21; 1 Thess 1:4; 2:1, 9, 14, 17; 3:2, 7; 4:1, 6, 10, 13; 5:1, 4, 12, 14, 25–27; Phlm 1:1, 7, 16, 20. Cf. Rom 9:3. Among the disputed letters of Paul: Eph 6:21, 23; Col 1:1, 2; 4:7, 9, 15; 2 Thess 1:3; 2:1, 13, 15; 3:1, 6, 13, 15; 1 Tim 4:6; 5:1; 6:2; 2 Tim 4:21.

40. Titus and Jude alone do not use sibling language (cf. Jude 1:1), and 1 Peter uses it infrequently (5:12).

41. See Meeks, *First Urban Christians*, 87n73; McCready, "*Ekklēsia* and Voluntary Associations"; Harland, *Dynamics of Identity*, 63–81.

42. Osiek, *What Are They Saying about the Social Setting of the New Testament?* Rev. ed. (New York: Paulist, 1992), 71.

43. Bill Bishop, *The Big Sort: Why the Clustering of Like-Minded Americans Is Tearing Us Apart* (New York: Houghton Mifflin, 2009); Wendy K. Tam Cho, James G. Gimpel, and Iris S. Hui, "Voter Migration and the Geographic Sorting of the American Electorate," *Annals of the Association of American Geographers* 103, no. 4 (2013): 856–70.

44. Lincoln, "House Divided Speech," Illinois Republican Party Convention, Springfield, Illinois, June 16, 1858.

45. Bonhoeffer, *Life Together*, trans. John Doberstein (London: SCM, 1960), 20.

CHAPTER 3: BEING A BODY IN A STRATIFIED SOCIETY

1. Pew Research Center, "'Nones' on the Rise: One in Five Adults Have No Religious Affiliation," Pew Forum on Religion & Public Life, October 9, 2012, https://tinyurl.com/llu8pa5.

2. Bruce J. Malina, *The New Testament World: Insights from Cultural Anthropology* (Louisville: John Knox, 1981), 30–32.

3. Mark Allan Powell, *Introducing the New Testament: A Historical, Literary, and Theological Survey*, 2nd ed. (Grand Rapids: Baker Academic, 2018), 31.

4. Warren Carter, *The Roman Empire and the New Testament: An Essential Guide* (Nashville: Abingdon, 2006), 10.

5. David Fiensy, "Ancient Economy and the New Testament," in *Understanding the Social World of the New Testament*, ed. Dietmar Neufeld and Richard E. DeMaris (New York: Routledge, 2010), 200.

6. Alan B. Wheatley, *Patronage in Early Christianity: Its Use and Transformation from Jesus to Paul of Samosata* (Eugene, OR: Pickwick, 2011), 6.

7. John H. Elliott, "The Jesus Movement was not Egalitarian but Family-Oriented," *Biblical Interpretation* 11 (2003): 173–210.

8. Roger Gehring, *House Church and Mission: The Importance of Household Structures in Early Christianity* (Peabody, MA: Hendrickson, 2004), 190–96; Richard Last, *The Pauline Church and the Corinthians Ekklēsia: Greco-Roman Associations in Comparative Context*, SNTSMS 164 (Cambridge: Cambridge University Press,

2016), 183–212; Peter Oakes, "Urban Structure and Patronage: Christ Followers in Corinth," in Neufeld and DeMaris, *Understanding the Social World*, 178–93.

9. Carolyn Osiek and Margaret Y. MacDonald, *A Woman's Place: House Churches in Earliest Christianity* (Minneapolis: Fortress, 2006), 144–63.

10. See 2 Cor 5:18–20; Eph 6:20. Robert Jewett, *Romans: A Commentary*, 2nd ed. (Minneapolis: Fortress, 2006), 101; Wayne Meeks, *First Urban Christians: The Social World of the Apostle Paul*, 2nd ed. (New Haven: Yale University Press, 2003), 131–32.

11. The twelve disciples: Gal 1:17, 19; 1 Cor 9:5; 15:7, 9. "False" apostles: 2 Cor 11:5, 13; 12:11; Rev 2:2. Coworkers and associates of Paul's: Barnabas (Acts 14:4, 14), Silvanus and Timothy (1 Thess 2:7; perhaps Apollos in 1 Cor 4:9), Andronicus and Junia (Rom 16:7), and Epaphroditus (Phil 2:25).

12. Paul uses "coworker" (*synergos*), "coworking" (*synergontes*), and "striving alongside" (*synathleō*) in reference to nineteen individuals: Prisca and Aquila (Rom 16:3–5); Urbanus (Rom 16:9); Timothy (Rom 16:21; 1 Thess 3:2); Apollos (1 Cor 3:6–9); Fortunatus, Achaicus, and Stephanas (1 Cor 16:15–18); Titus (2 Cor 8:23); Epaphroditus (Phil 2:25); Euodia, Syntyche, and Clement (Phil 4:2–3); Philemon (Phlm 1); Mark and Aristarchus (Phlm 24; Col 4:10–11); Demas and Luke (Phlm 24). Colossians adds Jesus called Justus (4:11). Paul depicts four women as significant workers "in the Lord" in the church at Rome: Mary, Persis, Tryphaena, and Tryphosa (Rom 16:6, 12). Colossians depicts Epaphras similarly (Col 1:7–8; 4:12–13).

13. For more on prophecy, see chapter 4.

14. So David E. Aune, *Prophecy in Early Christianity and the Ancient Mediterranean World* (Grand Rapids: Eerdmans, 1983), 338; Pheme Perkins, *Ministering in the Pauline Churches* (New York: Paulist, 1982), 56.

15. In the Gospels alone, Jesus is called "teacher" over forty times. See Matt 10:24–25; Luke 6:40; 1 Cor 4:17.

16. Thessalonica (1 Thess 5:12–13), Galatia (Gal 6:6), Corinth (1 Cor 12:28), Rome (Rom 12:7; see also "exhorter" in v. 8), Ephesus

(Eph 4:11–12), Antioch (Acts 13:1). According to Acts, the apostles teach in Jerusalem (4:18; 5:21, 25, 28, 42).

17. Civil service: Rom 13:4. Serving food: John 2:5, 9; 12:2. Waiting on tables: Acts 6:1–7; Philo, *On the Contemplative Life* 70; Josephus *Jewish Antiquities* 2.65; 11.163.166. Stewarding a collection of money: Rom 15:25, 30–31; 2 Cor 8:4; 9:1, 12, 13. Ministry for the sake of the gospel: Col 4:17; Acts 1:17, 25; 11:29; 12:25; 20:24.

18. Paul: Rom 11:13; 1 Cor 3:5; 2 Cor 4:1; 5:18; 6:3; 11:8. Stephanas: 1 Cor 16:15. So also Archippus in Col 4:17.

19. Christ: Rom 16:8; Mark 10:43; also 9:35. Paul and Apollos: 2 Cor 3:5–6; 6:4. Colossians also refers to Paul as a servant (1:23, 25), as well as Epaphras and Tychicus (1:7; 4:7).

20. H. W. Beyer, *"Episkeptomai, Episkopeō, Episkopē, Episkopos, Allotriepiskopos,"* TDNT, ed. Gerhard Kittel and Gerhard Friedrich (Grand Rapids: Eerdmans, 1977), 2:599–622, esp. 608–14.

21. See Andrew M. Selby, "Bishops, Elders, and Deacons in the Philippian Church: Evidence of Plurality from Paul and Polycarp," *Perspectives in Religious Studies* 39, no. 1 (Spring 2012): 79–94. On the broader historical development of the role in the Christian church, see Everett Ferguson, "Bishop," *Encyclopedia of Early Christianity,* ed. Everett Ferguson, Michael P. McHugh, and Frederick W. Norris, 2nd ed., 2 vols. (New York: Garland Publishing, 1997), 1:182–85.

22. Only occasionally in the NT does the word refer to authoritative representatives (e.g., of the Jerusalem church: Acts 11:30; 15:2, 4, 6, 22–23; 16:4; 21:18) the way "elder" language functioned in ancient Israel.

23. Cf. 1 Tim 3:1–7; Titus 1:5–9; also 1 Tim 4:14; 5:17–22.

24. "Leader" or "patron" (*proistamenos,* 1 Thess 5:12; Rom 12:8), the one who "labors" (1 Thess 5:12; also Rom 16:6, 12), and both "forms of assistance" (*antilēmpseis*) and "forms of administration" (*kybernēseis*) (1 Cor 12:28). See also "exhorter," "giver," and "the compassionate" (Rom 12:8).

25. "Women Clergy: A Growing and Diverse Community," *Religion Link,* May 15, 2015, https://tinyurl.com/y2tz36kr; David Masci, "The Divide over Ordaining Women," *Fact Tank,* September 9, 2014, https://tinyurl.com/y5nz3l3x.

26. Benjamin R. Knoll and Cammie Jo Bolin, *She Preached the Word: Women's Ordination in Modern America* (New York: Oxford University Press, 2018), esp. chaps. 5–8.
27. Sojourners, "Seven Reasons Why Men Should Not Be Pastors," April 5, 2016. Within two weeks the video had been liked by more than seventeen thousand Facebook users, generated more than 1,600 comments, been shared by more than thirty-four thousand people, and been viewed more than three million times (Knoll and Bolin, *She Preached the Word*, 2).
28. See Eldon Jay Epp, *Junia: The First Woman Apostle* (Minneapolis: Fortress, 2005); Rena Pederson, *The Lost Apostle: Searching for the Truth about Junia* (San Francisco: Jossey-Bass, 2006).
29. Luke 1:41–55; 2:36–38; Acts 21:9; cf. Rev 2:20. On women as prophets beyond the NT period, see Ute E. Eisen, *Women Officeholders in Early Christianity: Epigraphical and Literary Studies* (Collegeville, MN: Michael Glazier, 2000), 63–88. Eisen writes, "The number of [prophets] mentioned by name in early Christian literature is small. . . . In light of that fact it is especially striking that such a large proportion of those named are women" (70).
30. I deem 1 Cor 14:33b–36 either a quotation of Paul's dialogue partners at Corinth or a later (non-Pauline) insertion, based on its tensions with the rest of the letter (cf. 14:26–40; 11:2–16). So Joseph A. Fitzmyer, *First Corinthians* (New Haven: Yale University Press, 2008), 529–31; Gordon Fee, *First Corinthians* (Grand Rapids: Eerdmans, 2014), 699–705; Lucy Peppiatt, *Women and Worship at Corinth: Paul's Rhetorical Arguments in 1 Corinthians* (Eugene, OR: Cascade, 2015).
31. See Eisen, *Women Officeholders*, 89–115.
32. Though disputed, many ancient interpreters read 1 Tim 3:11 as implying women served as deacons: John Chrysostom, Theodoret of Cyrrhus, Theodore of Mopsuestia, Ambrosiaster, and Pelagius. See Kevin Madigan and Carolyn Osiek, eds. and trans., *Ordained Women in the Early Church: A Documentary History* (Baltimore: Johns Hopkins University Press, 2005), 18–21.
33. Eisen, *Women Officeholders*, 199–216; Elisabeth Schüssler Fiorenza, *In Memory of Her: A Feminist Theological Reconstruction*

of Christian Origins (New York: Crossroad, 1983); Carolyn Osiek and Margaret MacDonald, *A Woman's Place*, 144–63; Karen Jo Torjesen, *When Women Were Priests: Women's Leadership in the Early Church and the Scandal of Their Subordination in the Rise of Christianity* (San Francisco: HarperSanFrancisco, 1993).

34. Osiek and MacDonald, *A Woman's Place*, 250. See also Susan E. Hylen, *Women in the New Testament World*, Essentials of Biblical Studies (New York: Oxford University Press, 2019).

35. Bruce Malina, *Windows on the World of Jesus: Time Travel to Ancient Judea* (Louisville: Westminster John Knox, 1993), 71–78; Osiek and MacDonald, *A Woman's Place*, 144–63.

36. Lucy Peppiatt writes, "Men held most of the positions of power and influence. For most women, this would have meant that they were second-class citizens in terms of their status and their rights. They were born inferior, and they knew it." *Unveiling Paul's Women: Making Sense of 1 Corinthians 11:2–16* (Eugene, OR: Cascade: 2018), 18.

37. *Prophetic Jesus, Prophetic Church: The Challenge of Luke-Acts for Contemporary Christians* (Grand Rapids: Eerdmans, 2011), 184.

38. Meeks, *First Urban Christians: The Social World of the Apostle Paul*, 2nd ed. (New Haven: Yale University Press, 2003), 134; Andrew Clarke, *Serve the Community of the Church: Christians as Leaders and Ministers* (Grand Rapids: Eerdmans, 2000), 59–77, 103–41. Some of these (*archōn, archisynagōgos*), along with "high priest" (*archiereus*), appear prevalently in the New Testament.

39. S. G. Wilson, "Voluntary Associations: An Overview," in *Voluntary Associations in the Graeco-Roman World*, ed. John S. Kloppenborg and S. G. Wilson (New York: Routledge, 1996), 10.

40. 1 Cor 2:6, 8; Rom 13:3; Matt 20:18, 23, 25; Luke 8:41; 12:58; 14:1; 18:18; 19:2; 23:13, 35; 24:20; John 3:1; 7:26, 48; 12:42; Acts 3:17; 4:5, 8, 26; 13:27; 14:5; 16:19; 23:5. Paul once calls himself a "master builder" (*architektōn*, 1 Cor 3:10), and later NT voices depict Jesus as a leader (*archēgos*, Acts 3:15; 5:31; Heb 2:10; 12:2) and high priest (*archiereus*, Heb 2:17; 3:1; 4:14; 5:10; 6:20; 7:26; 8:1; 9:11). Paul also embraces the language of apostle, father, elder, and ambassador, which carry authority but are not

honorific (1 Cor 1:1; 4:15; Phlm 9; 2 Cor 5:20; see also "slave of Jesus Christ," Rom 1:1)

41. Vincent Branick, *The House Church in the Writings of Paul* (Eugene, OR: Wipf & Stock, 2012), 94.

42. See also Mark 9:35; Matt 23:11; Luke 9:48; John 6:15; 15:13.

43. Paul employed conventional leadership roles in some contexts (e.g., overseer, elder) and honored hosts and benefactors of church communities (Gerd Theissen, "Social Stratification in the Corinthian Community: A Contribution to the Sociology of Early Hellenic Christianity," in *The Social Setting of Pauline Christianity: Essays on Corinth*, ed. and trans. John H. Schütz [Philadelphia: Fortress, 1982], 95). What Paul stood against was associating church leadership with honor and status (Clarke, *Serve the Community*, 249–52).

44. Col 3:18–4:1; Eph 5:21–6:9; 1 Tim 2:8–15; 5:1–22; Titus 2:1–10; cf. 1 Cor 14:33b–36. See also 1 Pet 2:18–3:7.

45. For more on this, see Theissen, *Social Setting*, 121–74; John Chow, *Patronage and Power: A Study of Social Networks in Corinth*, JSNTSup 75 (Sheffield: JSOT Press, 1992), esp. 167–87; Andrew Clarke, *Serve the Community*, 209–47; Bruce W. Winter, *After Paul Left Corinth: The Influence of Secular Ethics and Social Change* (Grand Rapids: Eerdmans, 2001).

46. See, for instance, Livy, *History of Rome* 2.32.9–12; Josephus, *Jewish War* 4.4016; Marcus Aurelius, *Meditations* 7.13; Seneca, *Moral Epistles* 95.52; Epictetus 2.10.3–4.

47. This "same" language (*to auto*) appears elsewhere to emphasize communal sharing and unity among believers (Phil 2:2; Rom 15:5; 1 Cor 1:10; Acts 2:44; also Acts 2:42; 4:32–33; 1 Cor 11:20–21).

48. Pew Research Center, "'Nones' on the Rise."

CHAPTER 4: PRACTICING THE THINGS THAT MATTER

1. Edwin A. Judge, "The Social Identity of the First Christians: A Question of Method in Religious History," *Journal of Religious History* 11 (1980): 201–17; Ramsay MacMullen, *Paganism in the Roman Empire* (New Haven: Yale University Press, 1981), 1–48.

2. Gordon Lathrop, *Four Gospels on a Sunday: The New Testament and the Reform of Christian Worship* (Minneapolis: Fortress, 2011), 39. Lathrop suggests the same regarding "liturgy" for early church practices.

3. Didache 14.1; Pliny the Younger, *Epistle to Trajan.* 10.96.7 ("set day"); Justin, *1 Apology* 67. See also Ignatius, *To the Magnesians* 9.1; Barnabas 15.9.

4. Roman associations held sacrificial rites at most of their gatherings, and synagogue gatherings across the Mediterranean featured prayer and Torah-reading. S. G. Wilson, "Voluntary Associations: An Overview," in *Voluntary Associations in the Graeco-Roman World*, ed. John S. Kloppenborg and S. G. Wilson (New York: Routledge, 1996), 11–13.

5. So John Dominic Crossan, *The Birth of Christianity: Discovering What Happened in the Years Immediately after the Execution of Jesus* (San Francisco: HarperSanFrancisco, 1998), 423–44.

6. See Dennis E. Smith, *From Symposium to Eucharist: The Banquet in the Early Christian World* (Minneapolis: Fortress, 2003), 279–87.

7. Andrew McGowan, "Food, Ritual, and Power," in *Late Ancient Christianity*, vol. 2, *A People's History of Christianity*, ed. Virginia Burrus (Minneapolis: Fortress, 2005), 157.

8. Smith, *From Symposium to Eucharist,* 279.

9. Andrew McGowan, "The Inordinate Cup: Issues of Order in Early Eucharistic Drinking," *Studia Patristica* 35 (2001): 283–91.

10. Lathrop, *Four Gospels on a Sunday,* 44 . See also Paul F. Bradshaw, *Eucharistic Origins* (London: SPCK, 2004); Andrew McGowan, *Ascetic Eucharists: Food and Drink in Early Christian Ritual Meals*, Oxford Early Christian Studies (New York: Oxford University Press, 1999); Smith, *From Symposium to Eucharist.*

11. Cf. Jude 12; Did. 9–10; Ignatius, *To the Smyrnaeans* 7–8; Pliny, *Ep.* 10.96; Hippolytus, *Apostolic Tradition* 26.

12. See Andrew McGowan, "'Is There a Liturgical Text in this Gospel?' The Institution Narratives and Their Early Interpretive Communities," *Journal of Biblical Literature* 118 (1999): 77–89; Bradshaw, *Eucharist Origins,* 64–68.

13. Translation from R. C. D. Jasper and G. J. Cuming, *Prayers of the Eucharist: Early and Reformed*, 3rd ed. (Collegeville, MN: Liturgical Press, 1990), 29–30.
14. Matt 28:19–20; John 3:22, 26 (cf. 4:2); Acts 2:41–42; 8:12, 36–39; 9:18; 10:44–48; 16:15, 33–34; Heb 6:2; 1 Pet 3:21; Titus 3:5. See also John 3:5–8; 13:8–10; Acts 18:25; 19:3–5.
15. Lev 16:4, 24; 1 Qs 3:5–9; *The Sibylline Oracles* 4.165; Mark 1:4; Matt 3:5–6; Acts 1:5; 19:1–7; Josephus, *Life* 11; *Jewish Antiquities* 18.116–118; b. Yebam. 47ab. A non-Jewish example of water immersion is Apuleius, *Metamorphoses* 11.23 (washing at entry into the Isis mysteries).
16. John 3:22, 26; Acts 8:36–39; 16:15; Did. 7.1–2. See also Mark 1:4–11; Matt 3:1–17; Luke 3:1–22; John 1:24–34. Some events in Acts may suggest home settings (Acts 2:41–42; 10:44–48; 16:33–34).
17. It is explicitly named in Hippolytus's *Apostolic Tradition* 21.3 (third or fourth century). Ancient Jewish practices of immersion and early Christian art also suggest early baptisms involved the complete stripping of clothes. Wayne Meeks, *First Urban Christians* (New Haven: Yale University Press, 2003), 151.
18. 1 Cor 1:16; 16:15; Acts 8:36–39; 10:24, 44–48; 16:15, 33; 18:8. The *Apostolic Tradition* assumes children were baptized, including children who "cannot answer for themselves" (21.4).
19. C. K. Barrett, *A Commentary on the First Epistle to the Corinthians* (New York: Harper & Row, 1968), 327.
20. Philo, *Against Flaccus* 121–24; *On the Contemplative Life* 80–81, 83–89; 1QH; Mark 14:26. Phillip Harland, *Associations, Synagogues, and Congregations: Claiming a Place in Ancient Mediterranean Society* (Minneapolis: Fortress, 2003), 72–73.
21. 1 Thess 1:2–3; Rom 1:9–10; 1 Cor 1:3; Phil 1:3–5; Phlm 4–7; see also Col 1:3, 9–10; Eph 1:16; 2 Thess 1:3.
22. E.g., Phil 1:9–11; 1 Thess 3:12–13; 5:23–24; Phlm 6; Rom 15:5–6, 13; see also 2 Thess 1:11–12; 2:16–17; 3:5; Col 1:9–12; Eph 1:3–14, 17–19; 3:14–21.
23. See m. Tamid 4:3–5:1; m. Berakot 1.1–3.6; Deut 6:7; Asher Finkel, "Prayer in Jewish Life of the First Century as Background to Early Christianity," in *Into God's Presence: Prayer in the New*

Testament, ed. Richard Longenecker (Grand Rapids: Eerdmans, 2001), 43–65.

24. E.g., Gal 1:5; 1 Cor 14:16; 15:57; 16:22; 2 Cor 1:3–4; 8:16; 9:15; Rom 11:33–36; 16:25–27.

25. 1 Thess 4:17–18; Phil 4:6–7; 1 Cor 14:13–15; Rom 8:26–27 (cf. Gal 4:6–7); Jas 5:13–18. See also Acts 1:24–25; 2:42; 3:1; 4:23–31; 7:59; 10:2–3, 9, 30; 12:12; 13:2–3; 14:23; 16:25; 20:36; 21:5; 27:35.

26. 1 Cor 14:26–40; Rom 1:11–12; Col 1:28; 4:16; Acts 2:42; 20:7–12; 2 Tim 1:13–14. Later NT writings imply the centrality of Scripture for teaching: 2 Tim 4:13; also 3:16–17; Luke 24:26–27, 45–46; Acts 8:35; 13:13–47; 17:2–3; 18:28; 28:23.

27. 1 Thess 5:19–21; 1 Cor 11:4–5; 12:10, 28; 14:1–5, 24–25, 31–32, 39; Rom 12:7.

28. Christopher Forbes, *Prophecy and Inspired Speech: In Early Christianity and Its Hellenistic Environment* (Peabody, MA: Hendrickson, 1997), 308.

29. So Thomas Gillespie (following Ernst Käsemann), *The First Theologians: A Study in Early Christian Prophecy* (Grand Rapids: Eerdmans, 1994); Anthony Thiselton, "Meanings and Greek Translation Relating to 'Spiritual Gifts' in 1 Corinthians 12–14: Some Proposals in the Light of Philosophy of Language, Speech-Act Theory and Exegesis," in *Thiselton on Hermeneutics: Collected Works with New Essays* (Grand Rapids: Eerdmans, 2006), 335–47.

30. So David E. Aune, *Prophecy in Early Christianity and the Ancient Mediterranean World* (Grand Rapids: Eerdmans, 1983), 247–338, esp. 338. Cf. Forbes, *Prophecy and Inspired Speech,* 218–50.

31. Aune, *Prophecy,* 338. On Montanism, see 313–16.

32. The miracle of Acts 2:1–11 (Pentecost) is different than classical *glossolalia,* though there are similarities.

33. See also 1 Cor 14:2, 14–15, 23–25, 28. Acts attests to tongues, as a sign of the Spirit's presence and power (2:1–11; 10:44–48; 19:1–7). On ecstatic speech as emptying one's mind, see Philo, *Who Is the Heir of Divine Things* 265.

34. Sophocles, *Ajax* 231–44; Lucian, *Alexander the False Prophet* 13; Testament of Job 48–50; Apocalypse of Zephaniah.

35. See Mark 16:17; Irenaeus, *Against Heresies* 5.6.1; Eusebius, *Hist. Eccl.* 5.7.6; Tertullian, *Against Marcion* 5.8; Novatian, *On the Trinity* 2.9; Ambrose, *The Holy Spirit* 2.150. Cf. John Chrysostom, *Homilies on 1 Corinthians* 29. Christopher Forbes, *Prophecy and Inspired Speech*, 84.

36. For Pentecostal evaluations of tongues in NT Christianity, see Craig S. Keener, *Acts: An Exegetical Commentary*, 4 vols. (Grand Rapids: Baker Academic, 2012–2015) 1:804–31; Gordon Fee, "Tongues—Least of the Gifts? Some Exegetical Observations on 1 Corinthians 12–14," *Pneuma* 2, no. 2 (Fall 1980): 3–14.

37. Richard S. Ascough, Philip A. Harland, and John S. Kloppenborg, eds., *Associations in the Greco-Roman World: A Sourcebook* (Waco, TX: Baylor University Press, 2012), esp. 13–23; Wilson, "Voluntary Associations," 13–14.

38. Paul uses different language for this: "collection" (*logeia*, 1 Cor 16:1), "service" or "ministry" (*diakonia, diakoneō*, Rom 15:25, 31; 2 Cor 8:20; 9:1, 12, 13), "fellowship" (*koinōnia*, Rom 15:26), "gift" (*charis*, 1 Cor 16:3; 2 Cor 8:6, 7, 19), "generous gift" (*eulogia*, 2 Cor 9:5), and "lavish gift" (*hadrotēs*, 2 Cor 8:20).

39. Rom 15:19, 23–28; 2 Cor 8:13–14; 9:11–15. See David J. Downs, *Offering of the Gentiles: Paul's Collection for Jerusalem in Its Chronological, Cultural, and Cultic Contexts* (Grand Rapids: Eerdmans, 2016).

40. 2 Cor 8–9; Rom 12:13; 1 Tim 6:7–10, 17–19; Jas 2:1–7; Did. 4:5–8; Justin, *1 Apol.* 67.1; Irenaeus, *Against Heresies* 4.13.3; Basil, *On Avarices*; John Chrysostom, *Homilies on Romans* 7. See Charles E. Gutenson, *The Right Church: Live Like the First Christians* (Nashville: Abingdon, 2012), 81–95.

41. See, for example, Deut 15:4–11; Josephus, *Jewish Antiquities* 18.20; *Jewish War* 2.122; Aristotle, *Nicomachean Ethics* 9.8; Iamblichus, *Life of Pythagoras* 30.167; Pliny *Ep.* 1.4.3. On this, see Luke Timothy Johnson, *Sharing Possessions: Mandate and Symbol of Faith* (Philadelphia: Fortress, 1981).

42. Gal 2:10; 6:6; 1 Cor 9:3–14; Jas 1:27; Luke 11:41; 12:33; Acts 9:36; 10:2, 4, 31; 11:27–30; 24:17; 1 Tim 5:3–16; Did. 13.1–7. Within

Judaism, see Tob 1:3, 16; 2:14; 4:7–11; 12:8–9; m. Peah 1:1; Pirke
Aboth 1:2; Aboth de Rabbi Nathan 4; b. Ber. 5b; 8a; b. Shab. 156b;
b. Rosh Hashanah 16b.

43. Some associations in Egypt instruct special meetings where discipline is called for (Ascough, Harland, and Kloppenborg, eds.,
Associations in the Greco-Roman World, 180–88). Qumran attests
similarly to a council that oversaw matters of discipline (1QS 7).

44. Tertullian, *Monogamy* 10; *The Crown* 3. The Martyrdom of Polycarp attests to the practice early on for Christian martyrs (18:3).

45. Acts 1:14; 6:6; 8:14–17; 12:5, 12; 13:2–3; 14:23; also 4:24–31; 9:17;
19:6; 20:36.

46. 1 Thess 1:2–3; 5:16–18, 25; 1 Cor 1:4–7; Phil 1:4–5, 9–11; 4:6–7;
Rom 1:8–10; 8:26–27; 10:1; 15:30–32; also Gal 4:6.

47. The phrase "in Christ" appears eighty-one times just in the letters
attributed to Paul. See esp. 1 Thess 2:14; 4:16; Gal 1:22; 3:26, 28; 1
Cor 1:2; 15:18, 22; 16:24; 2 Cor 3:14; 5:17; Phil 1:1; 4:21; Rom 8:1;
16:7–10; Col 1:2, 28.

48. Richard S. Ascough, *What Are They Saying about the Formation of
Pauline Churches?* (New York: Paulist, 1998), 98.

49. Thucydides, *Hist.* 1.87; 6.8; 8.69; Deut 4:10; 9:10; 18:16; 23:2–3;
31:30; Judg 20:2; 1 Kgdms 17:47; 3 Kgdms 8:14; 2 Chron 6:3; Ezra
10:8; Jdt 6:16; Sir 26:5; Pss. Sol. 10:6. Josephus, *Jewish Antiquities*
12.164; 19.332; *Life* 268. Richard Last, "*Ekklēsia* outside the Septuagint and the *Dēmos*: The Titles of Greco-Roman Associations
and Christ-Followers' Groups," *Journal of Biblical Literature* 137,
no. 4 (2018): 959–80.

50. Paul occasionally uses "church" to refer to communities (vs. specific gatherings), especially in greetings (1 Cor 1:2; 2 Cor 1:1; 1
Thess 1:1). But even in these cases, the original settings for hearing
these words would have been particular gatherings (1 Thess 5:27;
Col 4:16).

51. See esp. 1 Cor 8:1, 10; 10:23; 14:3–5, 12, 17, 26; 1 Thess 5:11; 2
Cor 10:8; 12:19; 13:10; Rom 14:19; 15:2; 15:20. Also Eph 2:21;
4:12, 16, 29.

52. Jesus's ministry is similar. Despite the individualistic tone of "dis-
ciple" (*mathētēs,* "learner"), in the Gospels Jesus most often works

with multiple learners at once. Further, the narrative most deliberate about discipleship as a formation model—Matthew's Gospel—deems "the church" a critical context for living discipleship out (16:18; 18:15–20).

CHAPTER 5: BEARING DISTINCTIVE WITNESS

1. Many believe the synagogue originated during the Babylonian exile or shortly thereafter, but the earliest evidence of synagogue structures is from the third century BCE in Egypt (Fayyum) and the second century BCE in Palestine (Modiʻin). Eric M. Myers, "Synagogue," *Anchor Bible Dictionary*, ed. David Noel Freedman, 6 vols. (New York: Doubleday, 1992), 4:251–60.

2. Lee I. Levine, "The Second Temple Synagogue: The Formative Years," in *The Synagogue in Late Antiquity*, ed. Lee I. Levine (Winona Lake, IN: Eisenbrauns, 1987), 7.

3. Philip Harland, *Associations, Synagogues, and Congregations: Claiming a Place in Ancient Mediterranean Society* (Minneapolis: Fortress, 2003), 200–210.

4. Ascough, *What Are They Saying about the Formation of Pauline Churches?* (New York: Paulist, 1998), 20–27.

5. Peter Richardson, "Early Synagogues as Collegia in the Diaspora and Palestine," in *Voluntary Associations in the Graeco-Roman World*, ed. John S. Kloppenborg and S. G. Wilson (New York: Routledge, 1996), 90–109; Philip Harland, *Dynamics of Identity in the World of the Early Christians: Associations, Judeans and Cultural Minorities* (London: Continuum, 2010), 99–142; Richard Last, "The Other Synagogues," *JSJ* 47, no. 3 (2016): 330–63; Benedikt Eckhardt, "Craft Guilds as Synagogues? Further Thoughts on 'Private Judean-Deity Associations,'" *JSJ* 48, no. 2 (2017): 246–60.

6. In antiquity, several words were used to refer to an association: *collegium, secta, factio, thiasos, eranos, koinon, koinonia, philosophia, hairesis*. Stephen G. Wilson, "Voluntary Associations: An Overview," in *Voluntary Associations in the Graeco-Roman World*, ed. John S. Kloppenborg and S. G. Wilson (New York: Routledge, 1996), 1–7.

7. Wilson, "Voluntary Associations," 13; Ascough, *What Are They Saying,* 76; Wayne Meeks, *The First Urban Christians* (New Haven: Yale University Press, 2003), 31–32.

8. Wilson, "Voluntary Associations," 10–14; John S. Kloppenborg, "Collegia and *Thiasoi:* Issues in Function, Taxonomy, and Membership," in Kloppenborg and Wilson, eds., *Voluntary Associations in the Graeco-Roman World*, 23–27; Wayne McCready, "*Ekklēsia* and Voluntary Associations," in *Voluntary Associations in the Graeco-Roman World*, ed. John S. Kloppenborg and Stephen G. Wilson (London: Routledge, 1996), 63–64; Ascough, *What Are They Saying,* 77–78; Harland, *Associations, Synagogues, and Congregations,* 25–53.

9. Dennis E. Smith, "Meals and Morality in Paul and His World," *Society of Biblical Literature 1981 Seminar Papers,* SBLSPS 20 (Atlanta: Society of Biblical Literature, 1981), 319–39, esp. 323. See also Ben Witherington, *Conflict and Community in Corinth: A Socio-Rhetorical Commentary on 1 and 2 Corinthians* (Grand Rapids: Eerdmans, 1995), 243–44.

10. Pliny, *Epistles* 10.96.7; Origen, *Against Celsus* 3.23; Lucian, *The Passing of Peregrinus* 11 (calling Peregrinus a *thiasarchēs,* a *thiasos* leader). Tertullian also describes Christian gatherings using words equally fit for religious associations (*Apology* 39).

11. Richard Ascough, *What Are They Saying,* 32–33; Everett Ferguson, *Backgrounds of Early Christianity* (Grand Rapids: Eerdmans, 1987), 255.

12. Loveday Alexander, "Paul and the Hellenistic Schools: The Evidence of Galen," in *Paul in His Hellenistic Context,* ed. Troels Engberg-Pedersen (Edinburgh: T&T Clark, 1994), 60–83, esp. 81; Ramsay MacMullen, *Christianizing the Roman Empire* (New York: Yale University Press, 1984), 33–34.

13. See 1 Thess 2:3–8; 4:1–12; Phil 4:8–9. Abraham J. Malherbe, "Hellenistic Philosopher or Christian Pastor?" *Australasian Theological Review* 68, no. 1 (Jan. 1, 1986): 1–13; *Paul and the Popular Philosophers* (Minneapolis: Fortress, 1989); Steve Mason, "*Philosophiai*: Graeco-Roman, Judean and Christian," in *Voluntary Associations*

in the Graeco-Roman World, ed. John S. Kloppenborg and Stephen G. Wilson (London: Routledge, 1996), 47–48.

14. *Against Apion* 2.145–296. See also *Jewish Antiquities* 1.1–26 (esp. 18); 13.171–73; 18.11–22; *Life* 10–12; 4 Macc 5:5–13; Philo, *Hypothetica (Apology for the Jews)* 11.1–18; *Every Good Man Is Free* 75–91.

15. So also Athenagoras, *Dialogue*; *Epistle to Diognetus*; Clement of Alexandria, *Exhortation to the Greeks*.

16. In *Galen on Jews and Christians*, trans. Richard Walzer (Oxford: Oxford University Press, 1949), 15–16.

17. See also 1 Thess 5:26–27; 1 Cor 11:16; 14:33b; 16:1, 19; 2 Cor 1:1; 8:1–9:15; 11:8–11; Phil 4:22; Rom 1:8–10; 15:25–29; 16:1–23; Col 4:16; Eph 6:23; Jas 1:1; 1 Pet 1:1–2; 5:13; 2 John 13; Rev 1:4a. This largely contrasts with associations (and to a lesser degree philosophical schools). McCready, "*Ekklēsia* and Voluntary Associations," 63–64. Cf. Harland, *Associations, Synagogues, and Congregations*, 36.

18. Ascough, *What Are They Saying*, 95. See 1 Cor 9:15–23; 2 Cor 5:18–21; Rom 1:16; 11:25–32; 15:19–21; Matt 28:18–20; Eph 2:14–22; Luke 24:45–48; Acts 1:8; 17:22–31; 26:27–28; 28:30–31; John 1:1–18; 3:16; 20:30–31.

19. Meeks, *First Urban Christians*, 85–94; Carolyn Osiek, *What Are They Saying about the Social Setting of the New Testament?*, rev. ed. (New York: Paulist, 1992), 52–71; McCready, "*Ekklēsia* and Voluntary Associations"; Harland, *Dynamics of Identity*, 63–81.

20. Greeting with a holy kiss: 1 Thess 5:26; 1 Cor 16:20; 2 Cor 13:12; Rom 16:16; 1 Pet 5:14 ("kiss of love"); sisterly and brotherly love: 1 Thess 4:9; Rom 12:9–10, 16; 13:8–10; 1 Pet 1:22; 3:8; Heb 13:1; 2 Pet 1:7; 1 John 4:7–21; assisting one another's needs: Gal 2:10; Rom 12:13; 1 Cor 16:1–4; 2 Cor 8:1–9:15; Acts 2:44–45; 4:4:32–37; 11:29–30; mutual concern for each other's well-being: Rom 14:1–15:6; 1 Cor 6:7–8; 8:1–13; 11:33–34; 12:12–26; 16:19; Phil 4:21–22; loving one another: Gal 6:10; 1 John 4:7–21; Acts 2:42–47.

21. Trans. Justo L. González, *The Story of Christianity*, 2 vols. (San Francisco: HarperSanFrancisco, 1984), 1:34–35.

22. Eusebius, *Ecclesiastical History,* 2.25; 3.17; 6.39. Valerian (253–60 CE) may also be included.

23. Harold Remus, "Persecution," in *Handbook of Early Christianity: Social Science Approaches,* ed. Anthony J. Blasi, Jean Duhaime, and Paul-André Turcotte (Walnut Creek, CA: Alta Mira, 2002), 432. See also Elizabeth A. Castelli, *Martyrdom and Memory: Early Christian Culture Making* (New York: Columbia University Press, 2004); Judith Lieu, *Christian Identity in the Jewish and Graeco-Roman World* (Oxford: Oxford University Press, 2004); Robin Darling Young, "Martyrdom as Exaltation," in *Late Ancient Christianity* (Minneapolis: Fortress, 2005), 70–92.

24. See John 11:48–50; González, *Story of Christianity* 1:32; Remus, "Persecution," 431.

25. E.g., 1 Thess 2:14–16; Gal 5:2–12; 6:11–16; Phil 3:2–4a; Col 2:8–23; 1 Tim 1:3–7; 4:1–5; Titus 1:10–16; 3:9–11; Mark: 2:18–3:6; 8:15; 12:13; 14:1–2, 10–11; 14:43–15:15; Acts: 4:1–22; 6:8–7:60; 8:1; 9:1–2; 12:1–2; 13:50; 14:2, 4–5, 19; 17:5–6, 13; 18:12–17; 20:3; 21:27–36; 23:12–15; 24:1–9; 25:1–7; John 9:22; 12:42.

26. Mary Beard, John North, and Simon Price, *Religions of Rome, Volume 1: A History* (Cambridge: Cambridge University Press, 1998), 212.

27. Justin, *1 Apology* 4; *2 Apology* 2; Athenagoras, *Plea for the Christians* 1–2; Tertullian, *Apology* 1–3.

28. Among surviving sources, Roman authors call the Jesus movement's beliefs "evil," "sordid and abominable" (Tacitus, *Annals* 15.44), "novel and vicious" (Suetonius, *Nero* 16.2), "degenerate" and "extravagant" (Pliny, *Ep.* 10.96.8). Remus, "Persecution," 436.

29. Justin, *1 Apol.* 5–6; Athenagoras, *Plea for the Christians* 3.1; Tertullian, *Apol.* 6.10; Clement of Alexandria, *Miscellanies* 7.1; Arnobius, *Adv. Nationes* 1.29, 3.28, 5.30. At Polycarp's trial in the second-century *Martyrdom of Polycarp,* the crowd chants "Away with the atheists!" (3.2; 9.2–3).

30. See esp. 1 Cor 8:4–6; 10:21; Rev 2:14, 20; Acts 4:12; 17:17–34; John 14:6.

31. The edict of Galerius (April 30, 311 CE) officially permitted Christians to practice their beliefs, "as long as they do not interfere with public order" (Eusebius, *Eccl. Hist.* 8.17.6–10).

32. Mark 10:29–30; 13:9–13 (cf. Matt 24:9–14; Luke 21:12–19); Luke 19:41–44; John 15:18–16:4. See also Mark 13:14–23; Matt 24:15–28; Luke 21:5–11, 20–24.

33. 1 Thess 2:14–16; Phil 1:27–30; Pet 1:6–9; 2:11–25; 4:12–19; 5:9–11. See also Jas 1:2–4; Heb 12:1–29; 1 John 2:15–17; 4:4–6; 5:4–5, 19.

34. See 1 Tim 2:1–3, 9–10; 3:2–13; 2 Tim 2:22–25; Titus 1:5–8, 12; 2:3–12; 3:1–3, 14. See also Col 3:18–4:1; Eph 5:21–6:4.

35. Chart data based on Rodney Stark, *The Rise of Christianity: How the Obscure, Marginal Jesus Movement Became the Dominant Religious Force in the Western World in a Few Centuries* (San Francisco: HarperSanFranciso, 1997), 6–7; Keith Hopkins, "Christian Number and Its Implications," *Journal of Early Christian Studies* 6, no. 2 (1998): 193; Remus, "Persecution," 432–33. The "percent of empire's population" numbers assume a population of sixty million total.

36. Besides Paul and his colleagues named in the New Testament, only Pantaenus (of Alexandria) and Gregory (Pontus, third century) are known from history.

37. Alan Kreider, *The Patient Ferment of the Early Church: The Improbable Rise of Christianity in the Roman Empire* (Grand Rapids: Baker, 2016), 11–12.

38. González, *History of Christianity,* 1:98–99. Celsus criticized early Christians for sharing their "secret lore in the marketplaces" as opposed to at gatherings of intelligent men (Origen, *Against Celsus* 3.50).

39. See also 1 Thess 4:1–12; 5:12–24; Gal 5:13–26; 1 Cor 5:1–6:20; Phil 2:1–11; 4:8–9; Rom 6:1–23 (also 7:1–25); 12:1–2 (as well as 12:3–15:13).

40. See also 2 Thess 3:6–15; Col 3:1–4:6; Eph 4:1–5:20; Heb 13:1–19; 1 Pet 1:13–4:19 (esp. 1:13–2:12); Matt 5:14–16; 28:18–20; Acts 1:8; 1 Tim 3:1–13; 5:1–6:2; Titus 1:5–9; 2:1–15; 2 Tim 2:1–25.

41. Remus, "Persecution," 443. Cf. Stark, *Rise of Christianity,* 163–89.
42. Acts 2:44, 47; 4:33–34; 2 Cor 8–9; Rom 12:13; 1 Tim 6:7–10, 17–19; Jas 2:1–7; Acts 2:42–47; 4:23–31, 32–37; 5:1–11, 42; 6:1–6; 11:28–30; Did. 4:5–8; Justin, *1 Apol.* 67.1; Irenaeus, *Against Heresies* 4.13.3; Basil, *On Avarices*; John Chrysostom, *Homilies on Romans* 7.
43. Henry Chadwick, *The Early Church* (Harmondsworth: Penguin, 1968), 55–56.
44. Sharing with the needy: Acts 2:45; 4:34; 6:1–6; 11:28–30. Healing the sick: 3:1–10; 5:12–16; 9:32–43; 14:8–10; 20:9–10; 28:7–10. Taking in widows and orphans: Jas 1:27; Acts 6:1–6; 9:36–42; 1 Tim 5:3–16. Attending to those in prison: Acts 12:12; 23:16; Heb 13:3. Showing hospitality: 16:11–15; 20:1–16; 21:1–16; 28:14–15.
45. Larry W. Hurtado, *Destroyer of the Gods: Early Christian Distinctiveness in the Roman World* (Waco, TX: Baylor University Press, 2016), 144–48. See Didache 2.2; Justin, *1 Apol.* 27–29; Diogn. 5.6. Though no NT writing explicitly condemns discarding infants, later Christian writings speak of the condemnation as a longstanding one.
46. See 1 Thess 4:1–8; 1 Cor 5:10–11; 6:9–20; Rom 1:26–27; Gal 5:16–21; 1 Tim 3:2; Did. 2.2. Condemnations of pederasty appear in Mark 9:42–48; Didache 2.2; Justin, *1 Apol.* 27. Jewish writings also condemned many of these same practices: The Sibylline Oracles 5:388; Let. Jer. 42–43; 2 Macc 6:3–6; Test. Moses 8:3; Ps. Sol. 2:11–13; Philo, *On the Life of Joseph* 42.
47. Galen, *Summary of Platonic Dialogues* 3; Justin, *1 Apol.* 15; Minucius Felix, *Oct. 31.1*; Athenagoras, *Plea for the Christians* 32.5; Hippolytus, *The Apostolic Tradition* 15.6–7. See Hurtado, *Destroyer of the Gods,* 143–81; Krieder, *Patient Ferment,* 102.
48. 1 Thess 3:13; 1 Cor 1:2; 6:1–2; 14:33; 16:1, 15; 2 Cor 1:1; 8:4; 9:1, 12; 13:12; Phil 1:1; 4:21–22; Phlm 5, 7; Rom 1:7; 8:27; 12:13; 15:25–26, 31; 16:2, 15. See also Col 1:2, 4, 12, 26; 3:12; 2 Thess 1:10; Eph 1:1, 4, 15, 18; 2:19; 3:8, 18; 4:12; 5:3; 6:18; 1 Tim 5:10.
49. 1 Cor 1:2; 2 Cor 1:1; Phil 1:1; Rom 1:7. See also Col 1:2; Eph 1:1.
50. 1 Cor 15:49; 2 Cor 3:17–18; Rom 8:29. See also Col 3:9–11; Eph 4:11–13.

51. See also 1 Thess 5:5; Phil 2:14–15; Rom 13:12–14; 2 Cor 4:4–6; 6:14; Eph 5:8; 6:12; 1 Pet 2:9; Luke 2:32; 8:16; 11:33–35; 16:8; Acts 13:47; 26:17–18. Also Matt 6:23; Rev 21:24; 22:5. These metaphors have roots in the Hebrew Bible (e.g., Isa 42:6–7; 49:6; 60:1–3). The language "sons of light" appears in the Dead Sea Scrolls (1 QS 1:9–10; 2:16; 3:13, 24–25; 1 QM 1:3–16; 17:8).

52. John's Gospel depicts Jesus as the "light of the world," and the letters of John portray God as light. Both have implications for those who "walk in the light": John 1:4–5, 7–9; 3:19–21; 8:12; 9:5; 12:35–36, 46; 1 John 1:5, 7; 2:8–10.

53. The metaphor of bearing light continues in the ensuing centuries: Origen, *Ag. Cels.* 3.29; Ignatius, *To the Philippians* 2.1; 2 Clement 1.4. Other examples build on language from Isaiah 49:6 and 58:6–10 (Barnabas 3.4; 14.7; Justin, *Dialogue* 65; Origen, *Ag. Cels.* 53). See also 1 Clement 36.2; 59.2; Diogn. 9.6; Ignatius, *To the Ephesians* 19.2–3; *To the Romans* 6.2; Barnabas 18.1.

54. Becka Alper, "Why America's 'Nones' Don't Identify with a Religion," Pew Research Center Fact Tank, August 8, 2018, https://tinyurl.com/y9eknmwj.

55. Krieder, *Patient Ferment,* 12; see also 7–12, 91–130; Hurtado, *Destroyer of the Gods,* 186–89; Stark, *Rise of Christianity,* 209–15.

CONCLUSION: ON BEING ROOTED AND RENEWING

1. John B Crist, "Virtual Reality Church," December 11, 2018, https://tinyurl.com/y2q9apcl.

2. Igniter Media Group, "MeChurch," July 31, 2006, https://tinyurl.com/y5b4resg.

3. Carey Nieuwhof, "10 Predictions about the Future Church and Shifting Attendance Patterns," February 2015, https://tinyurl.com/yyqc3clu.

SELECT BIBLIOGRAPHY

Adams, Edward. *The Earliest Christian Meeting Places: Almost Exclusively Houses?* The Library of New Testament Studies. Bloomsbury: T&T Clark, 2013.

Alexander, Loveday. "Paul and the Hellenistic Schools: The Evidence of Galen." In *Paul in His Hellenistic Context.* Edited by Troels Engberg-Pedersen, 60–83. Edinburgh: T&T Clark, 1994.

Ascough, Richard S. *What Are They Saying about the Formation of Pauline Churches?* New York: Paulist, 1998.

Ascough, Richard S., Philip A. Harland, and John S. Koppenborg. *Associations in the Greco-Roman World: A Sourcebook.* Waco, TX: Baylor University Press, 2012.

Aune, David E. *Prophecy in Early Christianity and the Ancient Mediterranean World.* Grand Rapids: Eerdmans, 1983.

Bakke, O. M. *When Children Became People: The Birth of Childhood in Early Christianity.* Translated by Brian McNeil. Minneapolis: Fortress, 2005.

Balch, David L. "Rich Pompeiian Houses, Shops for Rent, and the Huge Apartment Building in Herculaneum as Typical

Spaces for Pauline House Churches." *Journal for the Study of the New Testament* 27 (2004): 27–46.

Balch, David L., and Carolyn Osiek, eds. *Early Christian Families in Context: An Interdisciplinary Dialogue.* Grand Rapids: Eerdmans, 2003.

Balch, David L., and A. Weissenrieder, eds. *Contested Spaces: Houses and Temples in Roman Antiquity and the New Testament.* Tübingen: Mohr Siebeck, 2012.

Banks, Robert. *Paul's Idea of Community.* Peabody, MA: Hendrickson, 1994.

Barentsen, Jack. *Emerging Leadership in the Pauline Mission: A Social Identity Perspective on Local Leadership Development in Corinth and Ephesus.* Princeton Theological Monograph Series 168. Eugene, OR: Pickwick, 2011.

Barna Group. "How Many People Really Attend a House Church? Barna Study Finds It Depends on the Definition." August 31, 2009. https://tinyurl.com/y3p57byl.

Bartchy, Scott S. "Undermining Ancient Patriarchy: Paul's Vision of a Society of Siblings." *Biblical Theology Bulletin* 29 (1999): 68–78.

Barton, Stephen C. "Living as Families in the Light of the New Testament." *Interpretation* 52, no. 2 (1998): 130–44.

———. "Paul's Sense of Place: An Anthropological Approach to Community Formation in Corinth." *New Testament Studies* 32 (1986): 225–46.

Beard, Mary, John North, and Simon Price. *Religions of Rome, Volume 1: A History.* Cambridge: Cambridge University Press, 1998.

Binder, Donald D. *Into the Temple Courts: The Place of the Synagogues in the Second Temple Period.* Society of Biblical Literature Dissertation Series 169. Atlanta: Society of Biblical Literature, 1999.

Bishop, Bill. *The Big Sort: Why the Clustering of Like-Minded Americans Is Tearing Us Apart.* New York: Houghton Mifflin, 2009.

Blasi, Anthony J., Jean Duhaime, and Paul-André Turcotte, eds. *Handbook of Early Christianity: Social Science Approaches.* Walnut Creek, CA: AltaMira Press, 2002.

Blue, Bradley. "Acts and the House Church." In *The Book of Acts in Its Graeco-Roman Setting.* Edited by David W. J. Gill and Conrad Gempf, 119–222. Vol. 2 of *The Book of Acts in Its First Century Setting.* Grand Rapids: Eerdmans, 1994.

Bonhoeffer, Dietrich. *Life Together.* Translated by John Doberstein. London: SCM, 1960.

Branick, Vincent P. *The House Church in the Writings of Paul.* Eugene, OR: Wipf & Stock, 2012.

Button, Bruce M., and Fika J. Van Rensburg. "The 'House Churches' in Corinth." *Neotestamentica* 37, no. 1 (2003): 1–28.

Cameron, Ron, and Merrill P. Miller, eds. *Redescribing Paul and the Corinthians.* Atlanta: Society of Biblical Literature, 2011.

Cappelletti, Silvia. *The Jewish Community of Rome: From the Second Century B.C. to the Third Century C.E.* Leiden: Brill, 2006.

Caragounis, Chrys. "A House Church in Corinth: An Inquiry into the Structure of Early Corinthian Christianity," In *Saint*

Paul and Corinth: 1950 Years since the Writing of the Epistles to the Corinthians. Edited by C. J. Belezos, 1:365–418. 2 vols. Athens: Psichogios, 2009.

Carter, Warren. *The Roman Empire and the New Testament: An Essential Guide.* Nashville: Abingdon, 2006.

Castelli, Elizabeth A. *Martyrdom and Memory: Early Christian Culture Making.* New York: Columbia University Press, 2004.

Chadwick, Henry. *The Early Church.* Harmondsworth: Penguin, 1968.

Chow, John K. *Patronage and Power: A Study of Social Networks in Corinth.* Journal for the Study of the New Testament Supplement Series 75. Sheffield: JSOT Press, 1992.

Clarke, Andrew D. *Serve the Community of the Church: Christians as Leaders and Ministers.* Grand Rapids: Eerdmans, 2000.

Cohick, Lynn H. *Women in the World of the Earliest Christians: Illuminating Ancient Ways of Life.* Grand Rapids: Baker, 2009.

Crossan, John Dominic. *The Birth of Christianity: Discovering What Happened in the Years Immediately after the Execution of Jesus.* San Francisco: HarperSanFrancisco, 1998.

De Vos, Craig Steven. *Church and Community Conflicts: The Relationships of the Thessalonian, Corinthian, and Philippian Churches with Their Wider Civic Communities.* Society of Biblical Literature Dissertation Series 168. Atlanta: Scholars Press, 1999.

Downs, David J. *Offering of the Gentiles: Paul's Collection for Jerusalem in Its Chronological, Cultural, and Cultic Contexts.* Grand Rapids: Eerdmans, 2016.

Eckhardt, Benedikt. "Craft Guilds as Synagogues? Further Thoughts on 'Private Judean-Deity Associations.'" *Journal for the Study of Judaism in the Persian, Hellenistic, and Roman Periods* 48, no. 2 (2017): 246–60.

Eisen, Ute E. *Women Officeholders in Early Christianity: Epigraphical and Literary Studies.* Collegeville, MN: Michael Glazier, 2000.

Elliott, John H. "The Jesus Movement Was Not Egalitarian but Family-Oriented." *Biblical Interpretation* 11 (2003): 173–210.

Ellsworth-Moran, Nadine. "What Makes Space Sacred?" *The Presbyterian Outlook*, March 1, 2017. https://tinyurl.com/y2al8bun.

Engels, Donald. *Roman Corinth: An Alternative Model for the Classical City.* Chicago: University of Chicago Press, 1990.

Epp, Eldon Jay. *Junia: The First Woman Apostle.* Minneapolis: Fortress, 2005.

Esler, Philip F., ed. *Modelling Early Christianity: Social-Scientific Studies of the New Testament in Its Context.* London: Routledge, 1995.

Fee, Gordon. "Tongues—Least of the Gifts? Some Exegetical Observations on 1 Corinthians 12–14." *Pneuma* 2, no. 2 (Fall 1980): 3–14.

Ferguson, Everett, Michael P. McHugh, and Frederick W. Norris, eds. *Encyclopedia of Early Christianity.* 2nd ed. 2 vols. New York: Garland Publishing, 1997.

Finger, Rita Halteman. *Roman House Churches for Today: A Practical Guide for Small Groups.* Rev. ed. Grand Rapids: Eerdmans, 2007.

Fiorenza, Elisabeth Schüssler. *In Memory of Her: A Feminist Theological Reconstruction of Christian Origins.* New York: Crossroad, 1983.

Forbes, Christopher. *Prophecy and Inspired Speech: In Early Christianity and Its Hellenistic Environment.* Peabody, MA: Hendrickson, 1997.

Gehring, Roger W. *House Church and Mission: The Importance of Household Structures in Early Christianity.* Peabody, MA: Hendrickson, 2004.

Gillespie, Thomas. *The First Theologians: A Study in Early Christian Prophecy.* Grand Rapids: Eerdmans, 1994.

Glancy, Jennifer A. *Slavery as Moral Problem: In the Early Church and Today.* Minneapolis: Fortress, 2011.

González, Justo L. *The Story of Christianity.* 2 vols. San Francisco: HarperSanFrancisco, 1984.

Green, Joel B., and Lee Martin McDonald, eds. *The World of the New Testament: Cultural, Social, and Historical Contexts.* Grand Rapids: Baker, 2013.

Harland, Philip A. *Associations, Synagogues, and Congregations: Claiming a Place in Ancient Mediterranean Society.* Minneapolis: Fortress, 2003.

————. *Dynamics of Identity in the World of the Early Christians: Associations, Judeans and Cultural Minorities.* London: Continuum, 2010.

Harrison, John, and James D. Dvorak, eds. *The New Testament Church: The Challenge of Developing Ecclesiologies.* McMaster Biblical Studies Series. Eugene, OR: Pickwick, 2012.

Harvey, Jennifer. *Dear White Christians: For Those Still Longing for Racial Reconciliation*. Grand Rapids: Eerdmans, 2014.

Heath, Elaine A. *Five Means of Grace: Experience God's Love the Wesleyan Way*. Nashville: Abingdon, 2017.

Hilton, Allen. *A House United: How the Church Can Save the World*. Minneapolis: Fortress, 2018.

Hurtado, Larry W. *Destroyer of the Gods: Early Christian Distinctiveness in the Roman World*. Waco, TX: Baylor University Press, 2016.

Hylen, Susan E. *Women in the New Testament World*. Essentials of Biblical Studies. New York: Oxford University Press, 2019.

Jeffers, James S. *Conflict at Rome: Social Order and Hierarchy in Early Christianity*. Minneapolis: Fortress, 1991.

Jewett, Robert. *Romans: A Commentary*. 2nd ed. Minneapolis: Fortress, 2006.

Johnson, Lee A. "Paul's Letters Reheard: Performance-Critical Examination of the Preparation, Transportation, and Delivery of Paul's Correspondence." *Catholic Biblical Quarterly* 79, no. 1 (2017): 60–76.

Johnson, Luke Timothy. *Prophetic Jesus, Prophetic Church: The Challenge of Luke-Acts to Contemporary Christians*. Grand Rapids: Eerdmans, 2011.

———. *Sharing Possessions: Mandate and Symbol of Faith*. Philadelphia: Fortress, 1981.

Judge, Edwin A. "The Social Identity of the First Christians: A Question of Method in Religious History." *Journal of Religious History* 11 (1980): 201–17.

Keener, Craig S. *Acts: An Exegetical Commentary.* 4 vols. Grand Rapids: Baker Academic, 2012–2015.

Klauck, Hans-Josef. *Hausgemeinde und Hauskirche im frühen Christentum.* Stuttgarter Bibelstudien 103. Stuttgart: Katholisches Bibelwerk, 1981.

Kloppenborg, John S., and Richard A. Ascough. *Greco-Roman Associations: Texts, Translations, and Commentary: Attica, Central Greece, Macedonia, Thrace.* Berlin: De Gruyter, 2011.

Kloppenborg, John S., and Stephen G. Wilson, eds. *Voluntary Associations in the Graeco-Roman World.* New York: Routledge, 1996.

Knoll, Benjamin R., and Cammie Jo Bolin. *She Preached the Word: Women's Ordination in Modern America.* New York: Oxford University Press, 2018.

Kreider, Alan. *The Patient Ferment of the Early Church: The Improbable Rise of Christianity in the Roman Empire.* Grand Rapids: Baker, 2016.

Lampe, Peter. *From Paul to Valentinus: Christians at Rome in the First Two Centuries.* Edited by Marshall D. Johnson. Translated by Michael Steinhauser. Minneapolis: Fortress, 2003.

Last, Richard. "*Ekklēsia* outside the Septuagint and the *Dēmos*: The Titles of Greco-Roman Associations and Christ-Followers' Groups." *Journal of Biblical Literature* 137, no. 4 (2018): 959–80.

———. *The Pauline Church and the Corinthians Ekklēsia: Greco-Roman Associations in Comparative Context.* Society for New Testament Studies Monograph Series 164. Cambridge: Cambridge University Press, 2016.

Lathrop, Gordon. *The Four Gospels on Sunday: The New Testament and the Reform of Christian Worship.* Minneapolis: Fortress, 2011.

Levine, Lee I., ed. *The Synagogue in Late Antiquity.* Winona Lake, IN: Eisenbrauns, 1987.

Lieu, Judith. *Christian Identity in the Jewish and Graeco-Roman World.* Oxford: Oxford University Press, 2004.

Longenecker, Richard, ed. *Into God's Presence: Prayer in the New Testament.* Grand Rapids: Eerdmans, 2001.

MacMullen, Ramsay. *Christianizing the Roman Empire.* New York: Yale University Press, 1984.

————. *Paganism in the Roman Empire.* New Haven: Yale University Press, 1981.

Madigan, Kevin, and Carolyn Osiek, eds. and trans. *Ordained Women in the Early Church: A Documentary History.* Baltimore: Johns Hopkins University Press, 2005.

Malherbe, Abraham J. "Hellenistic Philosopher or Christian Pastor?" *Australasian Theological Review* 68, no. 1 (January 1, 1986): 1–13.

————. *Paul and the Popular Philosophers.* Minneapolis: Fortress, 1989.

————. *Social Aspects of Early Christianity.* Rockwell Lectures of 1975. Baton Rouge: Louisiana State University Press, 1977.

Malina, Bruce J. *The New Testament World: Insights from Cultural Anthropology.* 3rd ed. Louisville: Westminster John Knox, 2001.

————. *Windows on the World of Jesus: Time Travel to Ancient Judea.* Louisville: John Knox, 1993.

Masci, David, "The Divide over Ordaining Women." *Fact Tank*, September 9, 2014. https://tinyurl.com/y5nz3l3x.

McGowan, Andrew. *Ascetic Eucharists: Food and Drink in Early Christian Ritual Meals*. Oxford Early Christian Studies. New York: Oxford University Press, 1999.

———. "The Inordinate Cup: Issues of Order in Early Eucharistic Drinking." *Studia Patristica* 35 (2001): 283–91.

———. "'Is There a Liturgical Text in This Gospel?' The Institution Narratives and Their Early Interpretive Communities." *Journal of Biblical Literature* 118 (1999): 77–89.

Meeks, Wayne A. *The First Urban Christians: The Social World of the Apostle Paul*. 2nd ed. New Haven: Yale University Press, 2003.

Murphy-O'Connor, Jerome. "The Corinth That Saint Paul Saw." *Biblical Archaeologist* (September 1984): 147–59.

———. *St. Paul's Corinth: Texts and Archaeology*. Collegeville, MN: Liturgical Press, 2002.

———. *St. Paul's Ephesus: Texts and Archaeology*. Collegeville, MN: Liturgical Press, 2008.

Neufeld, Dietmar, and Richard E. DeMaris, eds. *Understanding the Social World of the New Testament*. New York: Routledge, 2010.

Osiek, Carolyn. *What Are They Saying about the Social Setting of the New Testament?* Rev. ed. New York: Paulist, 1992.

Osiek, Carolyn, Margaret Y. MacDonald, and Janet H. Tulloch. *A Woman's Place: House Churches in Earliest Christianity*. Minneapolis: Fortress, 2006.

Pederson, Rena. *The Lost Apostle: Searching for the Truth about Junia*. San Francisco: Jossey-Bass, 2006.

Peppiatt, Lucy. *Unveiling Paul's Women: Making Sense of 1 Corinthians 11:2–16*. Eugene, OR: Cascade: 2018.

———. *Women and Worship at Corinth: Paul's Rhetorical Arguments in 1 Corinthians*. Eugene, OR: Cascade, 2015.

Perkins, Pheme. *Ministering in the Pauline Churches*. New York: Paulist, 1992.

Pew Research Center. "'Nones' on the Rise: One in Five Adults Have No Religious Affiliation." Pew Forum on Religion & Public Life, October 9, 2012. https://tinyurl.com/llu8pa5.

Remus, Harold. "Persecution." In *Handbook of Early Christianity: Social Science Approaches*, edited by Anthony J. Blasi, Jean Duhaime, and Paul-André Turcotte, 431–52. Walnut Creek, CA: Alta Mira, 2002.

Selby, Andrew M. "Bishops, Elders, and Deacons in the Philippian Church: Evidence of Plurality from Paul and Polycarp." *Perspectives in Religious Studies* 39, no. 1 (Spring 2012): 79–94.

Smith, Dennis E. "The House Church as Social Environment." In *Text, Image, and Christians in the Graeco-Roman World: A Festschrift in Honor of David Lee Balch*. Edited by Aliou Cissé and Carolyn Osiek, 3–21. Eugene, OR: Pickwick, 2012.

———. "Meals and Morality in Paul and His World." In *Society of Biblical Literature 1981 Seminar Papers*, 319–39. SBLSPS 20. Atlanta: Society of Biblical Literature, 1981.

————. *From Symposium to Eucharist: The Banquet in the Early Christian World*. Minneapolis: Fortress, 2003.

Stark, Rodney. *The Rise of Christianity: How the Obscure, Marginal Jesus Movement Became the Dominant Religious Force in the Western World in a Few Centuries*. San Francisco: HarperSanFrancisco, 1997.

Stegemann, Wolfgang, Bruce J. Malina, and Gerd Theissen, eds. *The Social Setting of Jesus and the Gospels*. Minneapolis: Fortress, 2002.

Storey, Glenn R. "The Population of Ancient Rome." *Antiquity* 71, no. 274 (Dec. 1997): 966–78.

Taylor, Walter F., Jr. *Paul: Apostle to the Nations*. Minneapolis: Fortress, 2012.

Theissen, Gerd. *The Social Setting of Pauline Christianity: Essays on Corinth*. Edited and translated by John H. Schütz. Philadelphia: Fortress, 1982.

Thiselton, Anthony. "Meanings and Greek Translation Relating to 'Spiritual Gifts' in 1 Corinthians 12–14: Some Proposals in the Light of Philosophy of Language, Speech-Act Theory and Exegesis." In *Thiselton on Hermeneutics: Collected Works with New Essays*, 335–47. Grand Rapids: Eerdmans, 2006.

Thompson, James W. *The Church according to Paul: Rediscovering the Community Conformed to Christ*. Grand Rapids: Baker, 2014.

Torjesen, Karen Jo. *When Women Were Priests: Women's Leadership in the Early Church and the Scandal of Their*

Subordination in the Rise of Christianity. San Francisco: HarperCollins, 1993.

Wagner, Walter H. *After the Apostles: Christianity in the Second Century.* Minneapolis: Fortress, 1994.

Walzer, Richard, trans. *Galen on Jews and Christians.* Oxford: Oxford University Press, 1949.

Wheatley, Alan B. *Patronage in Early Christianity: Its Use and Transformation from Jesus to Paul of Samosata.* Princeton Theological Monograph Series. Eugene, OR: Pickwick, 2011.

White, L. Michael. *Building God's House in the Roman World: Architectural Adaptation among Pagans, Jews and Christians.* Baltimore: Johns Hopkins University Press, 1990.

———. *The Social Origins of Christian Architecture.* 2 vols. Harvard Theological Studies 42. Valley Forge, PA: Trinity Press, 1990 and 1997.

Winter, Bruce W. *After Paul Left Corinth: The Influence of Secular Ethics and Social Change.* Grand Rapids: Eerdmans, 2001.

Witherington, Ben III. *A Week in the Life of Corinth.* Downers Grove, IL: InterVarsity, 2012.

ACKNOWLEDGMENTS

Although writing a book involves many hours alone, it is hardly a solo endeavor. Many have encouraged, informed, supported, and inspired me along the way. Without their presence and assistance, this book would not exist.

It has been a joy working with Fortress Press, specifically Neil Elliott and Scott Tunseth. Neil was discerning early on about potential options for the project and gracious in assisting them. Scott has always been remarkably supportive of my work, perceptive about ways to improve it, and gracious in all feedback. I am grateful to work with people of such character.

I am very thankful to Wartburg Seminary for its support throughout this process, giving me access to library resources and sabbatical time to finish. I especially appreciate how President Louise Johnson, Dean Craig Nessan, and my faculty colleagues have always believed in the relevance of this work for the church and its future.

Many friends have read chapters of this book and offered valuable feedback. I am grateful to the writers' group I meet with at Inspire Café in Dubuque—specifically people like

Susanna Cantu Gregory, Martin Lohrmann, Amanda Osheim, Chris James, Elesha Coffman, Jake Kohlhaas, and Susan Forshey. They have not only informed my thinking, they have been supportive friends in the journey of writing.

I am grateful to the people at Lord of Life Lutheran Church in Asbury, Iowa, who took time to read chapters and engage me in conversation. They have followed my progress closely, asking often, "How's the book coming?" I am also thankful to those who first encouraged me to pursue writing on early church community and its relevance for today. Pastor Ritva Williams raised the idea to me at an internship supervisors' gathering by simply asking why there were not more resources on the topic of early church community. Jamie (Jordan) Reising served as my research assistant the next academic year, digging up several resources to feed my thinking early on.

Finally, I am grateful to my family members for supporting and grounding me throughout this writing process, especially my wife, Maria, and my two children, Timothy and Teresa. This book is dedicated to my mother, Judy Troftgruben, who passed away this year. She raised me with deep roots in the Christian faith and life, enabling me to answer more faithfully Christ's call to adapt, innovate, and respond to a changing world.

WORD & WORLD BOOKS

THEOLOGY FOR CHRISTIAN MINISTRY

Informing and inspiring Christian leaders and communities to proclaim God's *Word* to a *World* God created and loves. Articulating the fullness of both realities and the creative intersection between them.

Word & World Books is a partnership between Luther Seminary, the board of the periodical *Word & World*, and Fortress Press.

Books in the series include:

Future Faith: Ten Challenges Reshaping Christianity in the 21st Century by Wesley Granberg Michaelson (2018)

Liberating Youth from Adolescence by Jeremy P. Myers (2018)

Elders Rising: The Promise and Peril of Aging by Roland Martinson (2018)

I Can Do No Other: The Church's New Here We Stand Moment by Anna M. Madsen (2019)

Intercultural Church: A Biblical Vision for an Age of Migration by Safwat Marzouk (2019)

Rooted and Renewing: Imagining the Church's Future in Light of Its New Testament Origins by Troy M. Troftgruben (2019)